George Steinbrenner's Pipe Dream

George Steinbrenner's

Pipe Dream

The ABL

Champion

Cleveland

Pipers

Bill Livingston

Black Squirrel Books™

Kent, Ohio

In memory of my mother and father,
who gave me so much.

BLACK SQUIRREL BOOKS™ ™
Frisky, industrious black squirrels are a familiar sight on the Kent State University
campus and the inspiration for Black Squirrel Books™, a trade imprint of The Kent
State University Press. www.KentStateUniversityPress.com.

All photographs appear courtesy of Mike Cleary.

Library of Congress Catalog Card Number 2014049080
ISBN 978-1-60635-261-8
Manufactured in the United States of America

Library of Congress Cataloging-in-Publication Data

Livingston, Bill.
  George Steinbrenner's pipe dream : the ABL champion Cleveland Pipers /
Bill Livingston.
      pages cm
  Includes bibliographical references and index.
  ISBN 978-1-60635-261-8 (Paper : alk. paper) ∞
  1. Cleveland Pipers (Basketball team)
  2. American Basketball League—History.
  3. Steinbrenner, George M. (George Michael), 1930–2010, owner.
  4. Basketball—Ohio—Cleveland—History—20th century. 5. Basketball—United
States—History—20th century. I. Title.
  GV885.52.C575L58 2015
  796.323'640977132—dc23
                                    2014049080

19 18 17 16 15   5 4 3 2 1

Contents

Acknowledgments

Special thanks to Elton Alexander; Steve Helwagen; The Michael Schwartz Library, Cleveland State University, and librarians Lynn Bycko and William Barrow; the librarians at the main branch of the Columbus Metropolitan Library; Julianne Livingston Thomas.

The book would not have been possible without the ABL survivors, especially the invaluable Mike Cleary. I would also like to thank for their time Dr. Jack Adams, Dr. Dick Barnett, Wayne Embry, Joe Gordon, Harvey Greene, Ron Hamilton, Fritz Kreisler, Jerry Lucas, Mike Roberts, Gene Shue, Tina Siegfried, Bob Sudyk, Tony Tomsic, and the always cooperative Gene Tormohlen.

My wife, Marilyn, put up with many outbursts as I struggled with retracing my steps to do chapter notes. My first editor, Rebekah Cotton, brought cohesion to the chaos.

My mentor John McEvoy and *Plain Dealer* friend Tom Feran, my companion on many cold-weather visits to the microfilm room at Cleveland State, were always encouraging.

Introduction

T he mark the American Basketball League (ABL) made on the sport
seemed to be no longer lasting than the masking tape a worker
was laying down to delineate the wider boundary of the free throw lane
and the unfamiliar curve of the three-point arc on December 1, 1961, at
Columbus's Fairgrounds Coliseum. No one else in all the world played
the game on such an oddly configured court, so the lines appeared and
disappeared with each game like mirages.

As John McLendon, coach of the Cleveland Pipers of the fledgling
ABL, pressed the tape to the floor in accordance with the visionary new
ABL rules, the sparse crowd, variously estimated at between 500 and
1,000 curious spectators, began to titter and whisper.[1] Surely, it was
beneath the dignity of a professional coach, even an African American
professional coach like McLendon, the first of an integrated team in
post–World War II America, to perform such a menial task.

The fans had no way of knowing that the coach stooping over the
floor had always sublimated his own ego for the greater good of his team
and had always done what was necessary when others either could not
or would not.

At Tennessee State, a historically black college in Nashville, McLendon's duties included sanding the basketball floor at Kean's Little Garden, the field house where he had cultivated the flower of small-college
basketball. Three straight times in the late 1950s, Tennessee State had

won National Association of Intercollegiate Athletics championships, the top small-college award in the country.

The Tigers' uninterrupted success led the Pipers' previous owner, Ed Sweeny, a plumbing supplies salesman, to hire McLendon to coach his new Cleveland team in a semiprofessional factory league that was an intermediate step between college basketball and the National Basketball Association. But now, under new management, driven by a fiery owner with a more grandiose vision, the Pipers were playing in the ABL, a professional league that posed a serious challenge to the NBA.

McLendon's burden was more than skin deep in that neutral-court game in Columbus. Such games were part of a barnstorming tour, an attempt to increase the popularity of professional basketball in cities as near as Cleveland's and as distant as Columbus.

McLendon had a team whose parts had meshed quickly because several of the players were former Tennessee State Tigers, now reunited with their old coach. They were all familiar with his fast-paced style of play.

McLendon had at his disposal some of the best talents in the ABL with NBA defector Dick Barnett, a former Tennessee State star, and the recently graduated captain of the Ohio State basketball team, Larry Siegfried.

But McLendon also had the most combustible and demanding owner in pro sports in George Steinbrenner. At the age of 30, the Cleveland native and future New York Yankees owner was making his first venture into professional sports.

Columbus was not just a potential market in the struggle to win fans between the Pipers and the NBA's Cincinnati Royals, it was also the home of Ohio State University, the dominant college team of the era, NCAA champion in 1960, and runner-up to the University of Cincinnati in 1961.

The state capital was where Jerry Lucas played, the best college player in the land, leader and star of the Ohio State Buckeyes, with future NBA great John Havlicek as his wingman. A white star in an increasingly black sport, Lucas was the most sought-after player in the country by both the insurgent ABL and the established NBA as he entered his senior season.

Given the essentially minor-league status of professional basketball in those days, including the NBA, Lucas was probably already playing on the nation's most popular team at Ohio State. Lucas was George Steinbrenner's heart's desire and irresistible obsession. Steinbrenner felt that Lucas was the one player who could guarantee financial solvency, assure championship contention for as long as he wanted to play in Cleveland, and possibly even secure admission to the NBA. That was the ultimate goal of Steinbrenner, who even then was as nakedly ambitious as he would be in the future as owner of the Yankees, the country's richest and most successful sports franchise.

But the young Steinbrenner lacked the one thing that assured his conquests with the Yankees—access to his family's Great Lakes shipbuilding fortune. That was controlled by George's imperious father. Without proper funding, the younger Steinbrenner's grand plans were only a pipe dream, insubstantial as the promises he made and empty as the lies he told as he ruthlessly pursued an unreachable goal.

By the end of the Pipers' one stormy season in the ABL, McLendon, a future member of the Basketball Hall of Fame, had been sacrificed in Steinbrenner's pursuit of a bigger name to coach the team. The players had revolted over missing paychecks and threatened to boycott a game. The ABL had come close to expelling the Pipers for breaking league rules. The team almost forfeited the fifth and final game of the championship series in a dispute over where it was to be played.

Bill Sharman, himself a future Hall of Famer as both a coach and a Boston Celtics guard, had replaced McLendon.

Lucas, despite the chaos surrounding the franchise, had signed with the Pipers, and the NBA had invited the team, eight years before the Cavaliers entered the NBA as a hapless expansion franchise, to join the league as the reigning ABL champions.

Although basketball historians contend that the three-point shot—adopted later by another NBA challenger, the American Basketball Association, and finally by the NBA itself— was the ABL's greatest legacy, it could have been far more than that in Cleveland.

Lucas, although he never played a game for the Pipers, was the city's greatest basketball star until LeBron James came on the scene over four decades later. The Pipers won a basketball championship that eluded

James in his first seven years as a member of the Cavaliers. In James's second tour with the team, beginning in the 2014–15 season, he was still striving to lead the team to Cleveland's first basketball championship since the Pipers in 1961–62.

The Pipers became champions in spite of the odds, many of them stacked against them by their very owner.

Just as the new lines on the floor created a new dynamic in the game, the Pipers were a team that needed a grander stage to accommodate Steinbrenner's ambitions. But they became a team, finally, that could not be saved because of him.

CHAPTER I

Castles in the Air

*I tell people that we won a championship in Cleveland
and LeBron James didn't. But nobody remembers the Pipers.*
—**Dick Barnett,** *Cleveland Pipers guard*

Outside, George Steinbrenner, heir to a Great Lakes shipbuilding fortune, saw the sky, the inland sea, and the future as he conceived it.

From the window of his 11th-floor corner office in the Rockefeller Building in Cleveland, he peered through a telescope at the captains of ore and grain boats who were wrestling their cargoes toward piers on the Lake Erie shoreline far below. It was a spring day in 1961 and young George watched the masters of his family's old industry.

The building served as the headquarters of shipping companies whose boats carried coal, iron, and grain—cargo that had been clawed and cut from the land—through wind and storm to brawny industrial cities such as Detroit, Cleveland, and Buffalo.

Born on the Fourth of July, Steinbrenner would be 31 years old when the skyrockets flew in the summer. He was a firecracker by both birth and inclination. He intended to become the captain of a new form of commerce, professional basketball. He had the goods at hand to do it too. Nothing was going to deter him from his goal, certainly not the truth.

In Steinbrenner's office was Mike Cleary, the general manager of the Cleveland Pipers of the fledgling American Basketball League. Cleary was only 27. "George and I were the young and the restless," he said.[1]

Joining them was Larry Siegfried, a second-team All-American at guard who had just graduated as captain of the 1960–61 Ohio State Buckeyes. George felt he needed Larry Siegfried as much as a helmsman needed good charts.

I

Kinsman Marine Transit was the family's shipping company. The Rockefeller Building on West 9th Street, built by John D. Rockefeller, an earlier mover and shaker from Cleveland, is listed in the National Register of Historic Places. From his office, Steinbrenner would try his damnedest to make his mark outside the family business.

Down the hallway from George's aerie was the office of his father, Henry.

While George would describe grandiose plans to Siegfried, they were only dreamy projections without money. Henry controlled the money in the real world. George could only control his spellbound listeners in the realm of fantasy.

George Steinbrenner probably had no inkling then, as he watched the boats moor and chatted with Siegfried, that he was about to repeat in basketball, at least in some ways, the family's history in shipping.

Like the Pipers, the shipping firm had flirted with economic ruin. Like the Pipers in their lone season, the shipping company had succeeded against all odds.

The family's involvement in Lake Erie shipping developed after the *Western Reserve*—a 300-foot-long steamer, the pride of the Great Lakes, built by the Minch Shipping Transit Company of Cleveland—sank in Lake Superior in 1892. The too-brittle steel of the *Western Reserve*'s hull split under the pounding of a fierce storm; then the two lifeboats failed. All but one of the 31 passengers and crew members drowned. All 11 Minch family members onboard died.

The tragedy left the family's patriarch, Philip Minch, grief stricken. The *Western Reserve*'s starboard lantern eventually washed ashore on the desolate Canadian coast. It was a battered remnant of the lost grandeur of the ship and the company that built it. The lantern burned in the front window of the Minch home for years afterward, like a searchlight, unable to find what was lost.

By 1901, Minch Shipping was in danger of foundering too. The husband of the former Sophie Minch, lawyer and businessman Henry Steinbrenner, agreed to try to save it. Renamed, because of Steinbrenner's in-law status, the Kinsman Marine Transit Company, the firm prospered under the stewardship of Henry's son, George II, and then under George II's son, the next generation's Henry.

That Henry took over the business in 1939, intending to eventually turn it over to his son, George III. Roman numerals proliferated in the family, just as they do with popes, kings, and queens of England, and given the dynamic of the relationship between Henry and George III, world wars.

Shipping always came first, Henry thought.

Henry sometimes walked across the street to a saloon called Hoty's, just so he could drink with his captains. George was on a first-name basis with the captains too.

Henry named the family home in Bay Village, a western suburb of Cleveland, "The Anchorage," placing a ship's anchor and capstan near the gate. Years later, George named his own home near the New York Yankees' spring-training facility in Tampa, Florida, "The Anchorage." The name was an obvious homage to Henry, whose denial of resources had fed George's determination. George simply had gone buccaneering in different currents and riptides.

As Steinbrenner gazed out the window, down at the melting ice that often mantled the shoreline in winter, perhaps he felt his basketball team could loosen hockey's iron grip on Cleveland, which was captivated by the sport.

The vast engineering project known as the Saint Lawrence Seaway opened in 1959, creating dreams of rich new markets by making the ports of Europe accessible to the cities of the Midwest. No telescope could see into the future, but could Steinbrenner have guessed even then, in the early days of his first venture into a different world, that sports, not shipping, would be the vehicle to carry his name far and wide? All George knew was that Siegfried was the blue ribbon, the grand prize, and the big headline. And Steinbrenner loved his publicity.

"Siggy" is what teammates called Siegfried. He was bright and hyperactive, a chatterbox, and he would end conversations on a selected topic by saying, "Follow me."

Everyone did at Ohio State. He was a year older than the team's precocious sophomores, Jerry Lucas and John Havlicek, in the 1959–60 season. So Siggy knew his way around.

Flushed with their victory over the University of California at Berkeley in the 1960 NCAA basketball championship game, the Buckeyes returned to their hotel in San Francisco, only to find its restaurant was closed.

"Siggy was our leader, so, when we found a bar-and-grill that still had its lights on, he knocked on the door," said Bob Knight, the future Indiana coach, who was a sophomore substitute on the team.[2]

The bartender said he was closing and told the players to go away.

"But we just won the national championship," said Siegfried.

"Of what?" asked the bartender.

"It was a different era," Knight would later say.

Steinbrenner was attracted by the glitter of Ohio State players. It did not matter that Siegfried was an unimposing physical specimen.

"Siggy was one of those guys who defied the scouting report. He might not have had the quickness and speed everyone looks for, but he was very competitive, and he knew how to play the game," said Wayne Embry, Siegfried's teammate on the Boston Celtics and later the general manager of the Cleveland Cavaliers and the Milwaukee Bucks.[3]

It did not matter that Siegfried was more of a defensive force than a glamorous scoring star. "Siggy is in his shirt!" Celtics radio broadcaster Johnny Most would shout to his radio audience years in the future.[4]

Obviously, Steinbrenner did not understand the nuances of basketball. But he understood box office. He understood that star power and publicity mattered. His fascination with big-name players who did not fit the team's style often put him at odds with coach John McLendon. Pointedly, McLendon was excluded from the meeting with Siegfried. The first black man to coach an integrated professional team in the United States, McLendon blazed his trail five years before Bill Russell became the player-coach of the Boston Celtics, 14 years before Frank Robinson managed the Cleveland Indians, and a stunning 28 years before Art Shell coached the Los Angeles Raiders of the National Football League.

It was also two years before Eugene "Bull" Connor, the Commissioner of Public Safety in Birmingham, Alabama, ordered his policemen to turn fire hoses on black civil rights protesters, including small children. It was three years before Lyndon Johnson signed the Civil Rights Act that partially resulted from that.

McLendon's teams were characterized by their fast pace of play, their superb conditioning, and their quickness. The coach also was ahead of his time in his belief in strength training. It was the opposite of the conventional thinking of the era.

McLendon was the first coach to win a national collegiate championship with an all-black team, winning three in a row, in fact, at Tennessee A&I (later called Tennessee State) from 1957 to 1959 in the National Association of Intercollegiate Athletics (NAIA) Tournament.

He coached the Pipers to the 1961 championship of the National Industrial Basketball League (NIBL), an intermediate stage between college basketball and the National Basketball Association. So well respected was NIBL basketball that its players often formed all or part of the U.S. Olympic teams in that amateur era.

McLendon was the first man of his race to coach an NIBL champion. It was a task made more difficult by the racial makeup of the league. Only two of the other eight NIBL teams even had black players. In the spring of 1961, McLendon added the Amateur Athletic Association (AAU) championship, the first-ever for an Ohio team.

That summer, soon after the East-West tension caused by the abortive invasion of Cuba at the Bay of Pigs, McLendon led an AAU team, made up primarily of the NIBL Pipers, to an eight-game sweep in the Soviet Union. No other black coach had ever led an integrated American team, or any team for that matter, in international competition.

Ohio State's Jerry Lucas, personally selected to the barnstorming team by Steinbrenner, was one of the greatest college players ever. A forerunner of Larry Bird in his all-around basketball excellence and future U.S. Senator Bill Bradley in his academic brilliance, Lucas was a white superstar in a game increasingly dominated by black players.

The tall, cerebral Lucas would become the ultimate expression of Steinbrenner's fondness for Ohio State and attraction to stars. At the end of the Pipers' short, stormy life as a professional team, their rise or fall—and Steinbrenner's salvation or downfall as a prominent mover and shaker in Cleveland—would depend on Lucas and the team's diminishing chances of, first, signing him and, more importantly, paying him.

Basketball was not, however, Steinbrenner's only tie to the Buckeyes. He served as an assistant football coach at Ohio State on Woody Hayes's first national championship team in 1954. (Steinbrenner also was an assistant coach at Big Ten rivals Northwestern in 1955 and Purdue in 1956.)

In Columbus, Steinbrenner became fast friends with the Buckeyes' 1955 Heisman Trophy winner, halfback Howard "Hopalong" Cassady.

Steinbrenner took credit for steering him to Ohio State and then convincing him not to transfer to the College of Wooster when Hayes refused to let Cassady play college baseball. In later years, Steinbrenner hired Cassady as a spring training conditioning coach, a scout for the New York Yankees, and a first-base coach for their farm team in Columbus, Ohio.

Steinbrenner's Buckeyes sports absorption was total. He was coach of the Lockbourne (later Rickenbacker) Air Force Base's baseball and basketball teams. The SkyHawks basketball team would prove to be the more successful one, posting a 100–19 record under him, including victories over West Virginia and the College of Rio Grande, for whom Clarence "Bevo" Francis, a future Piper for a short time, once scored 113 points in a game.

In Columbus, Steinbrenner became friends with Dr. Jimmy Hull, Ohio State's first basketball all-American in 1939, when the Buckeyes finished second in the inaugural NCAA Tournament. Hull would become the best man in the tempestuous sports executive's marriage to a suburban Columbus girl. Hull also invested in the Pipers later and was one of the voices in George's ear, urging him to consider moving the team to Columbus.

The Ohio State connection was deep and rich. In some ways, Steinbrenner probably considered McLendon's Tennessee State experience to be too small-time, compared to the colossus of Ohio State, with the thistles and hayseeds of the bush leagues clinging to clothes of the Pipers' coach.

With or, as he probably preferred even that early, without McLendon, Steinbrenner wanted to tap into the Buckeyes' popularity in the worst way. Steinbrenner was a great salesman. As emotionally abusive as he was, he could be warm and personable too. As he spoke to Siegfried, he threw one arm around the player's shoulder and pointed with the fingers of his other hand as he made his pitch. It was a habitual gesture, literally reaching out to those he needed and later misused.[5]

Siegfried had been the third pick of the 1961 NBA Draft, selected by the Cincinnati Royals. He eventually played 11 seasons, won five championships with the Boston Celtics, and averaged 10.8 points for his NBA career.

"Do you know what the third pick of the NBA draft would be worth today?" Siegfried, who died in 2010, had wistfully asked his wife, Tina. In the 2013–14 NBA season, under the terms of the Collective Bargaining Agreement between players and owners, such a player would earn $3,444,400 for his rookie season. Siegfried's salary in his rookie season with the Pipers was $13,000.[6]

Why would a player with Siegfried's credentials consider the ABL, a league with a comparative lack of them?

The determining factor for many ABL players was simply the lack of opportunity in the closed shop that was the NBA in that era. In 1960–61, the NBA consisted of nine teams, each with 12 roster spots. With a mere 108 jobs available, only the top nine players in the collegiate ranks, the first-round draftees, were assured of a spot. The 10th-best player in the world might wind up in the NIBL, a glorified factory league.

For his part, Siegfried was a farm boy who occasionally brought roast pork crackling from the family farm in Shelby, Ohio, to teammates as snacks after practice.[7] He was not only a homespun boy from central Ohio, he was an Ohio State boy.

"I could never sign with Cincinnati," said Siegfried. "They [the University of Cincinnati Bearcats] were our big rivals."[8]

The Pipers were also a strong and appealing team. In 1960, the NIBL version of the Pipers played a two-game series with the 1960 U.S. Olympic team. The latter was one of the greatest amateur basketball teams ever, headed by Oscar Robertson, Jerry West, Lucas, and Walter Bellamy, future Basketball Hall of Famers all.

Under McLendon's direction, the Pipers split the series, winning, 101–96 in overtime in Canton, Ohio, on July 10, 1960, and losing, 91–69, four nights later in Morgantown, West Virginia, where West had played collegiately. The loss in Canton was the only one suffered by the Olympic team.

That the Pipers fared so well against the Olympians impressed Siegfried. He and fellow Ohio State player John Havlicek had been told they were on the 1960 Olympic team, along with Lucas, before the politics of sports shattered their dreams overnight. Three Ohio State players, two of whom were not named Lucas, were too many. Both Havlicek and Siegfried were quickly dropped from the team. Siegfried called it one of the biggest disappointments of his life, along with not winning the national championship game against the Cincinnati Bearcats.[9]

The Pipers' roster in the game against the Olympic team included former Tennessee State players John "Rabbit" Barnhill and Ben Warley. Both were future NBA players. Dan Swartz, who was to be an ABL three-point leader and the league's top foul shooter, was already on the NIBL roster.

Before splitting with the Olympic team, the NIBL version of the Pipers played Oscar Robertson and a group of college all-stars in a highly publicized two-game series. The Pipers lost in Indianapolis, Robertson's hometown, before 6,000 screaming fans, but then won, 120–119, before 9,139 fans at Cleveland Arena. It was an attendance figure never to be threatened again, in either the Pipers' NIBL or ABL incarnations.

The Arena victory all but assured McLendon's position as Pipers coach, at least for the time being.

The biggest hurdle Steinbrenner had to clear with Siegfried was, in fact, dark, dingy, crumbling Cleveland Arena. It was the site of several of the Pipers' home games. The building had been built during the Great Depression in 1937. Arenas then were not the palaces of today. The most famous one, Madison Square Garden, then located between 49th and 50th streets on Eighth Avenue in Manhattan, was called the "Mecca of Basketball." The nickname was the grandest thing about the place. The rims were so loose that Jack McMahon, a former St. Louis Hawks guard who coached the ABL's Kansas City Steers, and other players called them "sewers." That was because, as McMahon said, "Everything went down them."[10]

"Knowing Jack, he would have found a beer at the bottom of the sewer somehow," said Cleary.[11]

"Larry didn't like Cleveland Arena," said Cleary. "He said the locker rooms were dingy. They were, but that was because the Barons' [minor-league hockey] owner owned the building, and we couldn't use their locker room. It wasn't as bad as some of the locker rooms at Cleveland Municipal Stadium. Some of the locker rooms there, you had to step outside to change your mind."[12]

Cleveland Arena was known as "The Icehouse" because it was the home of the American Hockey League's Cleveland Barons. Located on Euclid Avenue, several blocks east of the heart of downtown, the Arena was a seedy building with chicken wire shielding fans from wayward pucks in its hockey configuration. The ambient temperature fully lived up to its frigid nickname. The narrow wooden seats inside it were dilapidated. Showers in the locker room went from hot to cold with the flush of a toilet. Nobody ever said the place was about comfort for either fans or players.

Cleveland was a hockey town, with fans taking great pride in the Barons. In that era of the "Original Six" in the National Hockey League, the winner of the Calder Cup in the American Hockey League (AHL) playoffs was often called the "seventh-best team in hockey."

With the floor seating, the Arena could reach a capacity of 10,200. The view of fans in the balconies was often obscured by the pall of cigarette smoke that hung over the court. Moreover, the ceiling was low, so the noise had nowhere to go. The din was deafening when the Barons were skating into the corners and leveling the Hershey Bears and other rivals with savage checks.

By contrast, given the sparse crowds at Pipers games, fans' catcalls could clearly be heard by the players. So could an often red-faced Steinbrenner's denunciation of the referees.

Siegfried's Buckeyes, however, played in a new, state-of-the-art facility, St. John Arena, on the Ohio State campus. It was built specifically for basketball, unlike the multipurpose municipal arenas in big cities. No municipal building could match St. John Arena.

To overcome Siegfried's objections to the Arena, Steinbrenner laid out his own hasty blueprint, sketching majestic plans in the air with his hands. First, he pointed grandly to the empty land opposite Burke Lakefront Airport, a small facility for private planes. The land today is a Regional Transit Authority parking lot. In 1961, it was a weedy tangle that bordered the huge municipal parking lot near Municipal Stadium.

"Didn't you explain about the new 12,000-seat arena we're going to build there?" Steinbrenner asked, swiveling in his chair to glare at Cleary.

Taken aback, the general manager somehow did not let his eyes bulge and his mouth gape. "I hadn't had a chance to get to that," Cleary said.

"The way he explained it made perfect sense. The vacant land was at the eastern extremity of the municipal lot, used by 70,000 people for Browns games and Indians doubleheaders with the Yankees," Cleary said.

It was brilliant. The sunniness of George's vision shone on even the smallest detail. "It was going to be a state-of-the-art facility. Parking was taken care of. There would be a bus to the arena from the parking lot," said Cleary.

Siegfried was suitably impressed. "He was buying what George was selling," said Cleary. "You had to hand it to George. He could be creatively eloquent when he was wining and dining players."

After Siegfried left, Cleary said, "Why didn't you tell me this was in the works?"

"Because it's not," said Steinbrenner.

"He made it up out of the clouds above," said Cleary later.[13]

On May 24, 1961, Steinbrenner announced he had signed Siegfried to a no-cut contract. George won the battle with the Royals for Siegfried because he had his father's cutthroat competitiveness, explosive temper, and undiscouraged single-mindedness. The ancient Greeks got it right. It is the bad traits of fathers, not the good ones, which are usually passed on to their sons.

Unfortunately, daddy's money was not handed down in Steinbrenner's case. "George was a poor man's Mark Cuban," said Cleary of the stormy Dallas Mavericks owner.[14] With Siegfried, Steinbrenner must have felt that his castle in the air—the one he had simply made up, the one in his head, filled with fans cheering his team and shouting his praise—was close enough to touch. Such a brazen visionary had to have a great future in sports.

If he didn't wreck it.

CHAPTER 2

Ed Sweeny's Pipe Dream

The Pipers, the team with which McLendon broke the professional sports color barrier as a coach, were named for the pipes under your sink, not for the 11 pipers piping in the Christmas carol. If they had been named for bagpipes, a battle hymn would have been playing, given the relationship between Steinbrenner and McLendon.

The Pipers' original owner, an Irishman named Ed Sweeny, had been a plumber. His Hibernian heritage was why the "i" in the script "Pipers" on the Cleveland jerseys was dotted with a shamrock.

Sweeny was an engineer, strait-laced and with a crew cut, who dressed in accordance with the stereotype, all the way down to a pocket protector, bristling with pens. He loved basketball and, as an amateur boxer, the Sweet Science too. That was fitting for the sparring to come between Steinbrenner and McLendon.

So strong was the bond between the team's first owner and its groundbreaking coach that, on the day Steinbrenner forced McLendon out as Pipers coach, McLendon drove to Akron to thank Sweeny for all the old plumber had done for him.

As for the way the Pipers were built, Cleary said:

I wasn't a player in college at John Carroll, but I had a good eye for talent. Ed started thinking about having a team in the NIBL. So I got together a few local small-college players—John Hollis,

who had the career scoring record at Case Western Reserve, Jim
Dillings who played at Holy Cross with Bob Cousy, John Keshock
who was John Carroll's all-time leading scorer. We brought three
or four NIBL teams in and played them. We had a couple of ringers
like "Jumping" Johnny Green, who had been in the Air Force before
he played at Michigan State, and who played a couple of games
for us in 1959. We won a couple of games, so I told Ed that if we
could augment a couple of positions, we'd have a pretty good team.[1]

The biggest difference between the NIBL and ABL, said Cleary, "was
that we not only had young kids coming up the ladder, we had old ones
going down in the NIBL."[2]

One of the selling points of the NIBL was that it provided players
with a place from which to start business careers. It was considered an
intermediate step between college ball and the NBA.

"We had three off-season jobs for players with the Cleveland Recreation Department. The Carling brewery and Pepsi also chipped in [with
player jobs]," continued Cleary.[3] Before it relocated to Canada, Carling's
world headquarters were in Cleveland.

"Remember 'Hey, Mabel, Black Label'?" said Cleary, whistling before
repeating the old television commercial's words. "Mabel was a local girl.
She was from Cleveland."[4]

When the Pipers were readying to play in the NIBL, Tennessee State
was playing a game in Kentucky. Sweeny and Cleary drove down to
Villa Madonna College (now part of Thomas More College), located
just across the Ohio River from Cincinnati, to interview McLendon for
the job of Pipers coach.[5]

"Ed Sweeny and I had wound up signing six white guys and six blacks
for the NIBL Pipers," said Cleary. "We had the first black players in the
NIBL. One white and one black roomed together. That was John's rule.
Never two blacks or two whites.

"Four of the blacks were players from Tennessee State," continued
Cleary. "All of the whites were from south of the Mason-Dixon Line. Dan
Swartz was from Morehead [Kentucky] State, John Cox from Kentucky,
Gene Tormohlen from Tennessee, Jack Adams from Eastern Kentucky,

and Ralph Crossthwaite from Western Kentucky. We did John no favors."[6]

Only Cox would survive Steinbrenner's purges. Swartz and Tormohlen became leaders of the Piper's ABL playoff rivals, Washington/New York and Kansas City, respectively.

In 1959, the *Cleveland Press*'s Jack Clowser wrote that the Pipers of the NIBL "played the best basketball Cleveland has ever seen."

To assume control of this skilled basketball Utopia of racial enlightenment, Steinbrenner had sold his stock in Kinsman, the family business, to help raise the $25,000 needed by the group of investors he led. The sale and entry into the NIBL was approved on March 27, 1960.

"George was not buying any assets. We were deeply in debt," said Cleary. "He got together a bunch of little rich kids, Jim Stouffer and guys like that. George always thought he had the Stouffers' money [from their frozen foods empire] at his disposal. He was counting on all his friends to help, but they were all tied to their old men. And the old men had more sense than to throw money at a basketball team."[7]

The NIBL Pipers were a strong team from the outset, opening with a victory at the Akron Goodyears, whose team included Adrian "Odie" Smith, the 1966 NBA All-Star Game's Most Valuable Player while he was with the Cincinnati Royals. Eight future Hall of Famers played in the game, Smith's only All-Star appearance.

Smith grew up in poverty in Kentucky, in a house with no electricity and no indoor plumbing. He learned to shoot with a basketball made of his father's rolled-up socks.[8] With a thicker accent than most of his teammates at the University of Kentucky, where one of them was the Pipers' Cox, Smith almost *had* to let his play do his talking. On a Royals' flight, Smith once glanced idly out the window of the plane and then screamed, "Engine on fahrr! Engine on fahrr!" It took flight personnel a moment to realize he meant "Fire!" and then to land the aircraft safely.

Travel was an exotic adventure to many players in those days. Once, the NIBL Pipers landed in Seattle before playing the Buchan Bakers in the middle of the night. As the Pipers tramped wearily through the airline terminal, Cox saw an advertisement for flights to the 50th state of the union. "Hawaii—Only 4½ hours away by air!" the ad promised.

"How long do you think it would take to drive it?" Cox said.

"We have an off-day tomorrow," replied Tormohlen.[9]

The Pipers, however, also traveled by bus, an indignity to which NBA franchises now subject their young millionaires only for short trips, such as from Philadelphia to New York.

Actually, taking the bus was not always all that arduous, even in the NIBL. The Kansas City Steers, Cleveland's rival in two playoff series that each went the limit in the 1961–62 season, once toured with the Cab Calloway band, which served as pregame entertainment for three games between San Francisco and Los Angeles. The rigors of travel certainly did not harsh the musicians' mellow.

Calloway's band members brought their instruments, their tuxedos, their girdles to get into their tuxes, and their marijuana. Calloway, known as the "Hi De Ho Man" for the chorus of his hit song, "Minnie the Moocher," had previously recorded a song called "Reefer Man," about a man with a fondness for marijuana. In this case, life imitated art.

Clouds of smoke floated through the bus, smelling unlike anything the Marlboro Man would have enjoyed while riding through the purple sage. The basketball players were mystified by the sweet smoke. "Isn't that pretty funny smelling tobacco?" one said.

"They had no idea what it was," said Cleary, who—as we shall see, was found wanting by Steinbrenner through no real fault of his own— was fired and quickly hired by the competition.[10]

Despite recording the best first-year record in NIBL history in 1959–60, 24–10, losing in the postseason tournament to the eventual champion Peoria Cats (Caterpillars, named after the tractor company,) the Pipers' success did not guarantee that McLendon would still be their coach.

Sweeny, buried by debt, had released McLendon from his contract on April 6, 1960, but the coach told Chuck Heaton of the *Plain Dealer* that he wished to stay on and build "a club that can start the season out with a chance of winning the title."[11]

With Steinbrenner taking over the team, McLendon was reluctantly given the chance to do just that. It took George until April 22, 1960, 13 days after the victory at the Arena over Siegfried, West, and Robertson, to realize he had to live with McLendon as coach.

By 1961, so powerful were the Pipers that it seemed the only thing that could stop them was their new owner. The Pipers had already won the NIBL regular season championship, persevering amid travel rigors that would become commonplace in the ABL.

The NIBL championship tournament was supposed to conclude with a best-of-three championship format. In *A League of His Own,* an unaired, made-for-television documentary about McLendon produced by Cleveland State University, McLendon said Steinbrenner was unwilling to spend the money for such a prolonged series.

Although the Pipers were the regular season champions, the championship format was reduced to a single game, to be played in Denver.

The bigger box office receipts were a big consideration. The only competition for the sports fan's dollar in Denver was the quasi-major league American Football League's Broncos. The Pipers won anyway, 136–100. All five starters scored 20 or more points.

The Pipers followed that triumph by staying in Denver and winning the weeklong Amateur Athletic Union (AAU) national tournament. They were seeded second, despite dominating the NIBL.

"We won our first three games and had one to go when our expense account was cut off. Steinbrenner said we should drop out and come home. The players wanted to stay there and play whether they had jobs when they got back or not," McLendon said in the documentary.[12]

The Pipers moved into the YMCA, players and coach alike.

"McLendon was the only reason we could stay and play," said Ron Hamilton, a point guard on the NIBL Pipers. "He found a banker to loan him the money. We had prepared for the worst. We doubled up in the YMCA rooms. The thing is, Steinbrenner had done things like that before. Nothing was beneath George Steinbrenner. He was a crude man."[13]

With the loan of $722 to pay the hotel bill, despite all their privations, despite the interference of the team owner, the Pipers beat the Truckers, 107–96, before 10,500 screaming Denver fans.

If ever a home team was "homered," it was the Truckers in that game, Cleary concedes. The Pipers made 33 free throws, the Truckers only 18. Johnny Dee, the Denver coach, was in danger of losing his always hair-trigger temper. Dee had stormed onto the court in protest of a call in an earlier game. When told it would be technical foul for every step back to the bench, Dee had summoned two players to carry him off, like a minor despot being borne through the streets of a conquered city.

In the AAU championship game, when the Pipers were finally whistled for their first foul of the second half, Dee leaped to his feet, clutched his chest, staggered around, and fell to the floor, pretending to have a heart attack.

"Don't call your players to carry you, John," said the referee. "It's going to be the same [a technical foul] as when they carried you off the court before."[14]

The Pipers were the last NIBL champions. Escalating NBA salaries and the new ABL made it difficult for corporations to compete for the best college players. Although the Pipers had faced great distractions off the court, they had immense talent on it. Dan Swartz, the NIBL's Most Valuable Player in 1960–61, Jack Adams, Roger Taylor, and Ben Warley all made the 10-man AAU All-American Team.

"We won against all odds," said McLendon, recalling the travails of the week. "It was a miracle."[15]

CHAPTER 3

From Russia, with Fear and Grumbling

Because of McLendon's record in the NIBL, he was an easy choice to lead an All-Star team to the Soviet Union in 1961. The trip was delayed at the start by anti-American demonstrations in Moscow in the wake of the failed invasion by Cuban exiles of the Communist-controlled island at the Bay of Pigs in mid-April.

In the *Cleveland Press,* Clowser wrote, "[McLendon] typifies everything we hope to exhibit in international competition. This fine man has done honor to Cleveland with his mere presence the last two years. His magnificent sense of sportsmanship will make an indelible impression on the Russian people. The added, important factor is that he is a Negro. That gives our side an added propaganda weapon."

Adams, Barnhill, Warley, Swartz, and Roger Taylor, the Pipers' starting five, joined five other NIBL players and the handsome and erudite leading man of college basketball, Jerry Lucas. Only Lucas had had international experience, at the Rome Olympics in 1960.

The Americans won all eight games. The Pipers' Swartz led the scoring with 17 points in the first game, notable both for the dogged competitiveness of the Soviet National team in a 78–68 loss and the presence of cosmonaut Yuri Gagarin, who received a tumultuous ovation. The spaceman sat in the box at Moscow's National Sports Palace usually reserved for Premier Nikita Khrushchev and other Communist Party officials.

McLendon had to change tactics against the Soviets in the second game, a tense, 84–81 overtime victory. The Pipers only played perfunctory defense and simply tried to outscore the Soviets with their searing fast break.

There were only two problems in the Soviet homeland. The first was that McLendon was not a drinker. When the Russians were throwing down shots of vodka in the endless round of ceremonial toasts before each game, McLendon was surreptitiously watering every potted plant in the People's Paradise with vodka or substituting tap water for the alcohol and then taking hearty quaffs. The second and bigger problem was the pervasive air of suspicion that the Cold War fostered in the players.

Said Adams, the team's tough, hard-driving forward: "You have to remember the political situation then, Francis Gary Powers had been shot down in the U-2 spy plane the year before. The Bay of Pigs had just happened. We landed in Moscow and it took us forever to get processed through customs. When we got to the hotel off Red Square, we were told not to go anywhere, to stay in our rooms, not to mingle with the Russian people."[1]

Adams and his roommate, Swartz, both were country boys.

In Moscow, Adams and Swartz decided to step outside for a little fresh air. They didn't get more than a few feet from the door when they were surrounded by children, pushing souvenir pins at them, children with other tokens, 100 or more children in all, children behind them, in front of them, and all around them. It took Russian guards to rescue the American pair.

Told not to leave their room again, Swartz and Adams stretched out on their beds, talking about what had happened. Then the phone rang. On the other end of the line was, apparently, Natasha Fatale, spy, temptress, and arch-foe of Moose and Squirrel on the *Rocky and Bullwinkle Show* in the 1960s. The woman said she was from New York.

"She didn't sound like she was from New York, though," said Adams later.

"Be careful," Swartz had whispered.

Then, a moment later, as Adams stared uncomprehendingly at the phone, Swartz hissed, "Hang up!" Now they were really worried. Why were they getting called? Was it because they went outside against orders?

The phone rang two or three more times, but Swartz and Adams sat mute, staring at the instrument, afraid to answer. Then a knock sounded on their door. It was Natasha again, in the flesh. Neither player could understand what she was saying. When she finally walked off, her heels ringing on the floor, both sprang from bed and pushed all the heavy furniture in front of the door.

Then they sat behind their barricade, room lights blazing, frozen in fear, eyes locked on the door. "I don't think either one of us got much sleep," Adams said.

The next morning, they went down for breakfast. In the lobby, the director of their tour group said, "Why didn't you turn the lights off in your room? We called you about it several times and even sent the desk clerk up to tell you."[2]

Bigger problems loomed back home in Cleveland, Steinbrenner did not enjoy hearing the semipro team referred to as "amateurs" for propaganda purposes. The Pipers were not mentioned in game stories either.

He felt that if the team were to be presented as amateurs, amateurs they would be in fact as well as name, so he decided to withhold the Piper players' paychecks.

"I always had sort of a PR chip in me," Cleary said. "I would wait for the right opportunity and then tell George, 'You really don't want to do this.' He would never say, 'Well, maybe you're right,' but he would do what you suggested. He knew he looked bad after the Denver situation."[3]

"The best players got paid. I got paid. Barnhill got paid. Maybe the reserves that didn't play much didn't get paid," said Adams. "George took care of the best players."[4]

This did not mollify the player the *Plain Dealer*'s Chuck Heaton called "Deadeye" Dan Swartz. As a result of the paycheck dispute, Swartz, who would become a second team All-ABL player with the Los Angeles Jets and Washington/New York Tapers, was traded.

"Swartz was a real guy from Gooberville," Cleary said. "He chewed tobacco, so even when you were just talking to him, you'd get tobacco spit all over you."[5] The story goes that when George got rid of him, Swartz went in to see him, got jaw-to-jaw with him, and spat a chaw in George's face.

Peter Golenbock argues in *Wild, High and Tight,* a history of Steinbrenner and Billy Martin's years together with the Yankees, that the trade of Adams and Taylor in the second half of the ABL season was Steinbrenner's revenge for their complaining about paychecks on the Soviet Union trip.

At best, that is only partly true. Adams was part of a trade for six-foot-nine Connie Dierking, who filled a crying need for size in rebounding battles. Taylor was also traded for rebounding size in Ben Keller. At the same time, Swartz and, particularly, Adams, were angry about their pay.

"I know Steinbrenner is bidding exceptionally high for Larry Siegfried," Adams said before the Ohio State player agreed to terms. "He is willing to pay him much more than the other players who won a championship for him. I don't feel it is fair that he should do this at the other players' expense."[6]

For his part, McLendon returned to the United States, warning one and all that the Russians were a factor to be reckoned with in amateur basketball. In the most substantive of the columns he wrote for the *Cleveland Press,* McLendon spoke of the eagerness of Russian players and coaches to learn every technique at the clinics he conducted.

"I must admit an admiration for their extreme concern for the details of coaching. The same too for their attention to statistics. At least a half-dozen statisticians work on every piece of the sport that can be converted into figures," McLendon wrote.

Could modern "analytics"—the intricate use of metrics to track points per possession, to count fast break points and "second chance" (offensive rebound) points and points in the "paint" and other subtle measurements—have started in Russia? It's possible. The Russians had to catch up some way. Why not break each game down into quantifiable parts?

Thorough scouting certainly was used. McLendon marveled that the players and coaches from the Tbilisi Dynamo, who lost only 74–65 on an outdoor court in the southern part of the Soviet Union, flew to Moscow, 1,215 miles distant, to scout the two exhibition games there.

McLendon, however, was a modern Cassandra as he warned of the speed with which the Russians were coming. He would not be believed. American belief in supremacy even of college teams to seasoned international players came to a shocking end only 11 years later. After a finish that was so controversial the Americans refused the silver medal in protest, the Soviet Union beat a team of college players for the gold medal in Munich in 1972, 51–50.

The stakes became higher when the Pipers joined the fledgling ABL, giving Steinbrenner a bigger platform and a potential opportunity to wedge his team into the big time, the NBA.

Until McLendon died in 1999, however, the coach insisted that their differences sprang from competitive philosophy and not from racism. "I have been asked many times if George Steinbrenner was a racist," said McLendon. "No, he was not anti-black. He was anti-human. He treated everyone the same—like dogs."[7]

CHAPTER 4

George

The kidding was rough at the Round Table. There, the Pipers' AAU championship did not qualify as the miracle McLendon called it. The only miracles at Table 14 were the quantity of alcohol consumed, cigarettes smoked, rude jokes told, and deals made.

Although it was known as Table 14, it was not really a single table, but rather two small, Formica-topped tables that had been pushed together at the Pewter Mug at 207 Frankfort Avenue, just off Public Square in downtown Cleveland. The Mug aimed for an English pub atmosphere and was mid-priced. The clientele at Table 14, however, swung for the fences in the deals they made there. They were from big money.

As many as 60 onlookers could be standing around Table 14 at one time.

The regulars at The Table met probably 10,000 times over 40 years. Steinbrenner was a regular in the 1970s there and in the 1960s at the Theatrical Grill. The latter was a jazz club located at 711 Vincent Avenue, or "Short Vincent," as it was known. The downtown street was only 485 feet in length but far more extensive in local history.

According to Joe Mosbrook's *Jazzed in Cleveland,* Earl "Fatha" Hines, Gene Krupa, Wild Bill Davison, Oscar Peterson, Dorothy Donegan, Dizzy Gillespie, and Billy Butterfield played at the bandstand there, sometimes six nights a week, usually for a couple of weeks. Patrons included Edward G. Robinson, Victor Borge, Jimmy Durante, Judy Garland, Milton

Berle, Frank Sinatra, and Lorne Greene. Other celebrities were heavyweight champion Joe Louis, Hollywood bombshells Jayne Mansfield and Mamie Van Doren, actors Don Ameche and Yul Brynner, and sports figures Boog Powell, Blanton Collier, and that fistic night owl himself, Billy Martin.

Not that the Theatrical was hoity-toity. When a sign in the window said, "Closed for Alterations," regulars supposed that meant the employees were washing the glasses.

The business dynamic in Cleveland at the time was that of a fraternal network of hard-drinking, hard-driving young executives who got together to cut deals.

The recollections of Mike Roberts, a retired *Plain Dealer* city editor who later was editor of *Cleveland Magazine,* date from the 1970s sessions at the Pewter Mug. They are, however, the best way to experience vicariously the small, boisterous, clubby world in which lived Steinbrenner and the other luminaries of the city's sports and business world.

It was the same people, the same booze, and the same ambience as in the '60s. They just moved to another watering hole. Table 14 regulars at the Pewter Mug included Cleveland Browns owner Art Modell; Nick Miletti, who would eventually own the NBA Cleveland Cavaliers; and Steinbrenner. In later years, Richard Jacobs, future owner of the Cleveland Indians, would sit there, soaking up the lessons of arm twisting and sweet talking in negotiations.

Modell owned the most popular and successful team. But it was Steinbrenner who dominated the company. He was "King" George even then, first among equals.

"George was a very dynamic guy. I'd say he was the life of the party at The Table. He and Modell kidded each other all the time, in ways that you couldn't get away with today," said Roberts.[1]

"You're a Nazi!" Modell, a practicing Jew, would say to Steinbrenner.

"If I was, you wouldn't be around," Steinbrenner would retort.

One investor in the NIBL Pipers had been Sanford Gross, who owned Sheffield Bronze, a paint company that sponsored top-flight softball teams. One day, Steinbrenner was holding forth on sharp business practices, and the word "kike" came out of his mouth.

Gross said, "George, do you know what the definition of a kike is?"

Steinbrenner said no. Gross, rising from his seat, said, "The Jewish gentleman who just left the room." It was the only time Steinbrenner ever seemed embarrassed by what he said there.[2]

It was the era of "Mad Men." Alcohol flowed both at Table 14 and other haunts. (Steinbrenner was not a big drinker, although, in contrast to most of the others, he favored whiskey over beer.) Clouds of cigarette smoke twisted in the lights.

Frequently seen at table side was a prominent lawyer, Richard Lamb, who held a wedding party at Shaker Heights Country Club, running up a $25,000 bill in 1960s money. "Modell got so drunk he climbed into the backseat of his car to drive home," said Roberts.[3]

The rules at Table 14 were that each principal had to buy a round of drinks for all who were present. The round could cost more than a car payment.

"None of us reporters had any money. Al Bernstein, the owner of the Pewter Mug, used to treat us to a round," said Roberts.[4]

By getting out and meeting ordinary people, Modell and Steinbrenner were connected to the fans, probably more so than they would be by email or social media today. They would drive around, barhopping, finding out what was on the minds of regular fans.

The new generation of movers and shakers was made up of the scions of Cleveland's industrial titans. But at the start of the '60s, George could not tap into those resources, nor could most of his fellow Pipers investors.

Their fathers had been through a world war, the Depression, and shipwreck. They intimidated the younger generation. And no one was more intimidating than Henry Steinbrenner.

"One day, Jim Stouffer came into the Rockefeller Building, absolutely white-faced," said Cleary. "I asked him what was wrong, and he said he had seen George's father on the street and said, 'Hello, Henry.' He had never called him Henry in his life."[5]

The good impulses warred with the bad in the young Steinbrenner. Away from his father's scrutiny, George would prove in Major League Baseball to have no check on his temper, no governor on his voracious appetite for success, and no model for victory for years other than constant roster upheaval and front office purges.

"At the time I worked for him, he still had the old man to rein him in. That was one check on his behavior that was not around in later years," said Cleary.[6] The relationship between father and son was marked by volatility and by an undercurrent of competition. Shouting matches between the Steinbrenners occasionally erupted in the hallways outside their offices. The fights were often about getting the company's financial statements.

"I've got to have those sheets," the younger Steinbrenner, who needed the statements to determine his budget, screamed.

"I'll give them to you when I'm good and ready," shouted the elder Steinbrenner.

Other tenants stuck their heads out of other offices on different floors during a particularly loud decibel donnybrook between the two, wondering what was going on. After about five minutes of red-faced fury, the Steinbrenners ran out of steam.[7]

Basketball was George Steinbrenner's business only in his spare time. There wasn't much of it. Henry saw to that. Shipping was Henry's obsession. He was born and bred to the wind and waves and he was determined to make shipping George's obsession too. Once, when Henry barged into George's office and heard him discussing basketball, he strode straight to the desk and hung up the phone.

George's answer was not to confront his father, but to use deceit and subterfuge. A telephone on a separate line, which Steinbrenner had tucked in a drawer of his desk, rang feebly, because it was muffled by a pillow. Henry would sometimes leave George's office, wondering what caused the faint ringing in his ears.

With the secret phone allowing him to keep his schemes private, George rebelled against his domineering father and the business he ran.

Yet even after the ABL version of the Pipers moved their headquarters farther away, to the Union-Commerce Building on West 9th Street, Henry's opposition did not flag. Close proximity at the Rockefeller Building simply had made the fire burn hotter.

Cleary once went to see George about Pipers business in the Rockefeller Building and by misfortune ran into the guardian dragon, Henry. "I have him till five o'clock," Henry growled, dismissing Cleary.

The Pipers' general manager sat in the waiting room for 15 minutes, before wandering over to the accounting office. Whenever a Kinsman ship berthed in Cleveland, the captain would come to the accounting office and present a list of what he needed for his next voyage—sides of beef, potatoes by trenchermen's measure, and so on.

Ruth E. Webster, the firm's secretary, would give the captain the money for the provisions. "She wore a green eyeshade, like she was working for Scrooge and Marley," Cleary said. After one of the captains left, Cleary told her his sad story.

"Hmmm," she said, making only listening noises, as she punched the keys of an adding machine. Finally, she looked up. "If you think George's daddy is bad, you should have met *his* daddy. He was really something," she said.[8]

Above almost anything but victory, and maybe even more than that, George Steinbrenner valued loyalty. When Webster retired, he told the *Plain Dealer,* "She worked for our family for 40 years. That's the equivalent of 400 years with any other family."[9]

Soon he named one of the Kinsman vessels the *R. E. Webster* in her honor. That was George's sentimental side coming out.

Years later, he held a very successful benefit for Grambling football coach Eddie Robinson, not out of any ties to the great black coach, but simply because he admired Robinson and his record.

Steinbrenner's abusive side was the one that he more often presented in public. "He was the type of guy you had to stand up to," Cleary said. "He had a bully streak in him. Maybe it came from going to school away, at Culver Military Academy in Indiana, not to the Bay Village schools. Maybe it came from his dad being too busy or not being around."[10]

Like his father, George was a track athlete. George ran the same 220-yard low hurdles, a discontinued event today, as Henry did when he was a world-class hurdler at the Massachusetts Institute of Technology. George was fast at Williams College, a well-regarded liberal arts school in Massachusetts, but not world-class fast.

Henry did not tolerate second-place ribbons, nor did George. "George's father had been a great athlete," said Jack Adams.[11] Indeed,

Henry Steinbrenner won two national championships in the AAU, in the 110-yard high hurdles and the 220-yard low hurdles.

"His dad wanted George to be an athlete, but he lacked the ability to be a great one," said Adams to Peter Golenbock. "So his way of satisfying his father was to be an executive in sports. George was just part of an ownership group with the Pipers, but he sure liked everyone to know he was in charge."

"I know I say and do things I'm sorry for five minutes afterward," Steinbrenner admitted to Jack Clowser, the *Cleveland Press*'s astute basketball, golf, and Big Ten writer.

Steinbrenner's Piper years in the NIBL and ABL were the template for the employees he fired and rehired in later years—five times each for New York Yankees manager Billy Martin and the team's PR man, Harvey Greene.

It was a reflection of his desire, his need, to win, and that came with his gene pool as Henry Steinbrenner's son.

During his stint as Lockbourne Air Force Base's baseball coach, Steinbrenner gave Ohio State freshman first baseman Bob Sudyk, a member of the junior varsity team in 1953, his first look at the man he would cover on the Pipers' beat for the *Cleveland Press*. When the Ohio State team bus pulled into the parking lot at the Air Force base, Steinbrenner pounded on the doors with his fists, screaming, "Stay on the bus! Go home! We were supposed to play the varsity, not the JV scrubs!"

The "scrubs" won by a dozen runs. "It wasn't baseball, it was a nine-inning circus. With a baseball rulebook in hand to guide him, Lockbourne's screaming manager kept yelling at his players and berating the umpires," said Sudyk.

Afterward, the future newspaperman asked, "Who was that guy?"

"Lieutenant George M. Steinbrenner III," he was told.[12]

In Cleveland, George established a pattern of behavior for the people he broke and then tried to mend with money and belated kindness. The same affection Steinbrenner showed Ruth Webster would eventually go to Adams too.

"After he traded me, I was going to go back to Eastern Kentucky and get my Masters degree," said Adams, who eventually earned a doctorate in physical education. "George offered to get me a job on the basketball staff at Purdue with his connections there. But I wasn't going any place where they didn't want me, so I declined the offer."[13]

Perhaps it is best to think of the young George, on the cusp of his first plunge into professional sports ownership in the ABL, as a hurdler.

The hurdles serve as metaphor for overcoming the obstacles in life. The event is a daunting athletic test, requiring speed, explosiveness, balance, timing, and the ability to take a hit in clearing the barrier and keep going. The business side of sports requires the same qualities, sublimated to concerns of player acquisition, arena upkeep, and personnel manipulation. In today's track world, the so-called "rocker" hurdle, a lightweight barrier, can be hit and knocked down without the competitor losing his footing. In George's day, though, hurdles were wooden and heavy, and hitting them hurt. The effect was to disrupt timing and balance. When you hit a hurdle, you stayed hit.

George Steinbrenner stumbled over hurdle after hurdle with his temperament. He hit many others that Henry with his tight-fistedness put in his way. But in the young Steinbrenner's mental agility and his flexible concept of ethics, he always kept his eyes on the prize.

CHAPTER 5

John

From the hidden radio, its light keeping the monsters away from the little boy under the blanket, came a game that sounded like a joyous community festival. In some ways, it was.

Soft murmurs of incessantly pounded bongo drums, and a crowd singing and cheering as one, broke through the static. Blooming again were all the flowers of Kean's Little Garden, the gym at Tennessee State University, so called in honor of athletic director Henry Kean.

"When I was little, I was afraid of the dark, so my sister gave me her radio. I could put it under the covers and the soft orange glow of the tubes gave me the wizards of Tennessee A&I basketball," said Douglas Bates, a friend of the author of this book since their college days at Vanderbilt University.[1] (Tennessee A&I became Tennessee State in the 1960s, but for the purposes of this book, the updated name will be used.)

It is easy to love a team that is fashionable. The bandwagon always has room for more fans to climb aboard. It is harder to be a fan base of one. It is much harder still—and is largely a result of sweet, youthful innocence—to be a white fan in love with the black Tigers during the social apartheid of the South before the civil rights movement of the 1960s.

"In those days, the local newspapers did not cover this historically black school as they should have," said Bates, now a semiretired lawyer at the family firm in Centerville, Tennessee, an hour's drive west of Nashville. "But I remember reading in 1957 about the Tigers winning the

NAIA national championship. I knew they were black. I knew they were beating white schools. And I knew they were in Nashville. I knew they all had nicknames and played in a magical place called Kean's Little Garden.

"No one in my family or circle spoke of them. But I knew about them. It was as if I knew a secret, which was that over in some part of Nashville were men of magic who played in a little garden at home and on the road would travel so far away that no radio station could cover their games, and news of their victories would take a day or so to get to the papers, like news of a great naval victory that would finally reach the victor's home shores."[2]

It would take years before the secret of McLendon's genius in growing his Garden would be widely shared. But sports are a meritocracy, and it would belatedly happen.

Every year during February, Black History Month, stories crop up about the all-black starting five at Texas Western, which beat all-white Kentucky and its racist coach, Adolph Rupp, in the 1966 NCAA Tournament championship game. It was a landmark moment in basketball.

Yet McLendon had won his three straight small-college national championships in the 1950s, enduring bigotry of a much more pronounced nature. Majority-black schools were ineligible both for the NCAA and National Invitation Tournament, televised events with far higher profiles than the NAIA, until 1950.

In 1958, Converse sneakers' ambassador to basketball Chuck Taylor, whose name would become so synonymous with Converse All-Star shoes in the 1970s that they were called "Chucks," said after the 1958 NCAA final between Kentucky and Elgin Baylor's Seattle team in Louisville, Kentucky, "That little school down the road [Tennessee State] would beat both major-college finalists in the same afternoon."[3]

In the 1990s, during Black History Month, McLendon was the guest of Cleveland Cavaliers' general manager Wayne Embry at a home game.

By then, all the tempests Steinbrenner whipped up on basketball court were forgotten, turned, amid the spotlight George loved, on the Yankees, the most famous and successful sports franchise in American history.

By then, John McLendon was a respected cult figure in basketball, a racial and conceptual pioneer, honored on that night by Embry, the first black general manager in the NBA and thus a pioneer himself.

By then, McLendon had weathered the storms, and in 1978 had been enshrined as a "contributor" to basketball at Springfield, Massachusetts, the cradle of basketball, near the college of that name which he had almost attended.

By any measure, McLendon's story should be better known. But even in racially progressive Cleveland, with its string of racial pioneers in sports—from Marion Motley and Bill Willis with the Browns through Larry Doby and manager Frank Robinson with the Indians to Embry and former coach Lenny Wilkens with the Cavaliers in the first NBA front office with black leadership—McLendon and his Pipers are often overlooked.

To some extent, they were swallowed up in the cacophony of Steinbrenner's first venture into professional sports as a team owner.

"Dick Barnett and I have exchanged many emails on McLendon," said Embry of the Pipers' best player. "John is in the Hall of Fame as a contributor. We think he should be in as a coach too. His fast break philosophy alone makes him worthy. He learned the game from Dr. Naismith. Think about that! How many people can say something like that. And of course there was the racial pioneer aspect."[4]

John McLendon wasn't a big track and field fan, but he had cleared high hurdles all his life. McLendon was born in 1915 in Hiawatha, Kansas. As Milton S. Katz points out in his excellent biography *Breaking Through: John B. McLendon, Basketball Legend and Racial Pioneer,* McLendon's mother never let him smoke or drink coffee, tea, or alcoholic beverages. She never let him have a pillow either. She knew he wanted to be a coach, and she said, "Coaches should have straight shoulders."

For all her son's success, she never quite understood the value of basketball. "It's foolish to turn so much of your life over to what five people do with a ball," McLendon recalled his mother saying in *A League of His Own: The John McLendon Story*.

The last living protégé of Naismith, McLendon attended Kansas rather than Springfield College on the advice of his father, who noted that Naismith had invented the game and was teaching there. Basketball knowledge was unlikely to be stored in as impressive a fashion in the bricks and mortar of the Springfield campus.

At Kansas, McLendon integrated the swimming pool after several times being denied the chance to swim in the same water white students used. The pool would be drained overnight after his scheduled session. McLendon would swim again the next day. The pool would be drained. He would swim again.

Kansas finally gave up.

Throughout this time, he was supported by his campus adviser, Naismith, whose advocacy of integration has never gotten as much attention as the peach basket he hung on the Springfield balcony, although it certainly should.

"Naismith didn't know anything about color or nationality. Everything I did when I was coaching can be traced back to him," said McLendon.

McLendon was not an outstanding player in basketball. He was too small. Gymnastics was his sport in high school. Jarvis (Kansas) Junior College was the only varsity basketball team for which he played. A career-high 20 points on the fast break one day turned McLendon into a proponent of running basketball. His teams practiced three times a day, which led to a player rebellion in his last professional stop with the American Basketball Association's Denver Nuggets.

Strategically, he heeded Naismith's injunction to "follow the ball," attacking the basket when his team had it and disrupting the other team with a pressing defense when he didn't.

As fast as he liked to play, McLendon realized there were times when the foot had to be taken off the gas. He devised the "two in a corner" delay game, which became the seed of Dean Smith's famous "four corners" stall at North Carolina. McLendon said Smith took his idea "and made it a victim of inflation."

McLendon coached Basketball Hall of Famer Sam Jones of the Celtics and Charles "Tex" Harrison of the Harlem Globetrotters at North Carolina Central and Walt Frazier's backcourt mate, Barnett, at Tennessee State.

McLendon was one of the men who brought together North Carolina Central and Duke Medical School team in the famous "Secret Game" of March 14, 1944, the first integrated college game in the South. Tennessee State won, 88–44. In the Cleveland State documentary, McLendon admitted resentment of segregation led him to "double them up [on the scoreboard]." Afterwards, the teams played an informal scrimmage, with black and white players on the same teams.

Following his Pipers years, after a tour of popularizing basketball around the world for the U.S. State Department, McLendon coached the Cleveland State men's team, becoming the first black coach at a majority white college. His tenure was not a success. "Ohio State spends more money on the stadium grass than we had in our entire recruiting budget," McLendon said.[5]

Still, so respected was he in basketball circles that he actually got Julius "Dr. J" Erving to make a recruiting visit. Years later, when Erving played Kareem Abdul-Jabbar in a made-for-television exhibition, McLendon was on the sideline as Erving's "coach."

As different as were McLendon and Steinbrenner, the coach and the Pipers' first owner, Sweeny, were similar. "Ed hired him because John McLendon was Sweeney's kind of guy. By that I mean he was an open-hearted guy," Cleary said.[6]

In closed-door meetings with the sports editors of the *Plain Dealer, Cleveland Press,* and *Cleveland News* (the latter soon to close its doors), Sweeny heard a chorus of alarm. All of the opinion makers were convinced Cleveland was not ready for a black coach of an integrated team. It only made Sweeny more determined to go ahead with his plan.

In a *Plain Dealer Sunday Magazine* feature about McLendon, the main headline read: "New Coach with an Old Goal: Pipers Import from South Aims to Revive Basketball Interest Here."[7]

The story actually began with the dictionary definition of the sport:

"BASKETBALL—A game, usually played indoors, in which each of two contesting teams endeavors to toss an inflated ball into an elevated goal, originally an ordinary fruit basket, defended by the opponents. The game was invented in 1891 by James Naismith at the YMCA College in Springfield, Massachusetts."

The story said, "Cleveland is a tough basketball nut to crack, and McLendon knows it."

Professional basketball began in Cleveland in the Roaring Twenties with a team called the Cleveland Rosenbluths. Sponsored by a men's clothing store, the "Rosies" won three championships in the speakeasy era.

Their roster eventually resembled New York's Original Celtics, some of whose players simply relocated to the Midwest. It included Joe Lapchick, future Basketball Hall of Famer and coach of St. John's University and the New York Knicks. Also a "Rosie" was Dutch Dehnert, a pioneer of pivot play.

Said the story of flagging interest in basketball in Cleveland: "Something happened when the years caught up with Dutch Dehnert, Joe Lapchick, Carl Husta, et al."[8]

It was not revived by the Cleveland Rebels, who played the 1946–47 season in the Basketball Association of America, a forerunner of the NBA. The Rebels had Kenny Sailors, a star on the University of Wyoming's NCAA championship team, Most Outstanding Player of the 1943 NCAA Tournament for the champion Cowboys, a three-time All-American, and one of the first practitioners of the jump shot. Imagine the coverage across all types of media he would have gotten today.

Dehnert was one of the two coaches of the Rebels.

Their popularity was not boosted by the *Plain Dealer* sports editor Gordon Cobbledick's dislike of basketball and the constant reference he made to them as the "ugh! Rebels."

The Rebels posted a 30–30 record in the 1946–47 season. "They proceeded to lay a big, fat egg," charged Cobbledick in a column 15 years later, devoted to his lukewarm feelings about the Pipers.

Those "egg" layers and ugh-ers topped the Cavaliers in winning percentage 24 times their first 44 seasons.

Rabid basketball interest in Ohio was confined at the time to the southwestern corner of the state. The University of Cincinnati would be a great power in the late 1950s and early 1960s because of Oscar Robertson's presence on the roster in the first case and the Bearcats' two giant-killing victories in the NCAA Championship Game against Ohio State and Lucas in the second.

The close proximity of basketball-crazed Indiana and of Adolph Rupp's mighty teams at the University of Kentucky helped create this disconnect from the rest of football-mad Ohio. The *Plain Dealer* magazine story said McLendon and Ed Sweeny hoped "the germs of basketballitis, which makes maniacs out of the good citizens of Indiana and Illinois at certain seasons, are drifting this way on the prevailing wind from the west."

The article ended with an affecting scene that showed McLendon's humility: "In his years at North Carolina College, McLendon and his squad used to spend the holidays refinishing the gym's floors. Guess what he has been doing during his spare time this fall—helping to sand the boards at the Arena."[9]

Expectations for the Pipers were certainly low. McLendon had spent his entire life surprising people, however.

After the victory on April 9, 1960, at the Arena over "the Big O" (Robertson) and a college all-star team, the game that left Siegfried with such a negative impression of its creature comforts, Steinbrenner still delayed in hiring.

"George was not a racist, but he wanted a bigger name as his coach," Cleary said. "He was used to an Ivy League kind of coach. John was too country for George, not too black."[10]

In the *Plain Dealer*, Jimmy Doyle quoted "Talkative" Thomas Walsh, the PR man for the Harlem Globetrotters, beating the drums for Globetrotters-Pipers doubleheader early in the season. "Basketball is the truly American game, invented by the great Dr. Naismith," said Thomas, which ignores the fact that Naismith was a Canadian and thus not so heavily burdened with America's racial baggage. "Whereas baseball," Thomas continued, "derives from the old English game of rounders, soccer from rugby, Scotland gave us golf and so on."[11]

McLendon was a great figure in the society America was to become. His position as a racial pioneer and his quiet, dignified demeanor, combined with the racial progressiveness in Cleveland, made McLendon a popular figure among the newspapermen who covered him.

The *Cleveland Press*'s Clowser explored the roots of the coach's game-day deportment in a 1959 column. "Self-control is a very worthwhile discipline," McLendon told Clowser. "Years ago, I learned that if a coach pops off, throws his arms around and stomps the floor, he's setting a bad example for the student body. They often react with a show of booing for the official or the other team. In my early years, I often went to the [courtside] microphone to request order from the students. When [rival teams] started to call us the 'House of Sportsmanship,' I was extremely proud."

Containing his anger was one hurdle. The only time he openly surrendered to it was his admission that he ran the score up against the Duke medical school.

In general, McLendon clung to a benign view of the world, expecting people to reform over time. "I've reached the stage of experience where I'm no longer sensitive," McLendon told *Cleveland Press* sportswriter Ben Flieger. "My approach is to assume that everyone in any situation has intelligence. And that intelligence brings with it a certain amount of fairness."

Test after test would challenge that optimistic viewpoint.

"One of the places we played in the NIBL was in Oklahoma against the Phillips 66ers," said Cleary. "We couldn't even stay in the town of Bartlesville, Oklahoma, overnight. No hotel would have us. We ate in the executive dining room, reserved for Phillips 66's top executives. The players ate the best meals of their lives there, steaks cooked to order and everything."[12]

One of Phillips executives told McLendon, "Coach, that's the best bunch of niggers we ever had in here."

"John didn't say anything. He was from the South. He was used to it," said Cleary.[13]

It was a different world than the one Cleary knew. "I was in the navy in Georgia when my first child was born down there," said Cleary. "We went to a doctor in town who had a white entrance and a colored one. Same with the water fountains. Same with everything. But the races lived next to each other."[14]

The heady Jack Adams was an extension of his coach on the floor and off. Even more so was point guard Ron Hamilton.

Once, Adams took the team to Kansas City for a game. McLendon was going to scout another team the night before the game. "We got to the hotel and all the white players had nice rooms. The black players asked me to come up and look at their rooms. They were all on the top floor. No room had a TV in it and some didn't have a desk or a couch," said Adams. Hotel management was fearful the black players would steal the TV sets. "I went down to the desk in the lobby and said to move those players or we'd leave. They put the black players in rooms like everyone else," said Adams.[15]

Cleveland itself was not a hotbed of racial enlightenment in the 1960s, either.

The NIBL Pipers traded guard Roger Taylor, who was white and lived in an apartment around 117th Street and Clifton Avenue, on Cleveland's predominately white West Side. The female landlady wasn't going to let Taylor out of his lease. The players, however, hatched a scheme. Barnhill and Hamilton, both of whom were black, accompanied Taylor to a meeting with the woman, at which they claimed they had sublet the apartment from Taylor.

"These teammates of mine will take over the lease," said Taylor.

"The lease is no longer a problem," the landlady said, tearing it up.[16] These were the barriers McLendon had to clear even in a city with a reputation for tolerance, these the splinters of prejudice he tried to sand to smoothness.

Tormohlen said:

I grew up on a farm with parents who taught me better than to judge a man by his color. I was a tall guy anyway, but I always hoped I was bigger than any of that stuff.

There were times when I was the only white player at practice. Didn't matter. I was just part of the team. At that time, a lot of the brothers held it against you if you were white. Johnny never put up with any of that either.

We once played an exhibition game somewhere in the South. I went out to eat with three black teammates. The owner told me you had to have a reservation. There were maybe 100 empty tables. I didn't say anything. We just left. Some people still have feelings [racism] like that. But most have changed for the better.[17]

McLendon was an example to his players, even the white ones. "He was a father figure to us. That's the way most of us felt about him," said Tormohlen. Then, his voice breaking, Tormohlen said, "Oh, Johnny! May he rest in peace. What a fine man."[18]

CHAPTER 6

George and John

Cleveland Press editorial cartoonist Lou Darvas drew a small, elfin bagpiper in a kilt and tam o'shanter as the Pipers' mascot. In an NIBL program drawing, the unnamed musician stood knee-high to the towering player next to him. It gave a jaunty, heather-on-the-hill flair to a team named for plumbing equipment. But the real "pipes," the conduits of front office interaction, were always destined to burst, given the tension between McLendon and Steinbrenner.

"George traded me because he wanted big names," said Tormohlen. "George didn't want Johnny either because he wanted stars. The NBA has always been that way with some teams—the Lakers, for example, the Knicks right now too. Even now, you can't cross an owner. It's millionaires messing with billionaires now, but the principle is eternal."[1]

The situation worsened because the Pipers' coach and their owner were complete opposites in temperament. McLendon simply did not challenge bombast or rudeness. It rolled off the protective carapace he had built as a black man in the South. Steinbrenner was filled with the qualities McLendon had learned to avoid or to shed before they infected him.

In the 1960s, such athletes as Muhammad Ali and the Cleveland Browns' Jim Brown made strident protests against racism, creating new conversations on the national problem. McLendon, however was the same type of pioneer in basketball that Jackie Robinson had been in baseball.

"Are you looking for a Negro who is afraid to fight back," Robinson asked the Brooklyn Dodgers' visionary general manager, Branch Rickey.

Rickey exploded. "I'm looking for a ballplayer with guts enough not to fight back."[2]

McLendon learned to anticipate trouble and avoid it. A black man traveling through the Jim Crow South with a black basketball team had to be careful. McLendon knew which gas stations would allow his players to use the restroom and which would not. To avoid trouble at restaurants, the Tennessee State cafeteria prepared box lunches for the players before they left for away games.

In the NIBL, the team was on a bus, waiting to leave for a game one day, when a beautiful woman walked past. Forward Johnny Cox opened the window by his seat and shrieked the long notes known as a wolf whistle. "Now, Johnny. That's somebody's mother," reprimanded McLendon.[3]

The gentlemanly coach eventually got the nickname of "Mousy" from his players from his reluctance to protest even the worst of calls. His unobtrusive demeanor was a coping mechanism. "On the road, we never saw him except at the game or a practice," said Adams. "That was because of what John had gone through in Kansas and down in North Carolina. He stayed in his room. That way, he stayed out of situations that could have been trouble."[4]

A Plain Dealer story depicted McLendon as much as a moral exemplar as a coach. "Coach McLendon insists his pros lead lives conducive to staying power," it read. "They do not drink, smoke or gamble, and there is a curfew two hours and 15 minutes after the end of games—including those played at home."[5]

It's unclear if all McLendon's rules were obeyed. Dick Barnett, for example, was a dedicated card shark.

"He [McLendon] demonstrated directly the importance of personal character to his players," said Barnett. "When you look at the way he lived his life, the example he set and the roadways he took, they were a great influence on me. As a coach, he never raised his voice. He wasn't one to jump up and protest calls. He was trying to relay his self-discipline to others."[6]

For his part, Steinbrenner could never understand why McLendon did not leap to his feet and perform the sort of ruckus-raising "acrobatics" of which *Plain Dealer* sports editor Cobbledick accused Kansas City's coach, Jack McMahon. With every shouted protest and every aggrieved leap to his feet, McMahon showed everyone he *cared*.

The mystery to George was why McLendon didn't. The mystery to McLendon was why an owner so obsessed with victory, so obstructed it.

McLendon's Pipers were built to win now. They were not a traditional expansion team. On the roster were many of McLendon's Tennessee State players—John "Rabbit" Barnhill, so named for his speed, and Ben Warley, a strong rebounder, and reserve Rossie Johnson. Another substitute, Gus Guydon, later the coach at Morgan State, a historically black college, had played with Dick Barnett in high school.

Barnett himself had jumped from Syracuse of the NBA to the ABL Pipers because of the chance again to play for his old coach. The Pipers therefore had great cohesion because so many of the players knew McLendon's system.

The concept of "floor balance"—keeping a backcourt man out of the usual rebounding scrum in order to set up an early line of defense against the fast break—was not a big factor in that offensive era of astronomical scoring and corresponding shot totals.

Players crashed the boards to try to retain possession of the ball. This made them vulnerable to the devastating counterattack of McLendon's fast break. As long as the Pipers could get a decent share of the rebounds, they would win. That would become a critical weakness of the team in the ABL and a sore point in the discussions about tactical basketball between Steinbrenner and McLendon.

McLendon was a man with a strong sense of personal dignity that could not be outwardly affected by bigotry and racism. If he could not avoid a confrontation, he never let an antagonist see him sweat during it. His determination could not be drained away as easily as a swimming pool's water.

Steinbrenner was a man with no check on his temper, one who was subject to enormous mood swings depending on the bounce of a ball. He invaded the locker room, the preserve of his coach and players, to denounce players after losses, and then squired them out to victory meals at other times. Confrontation came as easily as breathing to Steinbrenner. Nakedly ambitious, he could drown common decency in the torrents of his invective.

Money, the need for it, the resolve to do almost anything to get it, had been the root of the pair's problems at the AAU tournament and during the tour of the Soviet Union. The need would become all consuming as Steinbrenner upped the ante in the ABL and then maneuvered to gain entry into the NBA. He always needed more, so there were always more withheld paychecks, more threats, and more insults.

"The bank we dealt with was on the first floor of the Rockefeller Building," said Cleary. "On payday, when I got that paycheck, I didn't wait for the elevator. I ran down the stairs. I knew there was only so much money in that till. I got my money before the players got theirs."[7]

Steinbrenner's financial troubles were the most obvious causes of his eventual breakup with McLendon. But it was never going to work, anyway. They were opposites that detracted.

CHAPTER 7

The League of the Extraordinary Aspiration

The American Basketball League was made of vision and delusion with more than a dash of spite. It lived and died amid the penury such a makeshift enterprise wrought.

Although Harlem Globetrotters owner Abe Saperstein was actually maneuvering to form a new league before the NBA transferred the Minneapolis franchise to Los Angeles, as Murry Nelson shows in his book *Abe Saperstein and the American Basketball League, 1960–1963,* the basketball impresario was angling for a Southern California franchise in the NBA too.

Saperstein stood at five foot three and was known as "Little Caesar" for his small stature and for the black sports empire he ran with the Harlem Globetrotters. Imagine his fury in 1960 when he did not get the new NBA franchise in Los Angeles. Saperstein thought he had been promised the West Coast market in return for his willingness to boost NBA teams' gate receipts by scheduling the Globetrotters as part of doubleheaders. After NBA commissioner Maurice Podoloff let Lakers owner Bob Short move his team to Los Angeles instead—and because preliminary explorations to form a new league were already underway—the ABL became Saperstein's response to the snub.

The emotional response was backed by the feeling Saperstein had that, with his marketing and promotional expertise, his new league could challenge the NBA after a year or two. It did not, however, last that long. Several teams in the NBA at the time were reeling financially.

The losses would mount without the lure of the Globetrotters to boost the gate. But the ABL hemorrhaged debt. In a war of attrition, its owner did not have deep enough pockets.

The ABL was, however, a fascinating league. It was visionary and short-sighted.

It was far-flung and tight-fisted.

It was very badly run and surprisingly well played.

It was plagued by owners who were both overwrought (such as Steinbrenner) and undercapitalized (Steinbrenner again).

It was a liberation movement, providing new jobs, opening professional basketball to more players than the NBA had room for. Yet the owner of the top ABL team, the Pipers, occasionally kept his players in unpaid servitude.

The ABL's rules were contradictory, encouraging finesse and force, marksmanship and mayhem. The ABL advertised the basketball of tomorrow with emphases on spacing on the court, ball movement, and long-range marksmanship, but it could only draw big crowds with black clowns—Saperstein's Harlem Globetrotters—playing racially stereotyped roles in doubleheaders.

It had a split season with first half and second half races in both East and West divisions. The winner of the midseason playoffs was guaranteed a spot in the finals. This is a format used mostly in minor league baseball. Major League Baseball borrowed it in the strike-shortened season of 1981.

Because of the collapse of the Los Angeles Jets and the transfer during the season of the Washington Tapers, the second half playoffs in the shrunken league involved every team still standing in a total of five sudden-death games until only one challenger was left to meet the first half champion in a final series.

It was a renegade league, reviving the glory days of big Bill Spivey, a Kentucky player, the tallest in the ABL at seven feet one, who was caught in the point-shaving scandal of 1951 and of St. John's Tony Jackson, ensnared in 1960's similar scandal.

Another such exile, Sylvester "Sy" Blye, a New York playground star, was playing at Seattle University, a power at the time. In need of money,

Blye was moonlighting under an assumed name with the Harlem Clowns, an ersatz Globetrotters team, whose players were paid.

There are two versions of how Blye was found out. One is that he was identified in a game photo. But the one that absolutely screams ABL screwiness—"There weren't a lot of Einsteins in the league," said Cleary[1]—is that, asked for his autograph after a game in Canada, Blye obligingly signed his real name.

The ABL left its mark in several ways:

- McLendon refuted racist stereotypes and commanded the respect of both his black and white players, the white sporting press, and virtually everyone except Steinbrenner.
- Bill Sharman, a Hall of Fame player who replaced McLendon in midseason with the team in a deep hole, coached the Pipers to the ABL's only full-season championship. It was the first of three he won in three different leagues—ABL, ABA, and NBA. Sharman eventually would be enshrined in Springfield, Massachusetts, as a coach too.
- The three-point shot, used at first solely as a comeback mechanism, began to exert a greater effect as players adjusted to the distance, showing the first signs of the transformative influence it would have on modern basketball.
- The most famous renegade of them all, the extravagantly talented prodigy Cornelius L. Hawkins, known as "Connie" to the sportswriters and as the "Hawk" on the playgrounds of New York, became a true superstar, although he was not recognized as such by most of the reporters who covered the ABL. Hawkins demonstrated conclusively that a teenager could possess such startling innate ability and instincts that he could play professional basketball at a very high level. The Hawk was the first LeBron James.
- Finally, the league featured Steinbrenner in all his loud, youthful fury. He already had most of the traits of the "Boss" whose New York Yankees dominated baseball when he was finally in possession of the family fortune.

The ringmaster of all this, although he almost never tamed his fractious team owners, was the diminutive Saperstein, a man whose girth rivaled his height. Saperstein is the shortest member of the Basketball Hall of Fame. In the 1950s, Abraham M. Saperstein was the most successful and influential executive in basketball. His Harlem Globetrotters, although founded in 1927, would not play an actual "home" game in Harlem until 1968. "Harlem" was an obvious code word, signaling that the players were black, and "Globetrotters" was a name that became both an itinerary for them and an omen for the eventual worldwide reach of basketball.

The Trotters' emphasis on ball handling, on sleight-of-hand fakes, and flamboyant passes anticipated the dribbling mastery and thread-needle passes of such white NBA stars as Bob Cousy and "Pistol" Pete Maravich, as well as the Pistons of Isiah Thomas, the Cavaliers of LeBron James, and the glitzy "Showtime" Lakers of Magic Johnson.

They and their patsies, the Washington Generals, would play the first game of NBA and, later, ABL doubleheaders. Fans would leave in droves before the real game, the second one, began. To lure casual fans, musical attractions such as Cab Calloway and others would perform. In a way, such entertainment foreshadowed the stage shows at Super Bowl half-times and the hip-hop party atmosphere of the NBA All-Star Game now. The counter-cultural music of the early 1950s—black, improvisational, and, like the Hi-De-Ho Man, pharmaceutically enhanced—was jazz.

Bill Veeck, the madcap promoter and owner of the Cleveland Indians' last World Series champions in 1948, had many imitators, but few equals. ABL owners certainly tried, though.

Wrote Sudyk, the former Ohio State JV first baseman who was then the 27-year-old beat writer for the *Cleveland Press,* "Now spectators at basketball matches can see Barnum and Bailey's best baggy-pantsed buffoons, tap dancers, acrobats, a husband and wife duo bopping a punching bag, fly casting, table tennis, badminton, hula dancers, rock 'n roll warblers, talking crows, fashions shows and community sings."

Sudyk noted that the Pipers had already featured "trampoline acrobats, a Japanese cyclist, a jazzy band, Cab Calloway and his review, a twist contest, indoor soccer, the Letter Carriers' band and baton twirling."

The last was curtailed "since one teenager lost sight of her spinning baton high up in the lights of Public Hall and got brained while a band played, 'Hey, Look Me Over.'"

Animal acts at the time were discouraged. This was probably a good thing. In the 1970s, Veeck disciple Pat Williams of the Philadelphia 76ers hired as halftime entertainment one Pepper, the Singing Pig. The show was not an artistic success. The *Daily News*'s headline read: "Williams Has His Own Bay of Pigs." The *Inquirer*'s headline: "Sixers Win; Pig Booed."

Few established NBA players joined the ABL, so it was mostly made up of players from the teams of the crumbling NIBL and the minor Eastern League.

The defending NBA champion Boston Celtics had only one rookie in 1961, top draft choice Tom "Satch" Sanders. Their leading Eastern Division challengers, the Philadelphia Warriors, had only two—Al Attles and Bill "Pickles" Kennedy. Only Attles played much.

There were similar stories around the league. Of the younger players who did jump leagues, Kenny Sears left the New York Knicks for the San Francisco Saints and Barnett after much litigation moved from Syracuse to Cleveland. In all cases, as Nelson notes, injunctions were obtained, countersuits were filed, and the cases were settled out of court. It was a strategy of attrition, bleeding the ABL owners dry through the courts.

Nat "Sweetwater" Clifton, a former Knick and a Globetrotter star, played for Saperstein's Majors. George Yardley, the first NBA player to score over 2,000 points (2,001, to be exact) with the 1957–58 Detroit Pistons, came out of retirement and played home games for the Los Angeles Jets. His engineering business kept him from going on the road.

Sharman renounced his retirement and played and coached in Los Angeles, then confined himself to the bench as coach only in Cleveland. A great player in Boston, Sharman's move to the new league infuriated Celtics owner Walter Brown.

In addition, there was faded college star Bevo Francis, who scored two points for the Pipers in his ABL career. Finally, athletic "crossovers" appeared in the ABL years before Bo Jackson or Deion Sanders, who played in both the NFL and Major League Baseball players in the 1990s.

NFL wide receiver, pogo-sticking, high-jumping R. C. Owens of the 49ers, who invented the lob-pass "alley-oop" play with quarterback

Y. A. Tittle, scored four points in four games for the San Francisco Saints. Owens had played basketball at the College of Idaho, where his room-mate was Elgin Baylor. Owens had also played on Seattle's NIBL team, the Buchan Bakers.

Washington/New York forward, six-foot-eight Gene Conley was a four-time All-Star as a pitcher in baseball and a former Boston Celtic.

As for the top players who had exhausted their collegiate eligibility, the only big name to sign with the ABL was Siegfried.

Except for Los Angeles, chosen because of Saperstein's personal animus to the NBA, and Chicago, selected because he lived there, the commissioner chose virgin territories for the ABL teams. Cleveland, Washington and San Francisco had no pro basketball at the time. All received NBA teams after the ABL folded. Kansas City got the relocated Rochester Royals, reincarnated as the Kings, then lost them to Sacramento. Pittsburgh almost got an NBA franchise (with Sharman as coach) before joining the ABL.

The ABL sprawled from Long Island (to which the Washington franchise relocated in the middle of the 1961–62 season) to Hawaii.

Saperstein raided the dying NIBL, convincing Steinbrenner, easily the most outspoken and controversial of the ABL's owners, and Paul Cohen, owner of the New York Tapers (named for Cohen's company, which made electronic tape) of the factory league to take their teams into the new league.

Cohen, for his part, appears to have been an impulsive sort. He briefly considered coaching the team himself after firing his NIBL coach, Elmer Ripley, a former coach at Cleveland's John Carroll University, among other schools.

Saperstein himself owned the Chicago Majors, which, in his position as commissioner, once put him in the ludicrous position of ruling on a protested game involving Chicago. All season, he shuttled players between the Globetrotters' roster and the Majors, creating in effect his own personal farm system.

Saperstein was also secretly involved in the ownership of other ABL clubs, including for a time San Francisco.

The other teams and owners were Art Kim's Hawaii Chiefs, Ken Krueger's Kansas City Steers, Len Corbosiero's Los Angeles Jets, George McKeon's San

Francisco Saints, and Lenny Littman's Pittsburgh Renaissance. Celebrity investors included Bing Crosby with the Jets and baseball's Stan Musial with Kansas City.

The Pittsburgh team was known in headlines and to their few fans as the Rens, despite Hawkins's resemblance in rebounding and scoring to the sculpting/painting multitasking of the Italian Renaissance master, Michelangelo.

Hawaii's Kim was a close friend of Saperstein. The structure of the league was, in fact, honeycombed with Saperstein loyalists. It probably contributed to the weak, vacillating way in which Saperstein ran the league. He had little experience with hard decisions, having always enjoyed the company of yes-men and basketball clowns.

Former pro players who coached in the ABL were Andy Phillip (Chicago, a Hall of Fame NBA player and a member of the University of Illinois's "Whiz Kids" of 1942–43); Red Rocha (a native of the 50th state and thus perfect for Hawaii); Jack McMahon (Kansas City, a former player for St. Louis across the state); Neil Johnston (Pittsburgh, who had been a hook shot artist with the Philadelphia Warriors); and Stan Stutz (Washington, after a playing career in an NBA precursor, the Basketball Association of America, or BAA).

The University of San Francisco's coach of the K. C. Jones–Bill Russell dynasty, Phil Woolpert, led the San Francisco Saints until he was fired early in the season.

Of those coaches, Johnston unretired for five games, scoring 19 points in one of them with his ambidextrous hook shots, and Sharman played in 19 games with the Jets as player-coach. One of the great free throw shooters ever, Sharman made 34 of 37, or 91.9 percent, in the ABL.

The ABL teams, perhaps because of the frantic, regionalized schedules and the sparse attendance almost everywhere, were nowhere near as dominant at home as is the usual case in basketball. The flexible definition of a "home" game, as teams barnstormed to try to draw new fans, hurt the emotional investment of those fans who did attend. The NBA used the same strategy, but not to the ABL's extent. Hawaii once played a "home" game in Jacksonville, Florida.

Uline Arena in Washington, D.C., renamed Washington Coliseum, was the most dilapidated building in the league with cracks in the boards of the basketball court, which let condensation seep through from the hockey ice that lay underneath. Players were always doing pratfalls on its floor.

The Tapers' midseason move to Commack Arena on Long Island was little better. Commack, 60 miles from New York City, was hard to find, and featured ramshackle bleachers more fitting for a high school game. It was more a part of the lucrative New York market than Hawaii or San Francisco, but not much more.

The Kansas City Steers played in Municipal Auditorium, a building that hosted three of the first four NCAA Final Fours and eight in all, more than any other arena. The Chicago Majors played in Chicago Stadium, the biggest and newest indoor facility in the city because of the lure of Saperstein's Globetrotters as part of doubleheaders. The expansion NBA team was shunted off to the International Amphitheatre near the stockyards and bore the appropriate name, the Packers.

Olympic Stadium, a boxing venue, was the home court of the Los Angeles Jets. A regulation basketball floor is 94 feet long. The cramped Olympic could only accommodate 80 feet. The 14 feet that were missing meant a shorter retreat to defuse fast-breaking teams like the Pipers.

San Francisco played in the Cow Palace, where Siegfried's Buckeyes won the 1960 national championship, to the surprise of the saloonkeeper who refused to feed them.

Hawaii played at the Honolulu City Auditorium on Oahu, Hilo Civic Center on the big island of Hawaii, and in Schofield Army Barracks at Pearl Harbor.

Due to conflicts in playing dates with the hockey Barons at Cleveland Arena, the Pipers actually played most of their games in 10,000-seat Public Hall, a post–World War I building. At one time the largest convention hall in the United States, it was the site of the 1924 and 1936 Republican National Conventions. It had no pillars to obstruct the view, but basketball had to seem incongruous in a building with a proscenium arch and raised stage.

A rent dispute during the Pipers' only season in the ABL between Cleveland Mayor Tony Celebrezze and Steinbrenner led to empty threats by the Pipers' owner to move the team to Columbus. The Pipers acceded to Celebrezze's asking price and agreed to pay the city either $750 or

15 percent of the gate receipts per game, in return for improvements to the venue for basketball at no cost to the team.

The Pipers played games in neighboring cities around Ohio to try to popularize the sport. In addition to three sites in Cleveland itself (one game was played at Baldwin-Wallace College), the Pipers played at Akron, Lorain, Sandusky, Ashtabula, Canton, and Columbus.

Two scheduled games in Columbus were canceled because of poor attendance. A game was canceled in Youngstown because a second pairing for the promised doubleheader could not be booked as a result of a feud between Steinbrenner and the San Francisco owner.

The Pipers also played road games at Milwaukee; Rockford, Illinois; New Castle, Pennsylvania; and Rochester, New York.

In the two halves of the ABL season, the Pipers had an overall record of 45–36. They recoded a 21–11 home record (15–7 at Public Hall, 6–3 at the Arena and Baldwin-Wallace College 0–1). They were 9–19 on the road and 15–6 at neutral sites. (Baldwin-Wallace is not considered a neutral site because the Pipers held training camp there, and it is located in Cuyahoga County, as is Cleveland.)

Their greatest dominance, oddly, was in regional games, on neutral floors, often with fewer fans attending than the disappointing turnouts in Cleveland. Their surprising record in the neutral-site games can probably be explained by the unique difficulties of the Pipers' season.

On the court and off, the Pipers had suffered, in the words of *Cleveland Press* beat writer Bob Sudyk, "more ups and downs than a basketball."

They had adapted to constant turmoil, late paychecks, a coaching change in midseason, Steinbrenner's tantrums, and a hectic and almost deranged work schedule. They could handle different lighting and new gym configurations in places only Rand-McNally knew about.

Once, they endured a bus ride of 371 miles, all the way back from Washington, D.C. Another time, the players got up at 5:30 A.M. to go to O'Hare Field to catch a flight, only four hours after getting to their hotel in Chicago following the late game of a doubleheader.

In all, the Pipers were scheduled to travel, said a midseason *Plain Dealer* story, 24,436 air miles, in addition to all the bus rides. The trip to Hawaii was 10,204 miles. These flights were on early 1960s commercial airlines, not jumbo jets and certainly not on chartered or team-owned planes.

"The trip to Hawaii, it is needless to say, doesn't count as part of the season's sufferings," said the *Plain Dealer* story. The Pipers played 91 games, counting playoffs, in 155 days, or just over five months. They played on average every other day.

To cut travel costs, ABL teams played baseball-type series. Familiarity breeds contempt in many of life's pursuits, and basketball was one of them. Players became sick of two- and three-game sets against each other—or four straight when visiting distant Hawaii. Tempers flared, and play went from hard, aggressive fouls to blunt-force trauma.

"We always hoped for a fight in the opener of a series," Cleary said. "It brought more fans out to the next game."[2]

Complaints arose during the season on all sides about the poor quality of officiating in the league. This was because the refs were selected from the home team's area and were disposed to give the benefit of the doubt on judgment calls to the team responsible for their employment. NBA and top college referees, fearing reprisals, were reluctant to work in the new league.

"Hawaii had refs that lived out there and just did the Chiefs' games. They were all Japanese. They probably had to go home if the visitors won. No wonder you couldn't win a game out there," said Cleary.[3]

Because of the folding of the Los Angeles Jets on January 10, 1962, teams played an uneven number of games. The schedule was changed at the snap of Saperstein's fingers, as he maneuvered the Globetrotters around to try to boost sagging attendance.

The Rens, trying to clinch the first half championship of the East Division, played two games on the West Coast against San Francisco, but only the first counted in the first half standings, lest Pittsburgh play more than the rival Pipers.

"Pro basketball—and I don't believe anyone will dispute this—has too many games too close together on its schedule," wrote Jack Clowser of the *Cleveland Press,* advocating a reduction from the scheduled 82 games to 65 or even 60.

The 18-foot-wide trapezoid-shaped lane widened near the rim and forced ABL teams to rely less on close-in shots because of the three-second rule that limited camping in the lane by big men. Instead, the premium was on cutting and passing. The Chicago Majors team was built to exploit the wider lane. (The amount of adhesive tape used in putting the three-point arc on the floor and the expanded and differently shaped lane could have bound up the wounds of a moderate military skirmish.)

As for the impact of the lane, Chicago coach Andy Phillip said of John Wessels, a six-foot-seven, 210-pound string bean, "John doesn't carry as much weight as we'd like, but with the 18-foot lane where speed and quick movements are so important, he's getting along well."[4]

The NBA began with a six-foot lane in the 1940s, which enabled centers such as George Mikan to establish position so close to the basket that they could almost score at will.

The lane was 12 feet after 1951–52, which still did little to restrain Wilt Chamberlain, who would average a stupendous 50.4 points per game and score 100 points in a single game in the 1961–62 NBA season. Three seasons later, in 1964–65, the NBA went to a 16-foot lane. But the wider flare near the basket of the ABL lane—used in international basketball until a rectangular configuration was adopted in 2008—was never used in the NBA.

The ABL shot clock was 30 seconds, not the NBA's 24, allowing more time for probing and testing defenses. Sometimes, though, the ABL rules were at cross-purposes. There was no "and one" free throw on a made shot if the player were fouled unless the "bonus" was in effect after five team fouls in a quarter.

This encouraged a style of play that amounted to mugging the game of basketball. David Wolf, author of Hawkins's biography *Foul!* theorizes that ABL was attempting to cash in on the violence of the NFL, which was quickly becoming the country's most popular sport. Certainly, many games devolved into free throw shooting contests.

In today's game, the ABL's legacy rests as much on its other new rule, the three-point shot, as anything. It debuted during the torrid noontime of post play, with Chamberlain acting as a one-man team in Philadelphia. The ABL three-pointer was 25 feet long except for a shorter 22-foot shot available in both corners.

The three-pointer was supposed to be basketball's answer to base-ball's home run, a sudden flick of the wrist that brought fans out of their seats, roaring. A half century later, it has almost becomes basketball's holy trinity. It has more than proven that the big man can be neutralized and forced to expand his offensive repertoire in a wide-open game of once undreamed of possibilities.

No one could have foreseen at the time that the real impact of the three-pointer would be in horizontal spacing—in clearing the lane of congestion because of the threat of "stretch bigs" whose threes had to be contested—and not in verticality.

In a column headlined "Saperstein Rules Too Big a Change," the *Cleveland Press*'s erudite and influential sports editor Bob August wrote, "The question is why do people who make their living off basketball always seem dissatisfied with the product. . . . Almost all basketball legislation amounts to punitive measures aimed at the tall man. There is reluctance to accept the fact that the 7-ft. tower of gristle is destined to dominate the game. He stirs up resentment and abuse."

Noting that Saperstein was "a small man himself," August said the new commissioner "wants to restore the dignity of the average-sized citizen on the basketball floor."

But that horse, a Clydesdale in all probability, was already out of the barn, argued August. "This is his game," August said of the big man and basketball. "These victims of frolicking glands have problems enough, and there should be one place where they can shine."

Still, the ABL would try to dim their lights. "We'd like to restore the small man to the place he used to have," Sharman said to *Plain Dealer* sports edi-tor Gordon Cobbledick, who, as we have seen, was hardly a fervent fan.

After humoring Cobbledick by absurdly saying, "We'll have a better game if we can get scores down to the 50s," Sharman added, "A happy medium is worth trying for."[5] He meant a balance between offense and defense, frontcourt and backcourt, power and finesse, big and small.

"We think people would rather see clever play-making than watch a lot of giants reach up and shove the ball through the hoop like a kid dropping a marble down an elevator shaft," Sharman said.[6]

Later in the season, Sharman addressed the defensive problems the long-distance shot caused. "The three-pointer means we have to pick up fellows like [Bucky] Bolyard and [Phil] Rollins [both of Pittsburgh] farther out and guard them tighter. It's tough to stop a fellow like [Chicago's] Tony Jackson because he's tall enough to shoot over our guards," the Pipers' coach said.[7]

The six-foot-five Jackson made an ABL record of 12 three-pointers against the Pipers in a 124–122 loss on March 15. His 53 points were the second-most ever scored in the ABL's only full season, behind Hawkins's 54.

On the season, Jackson, who made seven threes in three other games, led the ABL with 141. Next were the Rens' Bolyard with 104; the Chiefs' Herb Lee with 98; the Steers' Mantis and Rens' Phil Rollins, each with 89; and the Tapers' Roger Kaiser with 72. It was such a tempting weapon that only four players resisted trying at least one during the season.

Sharman, during his stint as a player/coach in Los Angeles, thought 25 feet was too far for the three-pointer. He proved his point by his lack of them, making only one of eight attempts. "[The players] adjusted fast . . . and have become so accurate it can be a decisive factor in a ballgame," Sharman said.[8]

A red light flashed at either end of the court when a three-pointer was made. In the early 1960s, as the discotheque era was getting underway, the Whiskey a Go Go nightclub on Sunset Boulevard in Los Angeles spawned imitators in sports. The "Go-Go" Sox in Chicago won the 1959 American League pennant with a game based on speed. ABL fans sometimes chanted, "Go-go-go for the long one!" and "Hit a home run! Hit a home run!"[9]

"Psychologically, it's a big weapon, especially when you're behind. And the spectators love it," said Sharman.[10]

Also digging the long ball was Doug Mills, the University of Illinois's athletic director and a member of the U.S. Olympic Committee. The Big Ten had tested the offensive foul rule, on which ball possession changed but no free throws were shot, and Mills urged it to experiment with the three-pointer in the coming season. If it improved the game, he said he would recommend it for the Olympics.

The Big Ten declined.

The key to three-point use is the effect of the extra point in a three-pointer. Making one-third of a team's three-point attempts—say, four of 12 for 12 points—is the equivalent of making half of 12 two-point field goals, with six equaling 12 points. The ratio increases from the minimum efficiency level of 33.3 percent. Fifty percent on threes (six of 12 for 18 points) equals 75 percent on shorter shots (9 of 12 for 18 points) and so on.

The chart below shows the ABL average in three-point shooting in 1961–62 versus the ABA average in 1967–68, the first season of the league that resurrected the 25-foot three-pointer, and the NBA average in 1979–80, the first time the trey was used in the established league—at a shorter distance of 23 feet 9 inches.

The ABL had eight teams; the ABA in its first season had 11; the NBA when it finally adopted the three had 22.

FGA means Three-Point Field Goals Attempted, FGM is Three-Point Field Goals Made, and 3 Pct. is three-point shooting percentage. All figures are averages for all teams in each league's inaugural season.

Year	League	3 FGA Avg.	3 FGM Avg.	3 Pct.
1961–62	ABL	177	583	30.4
1967–68	ABA	111	390	28.5
1979–80	NBA	64	227	28.0

Players in the ABA league, during its entire existence from 1967 to 1976, never shot better from the three-point line than the ABL in its one full season. It was not until the 1987–88 NBA season that its league-wide average, on a shot that was 15 inches closer, was better, at 31.6 percent.

Cleveland only attempted 5.2 threes per game, the league's lowest average, although the Pipers still hoisted 419 overall in 81 games. In the first year of the ABA, only three of 11 teams in that supposedly freewheeling league tried more threes than the Pipers' ABL low for a full season.

In the first year of the NBA three-pointer, only Boston with sharpshooting Larry Bird, tried more than the Pipers, 422 to 419. Only Boston (38.4 percent) and the San Diego Clippers (32.6 percent) topped the Majors' 32.5 percent.

Clearly, offensive conservatism had a tight hold on NBA coaches 18 years after the introduction of the ABL triple.

Not in the ABL. Saperstein wanted lights flashing and bells ringing, in a thin, indoor echo of Comiskey Park's "exploding scoreboard" salute to home runs by the Chicago White Sox. At the ABL commissioner's direction, a prizefight bell rang at every ABL scorer's table when a three-pointer was made.

Still, visionary and revolutionary though it was, the ABL's death knell was always just a matter of time.

CHAPTER 8

The Rivals

The ABL was a safe haven for Connie Hawkins, whose NBA ban was the result of a spasm of blanket condemnation and hasty retribution.

Hawkins had been ineligible as a freshman at the University of Iowa under the NCAA rules at the time; could therefore not have been involved in any point-shaving; and was only tangentially connected to the fixer at the heart of the conspiracy, Jack Molinas.

A 19-year-old from the streets of New York, Hawkins was soon to become the ABL's Most Valuable Player in Saperstein's league. "Oh, he did things you never saw before," said Jack Adams. "He had great body control and big hands. He had been in the point-shaving scandal at Iowa and I think he just loved showing what he could. He was a guy who was cheered wherever he played, even when he was on the opposing team."[1]

Yet in the best Hawkins biography, the chapter about his year and a half in the ABL was titled "Boss Man in a Bush League."

In the 1950s, the Globetrotters were almost a necessity for good box office returns in the NBA. The proud Hawkins, however, never could dismiss the clowning aspect when, still banned by the NBA until his victory in a court case years later, he played for the Globetrotters after the ABL folded.

"Tomming for Abe," meaning being an Uncle Tom in the confrontational rhetoric of 1972 when the book was published, was the title of the chapter in the Hawkins biography recounting his Globetrotter experiences. Saperstein, who liked to be known as the "Jewish Abraham Lincoln," would have been deeply hurt by Hawkins's feelings. Such a view was at the time a minority opinion, at least among whites. However, the *San Francisco Examiner*'s late sports columnist Wells Twombley, who was white, wrote in the 1960s, "They jabber like plantation slaves . . . they are grotesque . . . they belong to an era when blacks had no sense of purpose."[2]

Many Globetrotters would eventually be likened to Stepin Fetchit, the stage name of comedian Lincoln Theodore Andrew Monroe Perry. Then again, such roles were all that were available at the time to black actors, and Perry was the first black actor to become a millionaire.

But the clowning was years in the future for Hawkins.

Clearly, the Pipers did not know the force of the basketball firestorm that was coming their way on the courts of the ABL in the person of Connie Hawkins late in 1961. The Pipers did not prepare adequately for the increased quality of their competition in the ABL. Rather than playing exhibition games against other professional clubs as the Pittsburgh Rens and Kansas City Steers did, the Pipers played each other.

They held scrimmages, in between workouts at Baldwin-Wallace College, at Fairport Harbor, Cuyahoga Falls, Elyria, Berea, St. Ignatius High School in Cleveland, and in Westlake. They crushed the minor-league Gary (Indiana) Whips of the Midwest league in games played at Culver Military Academy in Indiana, Steinbrenner's high school, and again in Gary.

"We have some catching up to do and will have to do it in a hurry," McLendon said after an 87–82 opening night loss in Pittsburgh on November 5, 1961.[3]

The Rens were to be the Pipers' top East Division rivals. The Kansas City Steers of the West Division were their opponents in playoff series at the end of each half of the season.

The Pipers opened in Pittsburgh and then journeyed on to Kansas City. Games with these teams were like musical crescendos. Cymbals crashed and bodies collided. This was evident in the first "bars"—the first two of their many meetings with their two top rivals.

Incredibly, the Pipers began the season with nine straight road games. As a marketing tool, playing for over two and a half weeks on the road before a single home game was an idea so absurd it calls into question Saperstein's supposed promotional genius. Still, much now was expected of the Cleveland entry in the new league. The *Plain Dealer* summed up the sports year near the end of 1961 by declaring, "The basketball Pipers put together a fine team, coached by an old master, John McLendon, and won the NIBL and national AAU crowns, while fighting public apathy."

The fortnight on the road did little to combat the apathy back home. In Kansas City, the night after their opening loss, the Pipers claimed their first ABL victory, 110–106. Roger Taylor's 35 points led the way.

The first two games were a competitive template for the season.

The Pipers played Pittsburgh and Kansas City a total of 36 times, counting playoffs. Nine of their first 15 games were against either the Rens or the Steers. The Pipers' record on the season was, counting playoffs, 11–9 versus the Steers and 10–6 versus the Rens.

In addition, Cleveland took part in several doubleheaders against other ABL teams in Pittsburgh, which was called, because of the belching furnaces of the steel industry, the "Smoky City." The team's Ohio Turnpike tolls alone probably distressed Steinbrenner more than any smoke that got in his eyes.

Although the rivalries with both the Rens and Steers were heated, the nature of the matchups was different. Hawkins was something new—a player with a cult following, a word-of-mouth legend, a fixture at legendary Rucker Park in New York, who suddenly dropped into the professional ranks of what was still a gravity-bound sport, helping to transform it.

"He was already a legend in Brooklyn before he ever played in any league," said Embry. "He was such a presence in the Rucker League in the summer-time. He'd come up out of the subway, and he'd have a group of guys with him and a basketball in his hand, and when people saw him coming up those [subway] steps, they'd start screaming, 'Con-NEE! Con-NEE! and 'Hawk! Hawk!'"[4]

"Connie got started late in the NBA because of his alleged involvement with Jack Molinas, Once he got there, he was an elite player," said Joe Gordon, the Rens' publicity man, later their general manager, and still later a vice president of the Pittsburgh Steelers. "He was the first guy I ever saw could fly, who did what Dr. J did, what Elgin Baylor did," Gordon added. "Connie was the first one I saw who could skywalk. He had so many skills, he was so fluid. Not only a great scorer and rebounder, but because of his tremendous peripheral vision a great passer, and just a tremendous talent."[5]

To defend against Hawkins, who was six eight and spindly, many ABL teams used tactics worthy of the prizefight ring, all but rabbit punching him and rubbing with the laces in the clinches. McLendon did not think basketball was much of a game if its best players could be mugged. Nevertheless, he was a realist when theory failed.

Often McLendon used defensive specialist Dick Brott along with Nick Romanoff, his biggest man at the time, on Hawkins.

One night after Hawkins scored 40 points against the Pipers in a 97–91 Rens victory, Romanoff had success in a 137–94 Pipers rout, muscling Hawkins further from the rim than he liked and holding him to 17 points. It was an aberration, not the norm. Heaton admiringly described Romanoff in sinewy terms as "a rugged warrior who likes it rough."

In defense of strength training, McLendon often pointed to Romanoff, whom he first encountered when Romanoff was a 185-pound weakling. Now Romanoff was pushing former tormentors all over the court. "The idea that weight lifting tightens up the muscles of an athlete so that he loses his timing and rhythm is an erroneous one," McLendon said.[6]

Romanoff was a hardwood version of the fantasies of the scrawny teenage boys who, at least in advertisements in the back of magazines such as *Boys' Life,* had had sand kicked in their faces in front of their girlfriends by bullies at the beach. Such humiliation, leading to body reconstruction through a prescribed program and then to sweet revenge, were staples of Charles Atlas's bodybuilding ads.

Romanoff now weighed 240 pounds and looked like he had been chiseled by a sculptor and was about to mount a pedestal.

In a preseason story, Sudyk described Romanoff's daily, off-season dietary regimen, in which he ingested more than 60 protein pills, sunflower seeds, and wheat germ capsules. In addition to eating all his regular vegetable- and meat-rich meals, Romanoff also ate at least eight eggs and a dozen bananas per day and drank five quarts of milk. He eschewed potatoes. Nick Romanoff would have scoffed at Popeye and his can of spinach.

Rough and tumble was no substitute for good and big, though.

Early in the season, Sudyk wrote a story, casting the Pipers as giant killers. "Pipers Small, But on the Ball," read the headline. Accompanied by a Darvas cartoon of a small (white) Pipers player, staring up at a nameless towering (white) opponent whose head, Goliath-like, stuck through the bottom of the basket's net, Sudyk noted that the Pipers' roster "barely averages 6 ft., 3 in.," making them the smallest team in the league.

"At the top of the beanpole," he wrote, "is Los Angeles, with two men above seven feet and a team average of 6 ft., 8 in."

Such a disparity might not have been so pronounced had McLendon not traded Spivey before the season began, reasoning that the aging seven one center was not suited to the fast-breaking game he coached.

Tallest to shortest, the ABL teams stacked up like this: Los Angeles, Pittsburgh, Kansas City, San Francisco, Washington, Hawaii, Chicago, and the Pipers. Yet the Pipers held the third position in rebounds in league stats. In Darvas's cartoon, a referee, his hand clasped in shock over his mouth at this disclosure, exclaimed, "WOWIE!"

"We have to concentrate on it [rebounding] because we lack height. We are aggressive and determined under the boards and work on it in drills. We concentrate on position more than other clubs because we have to," said McLendon.[7]

Effective against players of bulk who lacked quickness, this tactic was no remedy for Hawkins, who was "long," in today's scouting parlance, in both limb and reach, high in jumping and, with his huge hands, discouraging in grasp. He swooped, soared, and held the ball in one hand like a grapefruit. "Someone said if I didn't break the laws of gravity, I was slow to obey them," Hawkins said.[8]

On the season, Hawkins scored 40, 42 twice, 49, and the league-record 54 against the Pipers.

Because of the Iowa scandal, Hawkins was consigned to a basketball purgatory, displaying his futuristic game in an obscure league whose scores were tucked into neglected corners of daily newspapers. "The best thing about the ABL was they had a team in Hawaii," Hawkins said, looking on the sunny side of competitive anonymity.[9]

Whoever the Pipers chose to guard Hawkins, he either punished the defender at the foul line, making 18 of 22 free throws on November 25 in a 97–91 Rens victory; or he fouled them out, three in all, on his way to 49 points in a 132–117 Pipers win on December 23; or he simply embarrassed them to the point of opponents saying, "No mas."

One of the most crucial additions to the Pipers' team after midseason was six-foot-nine Connie Dierking, a former Cincinnati Royal who came to Cleveland in a critical trade for Taylor and Adams.

In the Hawkins biography *Foul!* Leroy Wright, a Washington/New York Tapers forward who stood six nine, said: "With [Hawkins's] long arms and spring, there wasn't much I could do after a while. Connie Dierking was an NBA center, but he didn't want no part of Hawkins either. Every time we [Dierking was originally with the Tapers] were about to play Pittsburgh, Dierking got an upset stomach."[10]

As good as Hawkins was, he would have been better had Pittsburgh coach Neil Johnston helped him more. Inducted into the Basketball Hall of Fame after his death, Johnston owned an NBA scoring title, NBA rebounding title, and NBA championship ring (with the 1955–56 Philadelphia Warriors.) But he still harbored dreams of playing in the ABL. The urge only lasted five games, in which he averaged nearly 10 points.

Johnston was a very reluctant teacher with his promising pupil. When Hawkins asked if Johnston would teach him the hook shot, recounts David Wolf, the coach walked to the court, swished five hooks right handed, netted five more left-handed, then walked off, saying, "That's how you do it."[11]

At times, it seemed that the Pipers simply conceded Hawkins his big numbers and tried not to let the other Rens beat them. Before Hawkins's first 40-point game against the Pipers, McLendon said he would use Siegfried as a "stopper" on Bucky Bolyard, the Rens' outside shooting specialist.

It was remarkable that he played at all. Bolyard had a glass eye, having been blinded in a boyhood accident. He subsisted mainly on Pepsi-Cola and 5th Avenue candy bars. He reminded Hawkins of Will Stockdale, the naive bumpkin played by Andy Griffith in the popular 1950s movie *No Time for Sergeants*.

Bolyard was just the type of small man the three-point shot was designed to bring back to the game. There would have been no place for

Bolyard in the pro game without the added-value shot. When the ABL folded on New Year's Eve 1962, Bolyard was one of the players spurned by NBA scouts, who thought much of his effectiveness depended on the long ball.

Strangely, perhaps because Hawkins never played collegiately, reporters who covered the ABL seemed unable to grasp what a prodigy he was. Even the perceptive Fritz Kreisler, the *Kansas City Star* beat reporter who traveled with the Steers, was slow to see how dominant was Hawkins. Sudyk, however, picked up on the Hawkins boom after the first game in the second half of the season. It would, however, have been hard for him to have missed it. Listed as doubtful for the January 15, 1962, game against Cleveland, Hawkins not only played but grabbed 20 rebounds and scored his league-record 54 points.

Sudyk's "advance" before the Rens' next game in Cleveland only two days later, compared Hawkins to a ballet dancer and then to the "cool impassiveness and grace of a bull fighter." Rens owner Lenny Littman compared Hawkins to the Pirates' Hall of Fame slugger Ralph Kiner. "No fan left Forbes Field before a game ended when Kiner played here and basketball fans feel the same way about Connie," said Littman.[12]

A mysterious ABL owner, Sudyk wrote—presumed, but never confirmed, to be Steinbrenner—offered to trade his entire team for Hawkins and was summarily turned down.

"Littman placed a $3,125 an inch price tag on the brilliant Negro," wrote Sudyk. "Connie measures $250,000 or 6 feet 8 inches."

Hawkins was the future of basketball, going boldly where no man— well, other than Elgin Baylor—had gone before.

The Kansas City Steers were a more traditional rival. With the league's best record in both halves of the season, they were also the more potent threat. In the first 13 meetings of the Pipers and Steers, including the three-game first half playoff series, the point differential favored Cleveland by a mere nine points. The five-game ABL Finals distorted the differential because the first two games in Kansas City were blowouts due to the Pipers' fatigue.

In the broad view, they were two extremely closely matched teams. Cleveland led the ABL in offense at 109.3 points per game, but was next-to-last in defense at 106.3. The Steers led in defense at 99.4 points and were third, if the truncated Jets' season is discounted, in offense at 104.5. Actually, the statistics are somewhat misleading. The ABL was a league of parity. Almost everyone could beat everyone else. The Pipers rose and fell in the standings dramatically in both halves of the season in a short period of time.

The Pipers were the better team, though. Their best player, Dick Barnett, was ineligible until late December. The Steers' best player, forward Bill Bridges, was a hard-working future three-time NBA All-Star with the St. Louis/Atlanta Hawks. Bridges played all 79 games, often seeming indestructible.

"We had the best rebounder in the league in Bridges. But he was small. He was six-five," said Cleary. Drafted in the third round by the expansion Chicago Packers, Bridges, a star with the Kansas Jayhawks in college, signed with the Steers instead. "They offered him $7,800. He said flat out he'd like to stay here [near Kansas]. So we offered him $9,000," Cleary said. The Steers' players were in Cleary's word, "bland." So were most of the Pipers. Even Barnett was usually close-mouthed, other than his trademark "Fall back, baby!" cry.[13]

The Steers were also probably the best-run franchise. The first half champions, the Steers were assured of a spot in the ABL Finals. They could have protectively packed Bridges, Larry Staverman, Tormohlen, and their other standouts in straw, or wrapped them in old newspaper clippings and waited around for the Finals. Instead, the Steers ran away to the second half's best record too. They were thoroughly worthy adversaries.

Just as the Pipers' owner possessed the lion's share of the color and controversy in the franchise, so the Steers' coach garnered the same spoils of attention and notoriety. Jack McMahon gave the Steers instant credibility in Missouri because he had been a member of the St. Louis Hawks' 1958 NBA champions, the last all-white team to claim the title.

Unlike Cleveland, which had the Indians in Major League Baseball and the Browns in the NFL, Kansas City had only the baseball A's as competition to the Steers. Moreover, the A's, under the eccentric owner-ship of Charles O. Finley, were derisively considered to be a virtual farm team for the New York Yankees at the time.

Basketball was fertile ground in which to grow a fan base in Kansas City because of the NAIA and NCAA tournaments at Municipal Auditorium.

In a sport that needed the Globetrotters for crowd-pleasing entertainment, McMahon was his own one-man show. He had played on St. John's 1952 NCAA runner-ups, which lost to Clyde Lovellette's Kansas team. He also possessed an Irishman's ability to laugh at the absurdities of life, including big-time sports. He once told the author of this book about the job he had while playing at St. John's in New York, saying, "I had to be at a liquor store on Flatbush Avenue in Brooklyn by 8 o'clock on Saturday night to get my money." Asked what his job entailed, McMahon said, "I had to be at the liquor store by 8 o'clock on Saturday night."[14]

He was also very combative and would back down from no one. Forward Cliff Hagan, tiring of watching McMahon feed the ball to the Hawks' highest scorer, Bob Pettit, the team's other starting forward, once barked, "Why don't you bring the ball down my side of the court for a change?"

"Any more of that crap out of you, and the only way you'll see the ball is off the glass!" snapped McMahon.[15]

"He was a character. That league led to the development and nurturing of characters," said the Rens' Joe Gordon. "But Jack had a temper too."[16]

In the final minutes of an ABL exhibition game in Shawnee Mission, Kansas, a fight broke out between the Steers' Tormohlen and Pittsburgh's Jim Palmer.

As biographer David Wolf recounts, while backpedaling from two Steers players, Hawkins was suddenly punched in the small of the back by McMahon, leading Hawkins to wallop the coach in the nose. "Originally, when he first got to Pittsburgh, Connie was very shy and introverted," said Gordon. "That was understandable when you considered everything he'd gone through. He didn't know what kind of future, if any, he would have. But once he settled down, he was a very charming guy."[17]

Tell that to Jack McMahon.

"He never forgave me. He was cursin' me from the bench the rest of the season," Hawkins said.[18]

Charles O. Finley took note of McMahon's commitment to bench jockeying, and overly optimistic pugilism. He decided McMahon was just the man for him—as a baseball manager!

"He suddenly became enamored of us," said Cleary. "Charlie traveled around the country, watching our games. Come to find out, he wanted to hire Monte Moore, our radio broadcaster. And he finally did. Monte spent many years with the A's. Our next [Steers] play-by-play man was Merle Harmon. At least we had good announcers."[19]

Finley was dead serious too about hiring McMahon, who was to begin his managerial career with one of the A's minor league teams. McMahon said, "I don't know anything about baseball. Besides, I have a bar to run in St. Louis in the off-season."

Replied Finley, "But you know how to get the most out of your players." To McMahon's many sensible objections, Finley waved a dismissive hand.

"Oh, the pitching coach can handle the strategy and that stuff," he said.[20]

McMahon, however, stayed on the basketball bench, which he treated as a launching pad for his tantrums. Some were real, some were designed to spark his team.

After a 99–97 Pipers victory in Cleveland on November 29, 1961, the fiery McMahon stomped around the empty corridors of Public Hall, shouting, "Foul! Foul! Foul!"

McMahon cared deeply about foul shots, earning them and making them. In order to stoke his players' competitiveness, he held foul shooting contests at practice before a long trip. The ABL stipend for food was $12 per day. McMahon would take everybody out to the free throw line, throw all the meal money Cleary had given him on the floor, and each player would shoot 10 free throws. The game would continue for more rounds in case of ties. Whoever made the most got the most money. Whoever made the least got no money.

"We were a good free-throw shooting team," said Cleary. "It was not an accident."[21]

Not good enough after the Pipers' 99–97 victory, however.

A glance at the box score only increased McMahon's fury. "Lousy, rotten officiating cost us the ball game," he grumbled. "If the Pipers think they won this one, they're nuttier than the refs. We had 14 fouls shots and they had 34."

He then added the classic losing coach's lament, "We wuz robbed!"[22]

Flieger rose to the defense of the Pipers. "We had more than 300 [sic] free throws than the opposition in winning the [NIBL] title last year," the new general manager said, pointing to the Pipers' attacking style of offense.[23]

A free throw disparity in the Pipers' favor was common. When the team had ruled the NIBL, the Pipers were actually outscored from the field by a margin of 16 field goals (1,462–1,446), but they held a 1,000–769 lead in free throws made.

"Fouls naturally go with a fast break offense and our attack moves toward the basket," McLendon explained in the spring of 1961. "And in Dan Swartz and Jack Adams we have two experts in drawing fouls. I'm always trying to get players who drive in hard. I only wish our centers would too. But Ben Warley isn't strong enough, and the others never developed the habit."[24]

Despite the statistics, McMahon had not cooled down the next day, when the second game in the series was to be played in Cleveland. McMahon said the Steers would not play if the "homers"—Frank Sowecke of Huron, Ohio, and John Motsch of Bay Village, Ohio—worked that night's game. In a foreshadowing of the weakness of Saperstein as its commissioner, Phil Fox, the ABL's head of officiating, gave in. New referees, Dick Sheldon of Columbus and Tony Senopole of Ford City, Pennsylvania, were rushed to the game.

The heat of the rhetoric did not match the fire of the play, however, in a 109–102 Pipers victory. But McMahon's thermostat still had not been adjusted. The Press reported that McMahon charged onto the court to dispute calls three times and stomped his foot 16 times.

On the bright side, he remained shod. McMahon had stomped his foot down on the edge of the raised court in Kansas City earlier in the season, clipping the heel off his shoe and sending it flying. "That call was farcical!" spluttered McMahon, padding partially sock-footed and partially shod onto the court to protest. Unfortunately, his background as an English major deserted him in his rage and he pronounced the word as "FARSH-ull." "Jack, are you swearing at me?" said the puzzled referee, Hickman Duncan.[25]

In that era, players and coaches alike could quench their disappointment or celebrate their victory in the locker room with as many free beers, iced down in barrels, as they required. "One night, Jack took the beer can opener and put it all the way though the can. Every time he took a drink, it was running out the side of the can. I was standing behind him, trying not to laugh," Cleary said. "The players were looking at him, trying not to laugh," Cleary continued. "He was still oblivious. He was not getting any beer, and he was still yelling at them. The beer began to pour out the side. He had punched the can with the opener so vigorously because he was so mad that the beer was foaming out and streaming over his shirt, his tie and his jacket."

Finally noting that he had been basted in beer, McMahon growled, "Aw, you damn guys!" at the players and stalked off, unappeased, as well as un-dry.[26]

"That was the thing that first struck me," said the *Kansas City Star*'s Fritz Kreisler, now 82. "I got on the team bus the first time and Jack had a cooler of beer on it. I had been in the A's clubhouse a few times, but I had mostly been around high school kids. I couldn't believe the way things were in the pros."[27]

After the ABL, McMahon coached eight years in the NBA, including with the powerful Cincinnati Royals team of Robertson and Lucas, and the expansion San Diego team with Elvin Hayes. He coached two more years in the ABA. "He was a character, but his players loved him. He was their friend," Kreisler said.[28] The ABL was as close as McMahon got to drinking champagne after the last game of the season as a head coach, though. For such an experienced, respected, and flamboyant basketball man that was a shame.

Also, of course, for his dry cleaners.

CHAPTER 9

Controversies and a Star for Christmas

Usually a strong finishing team because of McLendon's emphasis on conditioning, the Pipers fell cold in the final quarter in the season opener at Pittsburgh. They were also hurt by foul trouble, which limited the play of captain Jack Adams, and by an injury to Warley, who crashed into the basket support after diving for a loose ball.

Probably, the players did not know how to react after a defeat. It was their first loss in 22 games, going back to before the exhibition tour in the Soviet Union, before the conquest of the AAU, and even before the NIBL tournament. Unusual as the loss was, Steinbrenner reacted punitively, sending nominal general manager Ben Flieger to McLendon with orders to enforce a midnight curfew. After Flieger said, "word has come from upstairs" about the curfew, McLendon said, "Well, you go right back upstairs and say I'll tell these players when I want them to report in." Then, turning to the team, the coach said, "I told you the time I want you in the hotel. You are to follow my orders. What I say goes."[1]

The confrontation is an example of why newspapers should not trim reporters' travel budgets, even in today's austere times. A reporter with an eye for flavorful detail or a sense of the personality polarities McLendon and Steinbrenner represented would have written an unforgettable story.

As it was, the curfew incident went unremarked in the Cleveland papers. Neither the *Plain Dealer* nor the more colorful *Press,* which did not publish on Sundays, national holidays, or even quasi-holidays, such as St. Patrick's Day, was a true paper of record on the Pipers.

The Pipers did what they had to do on the nine-game opening road trip. They survived it with a 5–4 record. The Pipers notched their first ABL victory in the opener of their two-game series at Kansas City, 110–106. Roger Taylor scored 35 points, dropping jumpers from the foul line to just short for the three-point arc. Warley added 24 and Cox 129. Bridges and Tormohlen posed the biggest problems for the Steers.

McLendon was gratified by the reception Barnhill and Warley, stars of Tennessee State's NAIA champions, received after their triumphs at the "Municipal" in their college days. The fans missed the legally embattled Barnett, the star of those teams. The Kansas Citians would feel less kindly about the Pipers' star by the springtime.

McLendon visited his parents in Kansas before a 101–100 loss to the Steers in the second game. Then the Pipers were off to the West Coast, a destination that was to become a sore point with Steinbrenner. They swept the Saints, 103–100 and 97–88, although five-foot-eight Joe Gardere, one of the shortest players in basketball, troubled them in the second game.

On the other end of the California coast, they were swept in turn by the Jets on their truncated Olympic Auditorium court. The Jets were a good team, expertly coached by Sharman, and they would have been a factor in the ABL race had better financing allowed them to stay the course.

Former Pipers Swartz and Spivey hurt Cleveland in the Jets games, as did George Yardley. The Pipers scored only eight points on the Jets' cramped court in the final quarter of the first game, a 109–99 loss. In the second game, a 106–90 loss, Rossie Johnson scored 38 points, which set the ABL's one-game scoring record at the seven-game mark. Like other offensive records that did not involve Cornelius L. Hawkins, it might as well have been written in pencil. Five of Johnson's baskets were threes, another record that was written on water.

Back in Cleveland to practice, McLendon said there was nothing wrong with the team that a few home games wouldn't cure. Before the home opener, however, the Pipers would make a second trip to Pittsburgh on November 17 for a game in which they beat the Rens, 111–94.

Driving to Pittsburgh in two station wagons, the Pipers had a flat tire in one of them. The incident and its aftermath had the effect of uncaging Steinbrenner's furies.

"John told us to go on to Pittsburgh and he'd get there when he could. He told me to coach," said Adams.

The Pipers were comfortably ahead by the time McLendon arrived.

"Go ahead. You've done a good job," said the coach to Adams.

At halftime, Steinbrenner stormed into the locker room, demanding to know what he was paying McLendon for. "Who's the coach of this team, anyway?" screamed Steinbrenner.

Laconically, McLendon pointed to Adams and said: "He is, for this game."[2]

McLendon could not understand what difference it made if the team was winning. He felt his trust in Adams was a signal to other players that his belief in them would always be strong. Steinbrenner could not understand how a coach, the central authority figure on the team, could not only delegate, but entirely abdicate, his responsibility, no matter what the scoreboard said.

The Associated Press story in the *Plain Dealer* did not mention Adams' "coaching," but Adams confirmed all the details of the story except the date in an interview.

The brief mentions of the incident in Steinbrenner biographies do not include the date of the game. But the November 17 game was Cleveland's only lopsided victory of the season over Pittsburgh on the road before McLendon resigned as coach. Thus it was the only game in which McLendon would have felt comfortable enough with the lead to delegate coaching authority after he arrived at the arena.

From Pittsburgh, the Pipers rode a bus to Washington, D.C., the next day to play the Rens again as part of a doubleheader. They squeezed out an 88–87 victory. Hawkins matched Rossie Johnson's 38 points in a losing cause.

In their long-delayed home opener on November 21 at Public Hall, the Pipers pounded the road-weary Hawaii Chiefs, who were 1–8 on their own season-opening odyssey, 91–74. Catering to fan interest, although the turnout was only 3,318, McLendon started Siegfried.

The Pipers won again the next night, 97–96, when some Piper or other who was dressed and in the building (Heaton said Adams; Sudyk credited it to Barnhill) saved the game with a tip-in in the final seconds before an announced 3,500 fans at Public Hall.

Heaton was on a tight morning newspaper deadline, and credit for tip-in baskets, with several hands flailing at the ball, often is hard to determine. Sudyk's afternoon paper deadline gave him more time to check the facts and get it right.

It certainly was a better story in Sudyk's version because "Rabbit" Barnhill was only six one, three inches shorter than Adams, and thus unlikely to soar so high. Rabbit, however, had serious hops, as he would prove in a critical moment in the decisive game of the ABL Finals.

The real excitement happened at halftime.

The *Plain Dealer*'s Heaton, a careful reporter, wrote in the last paragraph of his game story, in what is called a "shirt-tail," meaning a note which was not important enough for a separate story, "The Pipers announced before the game that Grady McCollum had been signed by Hawaii. An extra man on the Pipers who was not under contract, he was on the Hawaii bench and will fly to Honolulu with them."[3]

In Ron Thomas's book about black basketball pioneers, *They Cleared the Lane,* McLendon explicitly states that Steinbrenner traded McCollum to Hawaii at halftime of the game. "Red [Rocha, Hawaii coach] wanted Grady on the team and George decided it was time to make a little cash," McLendon said.[4] The sale price was $500. In a private meeting, Steinbrenner then ordered McCollum to suit up for the second half with the Chiefs.

McLendon, who like his team, was momentarily in shock at the callousness of the sale, told the tearful McCollum he did not have to play against his former teammates. McLendon told the distraught player, "Just go up and sit in the stands."[5]

"I'll take him to court," blustered McLendon, who soon realized he actually could not. As president of the team, Steinbrenner could do almost any autocratic thing he pleased with his playing personnel.[6]

The Hawaii series opened an eight-game stand in Ohio, on which the Pipers won six. The only losses were to Hawkins' Rens, thanks to a 40-point game by the teenager, and to the Jets, who split a series at Public Hall and at the Columbus Fairgrounds. The game in Columbus drew only an announced 2,201. *Columbus Dispatch* columnist Paul Hornung later claimed no more than 700 attended.

In the *Cleveland Press,* Gibbons noted that the game in Columbus drew only "a corporal's guard" and warned Steinbrenner "not to go up against Ohio State until Jerry Lucas has gotten his summa cum laude in basketball and other marks."[7]

Lucas, never far from Steinbrenner's mind, would come to dominate the college basketball season until his Ohio State team faltered in the biggest moment, just as he dominated Steinbrenner's plans for the future, until George too could not clear the last hurdle.

After the loss to the Rens at Public Hall, the Pipers moved to Cleveland Arena for the second game in the series. It was not a good night for the Renaissance men, as the Pipers ran away from them in a 137–94 rout.

The *Plain Dealer*'s Hal Lebovitz, taking a break from his "Ask Hal, the Referee" column, praised the bespectacled Brott's defense on Hawkins. For Brott, it was a novel experience. Steinbrenner had no appreciation for the limited game and shortened goals of a team player like Brott.

"Brott was a fighter, and I loved him. But Dick couldn't take what George was doing to him," McLendon said.

When Steinbrenner was not telling Brott he was a loser, he was trying to improve him by mandating an abstemious lifestyle. "When he signed me, he told me to stop smoking cigarettes, and I did," Brott told Peter Golenbock. "When he called me into his office, I started again. Imagine! He called me a loser!"

After that, Brott decided to resume puffing. "Might as well do something I enjoy," he said.[8]

Despite the cardiovascular demands made by basketball on players, many players smoked during the 1960s and '70s. Smokers included such stars as Billy Cunningham and George McGinnis, both of the 76ers, and Jo Jo White of the Celtics. Tom Heinsohn of the Celtics was a human chimney. Julius Erving bummed a cigarette from beat writers during an arduous 16-hour bus ride from Cleveland back to Philadelphia after a record snowstorm in 1978 closed airports throughout the Midwest and along the Eastern seaboard.

Cleary recalls guard Win Wilfong of the Steers racing directly to the locker room from wherever he was on the court or bench at the end of the half. By the time the other Steers arrived, Wilfong was already working on the dregs of his first cigarette.

In his story on the rout of Pittsburgh, Lebovitz lavishly praised Adams—comparing him to Wake Forest University coach Bones McKinney, a star in the BAA, and writing that Captain Jack "was a bear on defense, passed off beautifully, shot accurately from out[side] and often was the first man down on the debilitating fast break."

Lebovitz ended his story with the erroneous prediction that the three-pointer was destined to bring back the two-hand set shot. He noted that the Rens made two of the long shots using two hands, "something not seen since you and I were young, Margie."[9] (Margie was the "bride" Lebovitz mentioned in many columns.)

The crowd, estimated at 7,000 by Lebovitz and 6,000 by Sudyk, primarily came out to see the Globetrotters roll up another victory over the Washington Generals in the other half of the doubleheader.

Victories over Kansas City that included McMahon's aforementioned tirade about the referees, highlighted the remainder of the home stand.

The Pipers had won eight of their last 10 games when they went to Milwaukee to play Chicago on December 5. In the game, forward Ben Warley suffered what was described as a "rupture in the upper thigh and groin area," which would sideline him for three weeks and 10 games. Without him, the Pipers split the games, 5–5, ending any chance of a runaway in the East Division.

Warley, who died in 2002, was a slender, injury-prone six-foot-five, 200-pound forward player. He also had a very intriguing past. Officials at Seattle University, the 1958 NCAA Tournament runner-up to Kentucky, illegally paid for Warley's airline ticket on a recruiting trip. The coach, John Castellani, was fired. With the school facing NCAA probation, Elgin Baylor, who had transferred from the College of Idaho and was eligible for the NBA Draft, turned pro. Castellani said Seattle would have won at least two NCAA championships if Warley had gone there.

Warley was not a player looking for a free ride, however. He impressed Cleary with his scrupulous honesty. "When we tried him out for the NIBL, it was because he had played for John McLendon. I sent him $200 in Nashville, told him to catch a plane, grab a cab, and come on over to try out," Cleary said. "When he left, he handed me an envelope. There was $37.20 in it, which was what was left over from the $200, and every dime he spent was accounted for in receipts."[10]

Warley was the NIBL's Rookie of the Year in his lone season in the factory league. After the ABL, he played seven seasons in the NBA and the ABA, spending part of them in Philadelphia as Wilt Chamberlain's roommate. Warley's son, Carlin, played for St. Joseph's of Philadelphia after a high school career in which he broke Chamberlain's Pennsylvania state scoring records.

Sudyk called the elder Warley "only" six foot seven, but the authoritative research site ProBasketballReference.com says he was six five. Yet at the time he was injured, Warley led the ABL in rebounding. McLendon said Warley compensated for his lack of height with "the ability to jump well, pride in his ability and good hands." Then the coach added, "All the more credit to his pride, perhaps, because he is as small as some of these fellows go."[11]

At the time of the injury, Warley was sixth in the ABL in scoring with a 20-point average. He did not finish among the league leaders, ending with a 12.5-point average, third on the team behind Barnett and Johnny Cox.

The stunned Pipers, unable to adapt to the loss of Warley, lost the game to Chicago, 110–97. On the same day, Bill Sharman broke the middle finger of his shooting hand in a Jets' win over Hawaii. It was his last appearance as a player.

With Warley hospitalized for a week at Milwaukee's St. Luke's Hospital, the Pipers signed five-foot-ten, 175-pound Jimmy Darrow, one of the great players in Bowling Green State University history, to provide a scoring spark.

Darrow, a "BeeGee," as headline writers called any player from the school before the Brothers Gibb began recording songs, had led the Falcons to their first-ever NCAA Tournament berth in 1959. He averaged 25 points in his last season there, and his 52 points in one game is still the school scoring record.

Just four days after he signed, Darrow hit the shots in the final two minutes to tie Pittsburgh and then put the Pipers ahead to stay in a 107–102 victory at the Arena. It was only his second game as a Piper, but he finished with 16 points. On the season, Darrow would average 8.7 points, just below Siegfried's 9.0, in 55 games.

Darrow's points were the crucial ones, but the Pittsburgh game was an entertaining shootout between Johnny Cox, who scored 42 for the Pipers, and Hawkins, who had his usual big game with 36 against Cleveland.

"John wasn't playing full time and didn't have the feel of things," McLendon said. "With Warley out, Cox moved in and stayed there."[12]

During this win-one, lose-one, win-two, lose-two period without Warley, the Pipers seemed to have a different player each night take it upon himself to carry the scoring load.

Adams scored 42 in a 134–113 loss at Baldwin-Wallace to Pittsburgh, which was led by Hawkins' 42. The game was played on a Sunday afternoon and televised on tape delay back to Pittsburgh. The exposure still did little to boost the Rens' attendance.

Then it was 25 by Cox in a 99–84 victory at Washington, and Barnhill's 39 in a 117–95 win over the Majors at the Arena.

Warley returned and played briefly, scoring six points in a 113–112 loss to Chicago on December 21. The Pipers' foes that night were supposed to be the Kansas City Steers. But three different planes were crippled by mechanical problems, which kept the Steers in Kansas City until it was so late that the Pipers agreed to play Chicago in the first game of the doubleheader instead.

"But when Chicago unpacked to dress for the game," wrote Sudyk, "it was found that the Majors had left their playing shirts back in Chicago. Since the Majors could not play bare backed, the Pipers dug up some old red jerseys. The shirts were not uniform, however. Some had little numbers, some had large ones, some had one numeral, some had none."[13]

The *Plain Dealer* ran a photo of Barnhill scoring on a layup as "the Majors' Herschell Turner (7) and Kelly Coleman (no number)" looked on.

Meanwhile, back at the tarmac, the five Steer starters and sixth man boarded a 7:30 P.M. flight with the rest of the team catching one at 8:15. Both units got sirens-screaming police escorts after they landed.

Heaton mentioned only the switch in opponents, but Sudyk relished the "Comedy of Errors worthy of Will Shakespeare."

He said that "the seven-piece Dixieland Band scheduled to play at 7 P.M. started with a drummer, a trumpeter and trombone player. The banjo player, accordionist, bass and clarinetist had gone to Public Hall by mistake."

"All's Well that Ends Well; Pipers to Selves Were True," read the *Press*'s headline, echoing "Will's" Polonius. It was Sudyk's favorite game story of the antic season.[14]

Usually, Steinbrenner was the best show of all. He sat in the lower stands, which served only as launching pad for the explosive owner. Sometimes, he sat right next to the players on the bench. "It wasn't very comfortable. The fellows didn't like it," McLendon said.[15] Steinbrenner was in the team huddle during timeouts and in the locker room at half-time. McLendon told author Peter Golenbock he viewed Steinbrenner as a "spoiled brat of a millionaire's son."[16]

Steinbrenner once became so enraged at a foul call that was not called that he charged on to the court, wrenched the whistle that hung from the ref's neck toward his own lips, and blew the whistle furiously at him. Another time, he drop-kicked the game ball into the stands. Such a ball was unlikely to be returned.

"Kids would come to the games with the intent of stealing balls," said Sudyk. "They had whole rack of balls they could choose from. It was an organized plot, passing the ball up in the stands, then another guy would pick it up and run out the door. The cops were so surprised, they just stood there, watching."

One Pipers game was delayed because no game balls at all could be found.[17]

The lead Pipers' story was not about the Dixieland band's wand'ring minstrels, nor about the tirade Steinbrenner had unleashed in the locker room after the loss. That went unreported for days. It was about Stein-brenner's accord with the Nats, freeing Barnett to play for the team, not the Pipers' wacky loss to the Majors.

This would change almost everything about the team on the court.

CHAPTER 10

The Unorthodox Shot and Unexpected Life of Dick Barnett

"Skull" could always shoot.

Dick Barnett, the best player on the Pipers team and the driving force for their ABL championship, shaved his head at Tennessee State. His skeletal nickname became, said McLendon, a reflection both of his look and his game. For opponents, he was a death's head.

"I think he gave himself the nickname," McLendon told *New York Times* sports columnist William Rhoden. "He became so deadly on the court that it was a fitting logo for his activity."

The nickname had a strictly literal basis, but it had to seem metaphorical to Cleary too. To him, Skull meant death, curtains, the box in the ground, the dirt nap, the bell, and perhaps the whole carillon, tolling for him and the Steers.

Skull meant lingering death in the ABL's championship playoffs with a miraculous shot, which led to a stunning Pipers rally, averting a sweep by Kansas City Steers, where Cleary became the general manager after Steinbrenner fired him.

Skull meant sudden death as the Pipers' general manager too. Steinbrenner, at the height of his greatest triumph, as a result of his successful pursuit of Barnett, fired Cleary for spreading the news unintentionally.

Steinbrenner had secured a deal with the *Cleveland Press,* agreeing to give the paper the story of Barnett's jump from the Syracuse Nationals to the Pipers, in return for front-page play on the afternoon of August 17, 1961. He did not, however, tell Cleary, who sent out a press release announcing the signing and indicated that it was not to be made public until 6 A.M. August 18.

"It was all set up. 'Pipers Sign NBA Star' by the *Press*'s Bob August [the sports editor]," Cleary said. "But a new radio guy [future Cleveland Browns play-by-play man Gib Shanley] was in town and he was down at the Browns' camp at Hiram College. He saw the press release and didn't notice it was for p.m. release. So he ran with it and put it on the 11 o'clock news."[1]

"Mike, I've got to do something on it." The *Plain Dealer*'s Heaton said, after hearing the news.[2] Heaton's story ran on the fourth page of the sports section, under a one-column headline. After the premature disclosure of Barnett's signing, the *Press* didn't run the Barnett story on the front page either.

Carry Back, a three-year-old colt owned by Clevelanders, who had won the first two legs of Thoroughbred racing's Triple Crown in 1961, did not say much. But he enjoyed much better local coverage than did Barnett's signing. Of course, Carry Back was a local boy. Owned by Jack and Katherine Price of Dorchester Farms Stable near Cleveland, the horse was frequently featured in the Cleveland newspapers in an era when baseball, boxing, and horse racing were the meat, potatoes, and oats of the sports pages.

Cleary's penalty for failing to manage the news as Steinbrenner wanted, albeit in a free society, was to be scratched from the Steinbrenner futurity. "George fired me. I was the first in a long line of sports executives to be fired by George Steinbrenner," said Cleary.[3]

(Actually, Steinbrenner had already fired his sister, Susan, the team secretary, after she stepped out for coffee one morning and wasn't there when George needed her. She was back at work by noon, through her mother's intervention.)

Because the *Press* reneged on the deal, according to John Minco, an advertising executive in Cleveland and Steinbrenner associate, George called all his friends, urging them to cancel their *Press* subscriptions.

He also wanted them to call 15 more friends with the same exhortation. He ordered his players to do the same thing. It was a reverse pyramid scheme, dismantling the structure from the ground up. It never got far.

"It was ridiculous. George didn't have the power to make people do that," said Cleary.[4]

Meanwhile, back at the madhouse on E. 9th Street, Ben Flieger quickly took Cleary's place. "How can you even think about doing this?" Cleary said to the former *Press* reporter. "You know what George is like."

"I've always wanted to work in pro sports," said Flieger.

Cleary called Bob August, Flieger's former boss at the *Press*.

"Augie, sit him down and have a heart-to-heart with him," Cleary said. Nothing worked.

"Ben was going to be the guy who changed George," Cleary said.[5]

Steinbrenner also never paid Cleary—who soon accepted the Kansas City general manager's job he been offered months earlier—his salary for his last two-week period of work.[6]

The first time the Pipers went to Kansas City, in the season's second game, Cleary withheld his two weeks' salary from the Pipers' 20 percent share of the gate receipts. He also deducted two weeks' severance pay.

"You inadvertently neglected to pay me this. Knowing how magnanimous you are, I'm sure you would have wanted to give me two weeks' severance pay too. So I'm withholding four weeks' salary from your gate receipts," Cleary wrote in a note to Steinbrenner.

In the sealed envelope, along with the note, was "the $28.50 that remained [of the box-office take]," Cleary said.

"You SOB, you got me," Steinbrenner said.[7]

But it was Steinbrenner who got Barnett, even though it was without trumpets blaring and flags flying in the media.

Skull was an original—self-taught in his contorted shot and disdainful for much of his life of other types of learning. He converted to academics late in life, eventually becoming a college professor. Dreams don't get much more implausible than that.

Barnett learned to shoot in the night on the playgrounds of the tough steel town of Gary, Indiana, taking aim with cats' eyes that could see the rim in the heart of darkness. The first time McLendon met him, when he was told Barnett was shooting at the playground, the coach simply followed his ears, drawn by the snap of a net followed by the thump of a ball.

Barnett had developed his strange shot over countless repetitions. He rattled the chain-link nets on outdoor rims that were built to withstand shots that clashed instead of swished nylon. He sank silent shots on rims with no nets at all that hung like halos above his head. He shot, and he shot some more, and he shot some more after that, until he had developed an inner gyroscope that kept his game in balance for all the shot's contortions.

It was a shot so unorthodox as to mock the ideals of body alignment and economy in motion, the usual staples of a good outside shooter. Back tilted, legs kicking backward, almost as if they provided the impetus to the ball and not Barnett's left hand—Barnett would loft a shot that was soft and high arching.

McLendon had the good sense not to tinker with it.

"It was a layback. He would go up and back at a 40-degree angle," McLendon told Rhoden. "When he'd hit the floor, he was often off-balance. Sometimes, he'd exaggerate it. One time, he fell clear up in the second row after the shot."

"Fall back, baby!" Legend credits Barnett with yelling that while the ball was in midflight before it slipped into its bed of nylon cords. McLendon claims he would do it in phantom games, played against spectral opponents, alone, in Kean's Little Garden.

According to William Leggett of *Sports Illustrated* in the January 10, 1968, issue in a feature called "A New Knick With a Knack," "When [Barnett] popped a jump shot that he felt was sure to go in or saw teammate take a shot that looked good, he would yell: 'Let's go back!' urging his teammates on the Los Angeles Lakers at the time to retreat on defense."

When Elgin Baylor told Lakers play-by-play broadcaster Chick Hearn about it, Hearn "began to holler over the radio with each of Barnett's jump shots, 'Fall back, baby!' and now fans everywhere have taken it up."

"Jerry West in our league would clap his hands and run off the court while it was still in the air [on game-winning shots at the end of games]," said Wayne Embry. "But Dick was the first to call his shot, so to speak. As trash talk goes, it was pretty mild."[8]

"He was saying 'fall back, baby' in the ABL," said Gene Tormohlen. "I didn't know what trash talk was until I met him. He was known for his shooting, but Johnny McLendon had been his coach in college and, let me tell you, Skull could defend too."[9]

Barnett initially went to Tennessee State because of the close relationship between his high school coach, J. D. Smith, and McLendon.

Twice, Barnett was the Most Valuable Player of the NAIA Tournament, in 1958 and 1959. He was a very talented player, who was often overshadowed by some of the all-time greats with whom he played— Wilson Eison, an All-Big Ten player at Purdue at Gary's Roosevelt High School, Jerry West and Elgin Baylor with the Lakers, Walt Frazier and Willis Reed with two championship Knicks teams, and Dolph Schayes and Hal Greer in Syracuse with the Nats.

Whether he would stay in Nashville or not, keeping the night light on in Doug Bates's tent under the blankets, was another matter.

In Katz's biography of McLendon, *Breaking Through,* he makes the point that McLendon's reputation for passivity was undeserved. He could be firm. He just didn't make a public show of berating players at games or in front of teammates.

Barnett came from a tough neighborhood and had trouble coping with McLendon's firm, but understated discipline. Barnett was in trouble so often in college that McLendon told him to go to the bus station and find a way back home.

The school president at Tennessee State, Dr. Walter Davis, interceded.

"I did not understand that academics and athletics could peacefully and productively coexist," Barnett said in an interview with New York Knicks broadcasters.

To columnist Rhoden, he said: "It wasn't that I wasn't capable. I just didn't have the commitment; I didn't have a focus. I knew I wanted to play basketball. Beyond that, I had a blunted vision. [College] was just something to do at age 18 to stay occupied in basketball and having fun."[10]

With McLendon as the Pipers' coach, Barnett was an easy sell for Steinbrenner. Getting Barnett eligible would be another matter.

Hal Greer, an African American, was already starting at guard for the Nationals. There were unwritten, but always understood, racial quotas at the time. No more than two black starters and certainly no more than three—and only then when they were behind on the scoreboard—could be on the floor at one time.

"I wasn't happy with the minutes I played," said Barnett in a telephone interview. "I also wasn't happy with the social environment. It was a very different atmosphere than in Nashville. It was a radically different world."[11]

He was more outspoken in Leggett's *Sports Illustrated* story, saying, "Ever been to Syracuse, darlin'? It's out to lunch. As soon as I got there I took a little walk around town to see what it was like. When I found that I could go from one end of the town to the other and back again without ever having to raise my arm for a taxi I said, 'Oh, oh, Dick darlin', forget it.'"[12]

The cosmopolitan nature of that comment shows a different player from the one the Pipers acquired after a two-month legal fight.

Sometimes, it seems as though there are two Barnetts, a quiet, shy player who tried to present more confidence off the court than he really felt, and "Fall back, baby!" the man who called his shots on it.

"By the time he was out of Tennessee State, he was probably at the level of a college sophomore, academically," said Mike Cleary. Katz's McLendon biography supports that, calling Barnett an "upper sophomore" at the end of his college eligibility.[13]

Cleary said, "Barnett and John Barnhill used to sit together on plane trips. They always had a chess board between them." Asked which player usually won, Cleary said, "Neither knew how to play. But they thought it made them look smarter."[14]

McLendon said, "[Barnett] is a sociable fellow, but not what you'd call verbose. At Tennessee we used to make some of our trips by auto. I've driven 400 miles in with him and never heard him say a single word."

In an early game with the Pipers, Barnett struck up a conversation with a referee during a break in action. "The referee was in a state of shock," McLendon said.

"Barnett actually started a conversation with me. How about that?" the official said to McLendon.[15]

Barnett signed for $7,000 in 1959–60 with the Nats and played for

$8,500 the next season. He refused a raise to $11,500 for the 1961–62 season, instead agreeing to play for the Pipers for $13,000.

"Dick had a comfort zone with John McLendon," Cleary said. "He was his old college coach. Some of his teammates from Tennessee State were on the team. And we were offering more money. I imagine we outpaid Syracuse by 20 bucks or so. It really was almost about that kind of money then."[16]

Underpublicized as the Barnett signing was, it still was the culmination of a long legal battle. Syracuse had not let him go without a fight. The Nationals obtained a court injunction on October 27, 1961, keeping Barnett from playing for the Pipers, arguing that the "reserve clause" in the contract he had signed the previous season gave the Nats the option to retain his services.

This was a standard fixture of player contracts at the time in all major professional sports. It allowed a team to renew a player's contract for what amounted to perpetuity.

As Barnett's legal fate was being determined, the *Press*'s Sudyk spoke with the Pipers' exiled player, who had been the team's top scorer in several exhibition games. At the time, Barnett was in limbo, playing with former high school and small-college stars and out-of-shape businessmen at Cleveland's Fairfax Recreation Center, where he also conducted clinics for children.

"With the enthusiasm of a sharpshooter who practices with blank cartridges or a fighter who prepares for his next opponent by shadow boxing, Dick Barnett tries to stay sharp in a sport that has him in temporary exile," Sudyk wrote.

"I'm not even allowed to associate with the Piper players off the court. I don't know anyone in Cleveland, so I kill time watching television and going to the movies. This is a lonesome and nerve-wracking life," said Barnett. "Just sitting around wondering who I'll play with or if I'll play at all this season is rough."[17]

During testimony in Barnett's trial, Jim Palmer, a player with the Los Angeles Jets and a former member of the Cincinnati Royals and New York Knicks, testified that Barnett was not a first-stringer in the NBA. Palmer charged that Barnett "looked lost" as a guard with Syracuse and was not a good playmaker."[18]

This assessment was at variance with other assessments. Steinbrenner said, "Bill Sharman told me, in fact, that Dick could be as spectacular as Elgin Baylor if given the chance."

The Pipers' legal argument was based on the precedent set in a California court, which had declared a reserve-clause contract invalid in the Ken Sears case.

"We did not seek out Barnett," said Steinbrenner. "He came to us, mainly because he didn't feel he was playing enough. And we're overjoyed that he did. He was one of the coming superstars of that league [the NBA]."[19]

On December 21, 1961, Common Pleas Judge Saul S. Danaceau granted the Nationals a permanent injunction, preventing Barnett from playing for the Pipers at least until the 1962–63 season. "Professional players have unusual talents and skills, or they would not be so employed. Such players are not easily replaced," said Danaceau.[20]

The next day, Steinbrenner began selling as he had never sold before, not even to Siegfried. He quickly reached an out-of-court settlement with Syracuse owner Danny Biasone. The path to the accord was smoothed by the $35,000 Steinbrenner agreed to pay Biasone.

"George overwhelmed the Syracuse people," Clowser wrote.[21]

The connection with Biasone would surface again as Steinbrenner maneuvered to gain an NBA franchise.

At the moment, however, it was enough that Steinbrenner had cleared every obstacle—his tight-fisted father's objections, his rebel league's lack of reputation, the towering legal obstacle of the reserve clause—and had poured every bit of the persuasiveness he possessed into his sales pitch, and it had resulted in a deal.

Steinbrenner had signed the player who would take the Pipers to the summit of the ABL. This launched the fiery owner on a path on which he almost took a team he had bought when it was busted into the NBA. Such tornadic energy could also be turned on scapegoats and bystanders when Steinbrenner did not get his way. But when he did get his way, he almost got more than seemed humanly possible.

Sudyk's story reflected the excitement over the signing, quoting an unnamed NBA scout as saying "Barnett is as good as Oscar Robertson, now with the Cincinnati Royals, and he is as good a shot as anyone in pro basketball today."[22]

This was the same 1961–62 season in which Robertson averaged a still unmatched season-long "triple-double" (double figures in points, rebounds, and assists), so the Robertson comparison is so far over the top that it needed a rope so it could rappel back down.

"Barnett is a great crowd-pleaser, a fine ball-handler and has a flair that will win him a lot of fans here," said a more realistic McLendon.[23]

In years to come, Barnett's personality did not so much develop as effloresce. Barnett's success with the Pipers, beginning with the very moment when he was freed to play basketball again, seems to have been the start of the transformation. More money is also apt to elevate a man's confidence.

With the Lakers, he roomed with Jerry West. Once in New York, Barnett came back to their room, excited about some shirts he had bought from a vendor on the street. The only problem was they had no sleeves. Barnett, still something of an innocent, had never opened the cardboard box to check them out.

Barnett was a snappy dresser when his shirt sleeves were attached, however. He favored ensembles that included spats and top hats.

He was also an inveterate card player. Barnett carried a small toy trumpet on which he once played "Taps" when Elgin Baylor, a loser in the team's poker game at a hotel the night before, boarded the team bus.

Developing an eccentric, engaging persona, Barnett took to calling strangers, teammates, and much of the world "darlin'."

"When the Lakers traded him away in 1965, I was incredibly disturbed that they would part company with a player of his ability," wrote West in his autobiography, *West by West*.

In the book, West picks two 11-man rosters for his Dream Game, matching players of different eras in their prime. He also came up with a list of 18 players "I particularly admired and whose contributions I felt were undervalued, underappreciated, underrated or all three."[24]

Second on the list, behind Walt Frazier and ahead of such players as Moses Malone, Kevin Garnett, Bill Walton, David Thompson, John Havlicek, and Scottie Pippen, was Barnett.

That was just the beginning of the underestimation of Dick Barnett, however. The little trumpet should have been playing "Charge" instead of "Taps."

Shaken by a serious injury in 1967, Barnett returned to school, realizing he needed a life beyond basketball. Rhoden makes the point in his Barnett essay that education was what Barnett really learned to "fall back on."

Although Barnett never graduated from Tennessee State, he earned a bachelor of science at Cal Polytechnic College in Pomona, making a 150-mile round trip to class while he was a member of the Lakers.

During his years with the Knicks, Barnett earned a master's degree in Public Administration from New York University and followed that in 1991 a PhD from Fordham in Education. He became a college professor at St. John's in New York.

"I long ago determined that I was just as smart as anybody else," he said in the Knicks' video.[25] Today he politely corrects anyone who refers to him as "Mister Barnett," saying, "Doctor."

Barnett joked with sportscaster Howard Cosell after helping the Knicks to the 1970 NBA championship in an epochal series with the Lakers. It was a huge moment in pro basketball history, making the Knicks fashionable in the nation's top media market.

When Cosell praised him for his high-arching, left-handed layups over the Lakers' Chamberlain, Barnett had a ready quip. He had known payday shortages with the Pipers. "I saw dollar signs up there on the backboard," he said.[26]

The stress should be on the shot's trajectory and not the pot of gold at the end of the arc. It had started out as a shot in the dark, but Barnett learned to aim far higher than at a basketball goal.

CHAPTER II

Cage Fight

After the loss to Chicago, the Pipers had a 14–9 record. They lost five of six games in the stretch just before and after Christmas, including two out of three on the road to the cellar-dwelling Washington Tapers.

Steinbrenner, fuming at home, took note of those losses and brought them up in an angry attack on McLendon in a public forum before the year was out.

On December 27, in a column with the headline "Trouble at Top Endangering Pipers," Clowser divulged that Steinbrenner had charged into the locker room after the December 21 loss to Chicago. "I don't want to tell you how to run your team," Clowser quoted Steinbrenner as saying. He then promptly did just that. The furious owner screamed that, among other things, the effort that night was poor because the players were more interested in going out on dates after the game than playing basketball.

Clowser cited injuries to Warley, Barnhill, and Siegfried, and declared that the players had worked so hard to make up for such losses that "they should be receiving front office plaudits, not criticism."[1]

George Steinbrenner's store of plaudits, however, was usually restricted to those he was wooing and did not have under contract. He had no facility for channeling his anger into anything but castigation or his disappointment into anything but derision.

"The current Pipers . . . will continue as championship contenders ONLY IF [Clowser's capitals] their morale isn't dampened by the misguided actions of the club president," the columnist wrote.[2]

It was the right lecture, but it fell on the wrong ears. Steinbrenner's voracious need to win was so all-consuming that it almost devalued victory. It certainly made considerations of team morale meaningless.

What George had really wanted for Christmas, it seemed, was a new coach. That, or the opportunity to return the one he had.

In basketball's early days, players were called "cagers" for the simple reason that games were played inside chicken wire strung around the court. The "cages" the wire resembled were designed to keep spectators and players apart and to remedy the sport's disastrous first out-of-bounds rule.

In 1904, the ball was simply awarded to the first team touching it after it rolled out of bounds. This led to ferocious, football-like piles of clawing, punching players. If a ball bounced off the cast-iron rim of the basket (used instead of peach baskets as early as 1893) and flew into a balcony, players would stampede upstairs to try to retain possession. Some teams even bodily lifted a lightweight player up to the balcony, shortcutting the stairs entirely. That rule was changed in 1913 so that the team that touched the ball last on the playing floor lost possession.

The cages actually proved dangerous. Players shoved opponents into the wire, much as hockey players "board" rivals. The wires left a crosshatching of cuts, some of which became infected if the fencing was old and rusty. By 1933, the cages were gone too. Still, the term "cagers," which fit neatly into headlines, was used for decades afterward.

The Cleveland Cagers Club met downtown on December 27, 1961, to hear Pipers president George Steinbrenner discuss the state of the team. At the meeting, Steinbrenner burst completely out of the fragile cage in which he had tried to pen his simmering emotions.

It wasn't a speech that he gave that day, it was a scathing indictment of his coach. Like the cage wire, the remarks were cutting and capable of leaving scars. It was the verbal equivalent of a mixed martial arts fight inside the sport's eight-sided cage called "The Octagon."

Heaton provided the most thorough coverage of Steinbrenner's trademark style of threats and bombast, followed by a tepid attempt at tempering the criticism. "John selected the players, and he knows what's expected of him—a first half championship," Steinbrenner said. "We should be waltzing away with the title. I won't accept second place."[3]

Such an ultimatum is usually delivered in private, much as a good coach spares players a public reprimand, for all that he might blister the office walls in a closed-door meeting. This was not Steinbrenner's style. He would bulldoze this hurdle if necessary. Admitting he had underestimated the difficulty of the jump from the semi-pros to professional basketball, he made a passing reference to the team's injuries but quickly returned to the problem, as he saw it, of McLendon.

"Injuries have hurt us, but that shouldn't be an excuse. John is bumping up against some real good coaches, as good as he is," Steinbrenner said.[4]

With a limited background in basketball, Steinbrenner had decided his team was too one-dimensional. "Racehorse basketball won't go in this league, though," he said. "The players are too experienced."[5]

The remedy, said the owner, was simple: "You have to set plays, set some patterns."

This was the antithesis of the rapid pace at which McLendon wanted his team to play. A fast break team should get more wide open shots than a more deliberate offensive team, both because of the manpower advantage the fast break can create and because the defense is not organized.[6]

After Steinbrenner told the crowd that he felt some of the players didn't mind losing, he said, apparently seriously, "I will never stick my nose into coaching. I will never be a good loser, either."[7]

The *Press* quoted him more briefly, but also more bluntly: "[McLendon] hand-picked all his players, and we obtained them for him. The job is to mold them into a team. I have been attacked for criticizing John McLendon. Goodness, he's not God Almighty."[8]

It is almost possible to sympathize with Steinbrenner. The coverage of McLendon by Clowser certainly was as admiring as the gushy series he would soon write about Jerry Lucas.

Steinbrenner had a legitimate point in his emphasis on adding size, with which McLendon, champion of the smaller, swifter, and fitter, eventually concurred.

But with George, it always came back to names (bigger) and money (littler).

"Coaches like Neil Johnston of Pittsburgh with years of experience have the jump on John. He has a lot of catching up to do," Steinbrenner said to the *Press*. "We've paid out a lot of money to give Cleveland the best obtainable [players]. Our payroll is over $100,000, twice that of Pittsburgh."[9]

He also gave a figurative, flirtatious wink to the NBA, saying how impressed he had been with NBA officials during the settlement of the Barnett case.

Finally, further depressing the Cagers Club audience that had probably expected peppy discussions of a happy new year on the hardwood in 1962, Steinbrenner said of the Pipers' flagging attendance, "We'll get through the season. The ABL will function next year, but I don't know where we will be."[10]

Reached by telephone, McLendon tersely told Heaton his concentration was on winning the Tapers game in Washington, D.C., that night and that there would be ample time to discuss Steinbrenner's remarks when the team returned home.

Reports of those remarks did not act like a revitalizing tonic on the Pipers players. For the third time in the four games between the teams thus far, the Pipers lost to the last-place Tapers. The Pipers blew an early 19-point lead in a 123–106 loss, a turnaround of a staggering 36 points that did nothing to mollify their owner.

At that point, Cleveland's record was 17–17, tied for the East lead with the Rens, a one-man team. Despite the lackluster mark, the Cleveland writers rose as one in defense of McLendon. After the next game, a 124–98 rout of the Tapers in Public Hall on December 29, which was led by Barnett's 25 points, Heaton wrote, "It may have been Coach John McLendon's answer to President George Steinbrenner of the Pipers."[11] Heaton indicated that "racehorse" basketball had certainly worked for the night, at any rate.

Clowser wrote in the *Press,* getting near the probable motivation of the owner, "The team played scrappy basketball all the way. If Steinbrenner wanted to ignite a bigger spark in the squad, his efforts seem to have been successful." Clowser also noted that Warley, who got what today would be a stupendous 26 rebounds in the game, was finally starting to look like himself.

At this time, another of the interminable ABL squabbles arose. They seemed to follow Steinbrenner around like thunder on the heels of lightning.

Although Pittsburgh had announced its intention to sign six-foot-eight Archie Dees, who had been released by the NBA's St. Louis Hawks, Steinbrenner had signed him instead.

At ABL meetings in Saperstein's Chicago office on December 29, the Pipers, possibly on the principle of the squeaky wheel's tendency to get the grease, emerged with the services of Dees, a former Indiana University standout.

Dees scored three points, playing briefly in the fourth quarter during a 124–98 victory in Cleveland the same night over the Tapers.

Heaton wrote that it was "undoubtedly a coincidence" that, no sooner had Steinbrenner taken his seat, after returning from Chicago in the third quarter "than the team went as frigid as the weather outside."

A 118–104 victory on December 30 left the Pipers with six games remaining in the first half schedule, to be played the next year in its first nine days.

After sitting mutely before his typewriter as Steinbrenner's eruptions became almost as regular as those of a geyser, Gordon Cobbledick, the *Plain Dealer*'s basketball-averse sports editor, weighed in on the controversy. Actually, Cobbledick used the words of a reader, John Braucher of St. Ignatius High School, to make points that he merely seconded.

An employer criticizing an employe [*sic*] is nothing new. But in this case it seems to be in particularly bad taste. Apparently the president of the Pipers does not want a Negro, a gentleman and a peerless basketball man to be his coach. As for his coaching ability, the record speaks for itself.

John is a gentleman. No one who has met him, heard him speak or seen him on the sideline can deny it. He also shares his knowledge willingly with younger, less experienced coaches.

The president must decide whether he wants a basketball team or a circus . . . If there must be a sideshow, it should take place between halves.

If coach McLendon is replaced by the kind of showboat coach the president seems to prefer, the Pipers and the City of Cleveland will feel the loss.[12]

Replied Cobbledick in his column:

For what it's worth, I'm with you. I felt strongly that George Steinbrenner was out of line when he let go his recent blast at McLendon in the hearing of the players.

If he wants to fire the coach, it's his right. But it's an established principle in the business world that you don't chew out the foreman when the mill hands can hear you . . .

Steinbrenner's insistence on a first half championship as a condition of McLendon's employment put both coach and team in an impossible situation. I can't recall another case in which a club owner stated publicly that the manager would be fired unless he won the pennant.[13]

Cobbledick chose to refer to the sport of basketball by a feminine pronoun in his conclusion, which probably indicated how he felt about the game. "As something less than a truly dedicated follower of basketball as she is played in this city in this day of astronomical scores," he admitted he lacked the tactical knowledge to comment on McLendon's coaching moves. "[But] As between the two [Steinbrenner and McLendon], I have to go with the man who has devoted his adult life to coaching, just as I am obliged to believe that Paul Brown knows more about football than the Joe Blows who pan his strategy.

"McLendon is a credit to Cleveland. I don't want to lose him. Will you, therefore, join me in hoping the Pipers will win the first half championship so he can keep his job?"

He then initialed the column "G.C.," as if it were a personal letter, answering that of the fan.

Steinbrenner soon would resort to a letter-writing campaign of his own, although it was written by him and signed by unpaid players under pressure of being fired.

CHAPTER 12

The Amazing Jerry Lucas

As the season got stormier, Hurricane George moved inland off the
Great Lakes, with its tongue lashing everything in its path. Through
all the roof-rattling and window-shaking, Steinbrenner still clung to the
hope he could sign the one player to provide the commercial success
that Barnett was to supply artistically—Jerry Ray Lucas.

Lucas's Ohio State Buckeyes, in this, his senior season, were again
unbeaten and ranked in their customary spot at the top of the national
wire service polls.

There are few student athletes like Jerry Lucas—whether his name is
spelled J-e-r-r-y L-u-c-a-s or e-J-r-r-y a-c-L-s-u, with the letters alphabet-
ized, a trick Lucas's facile brain could turn in an instant. And so it is hard
to grasp the place he occupied in the American sports consciousness in
the early 1960s.

He was smart, prodigiously gifted at his game, studious, and patriotic.
He was the best player on the best college team in the country for most
of his last three seasons, the only ones in which he was eligible in those
days when freshmen were actually allowed a year in which to acclimate
themselves to college life.

He got his degree in marketing at Ohio State with election to Beta
Sigma Gamma, the School of Commerce's equivalent of Phi Beta Kappa.

He dropped out of school against the wishes of his coaches to make
the Russian trip with the Pipers, enjoying what he called the most

interesting weeks of his life. His wife, Treva, dropped out in the winter quarter of 1961, working at a bank to support the couple.

"I'm determined she's going to finish up and get her degree too. If anything happened to me, she would have her education—and the better educated we all are, the better will be the contributions we all can make to society," Lucas told the *Press*'s Jack Clowser in the second part of a four-part series titled "Jerry Lucas—All-Around All-American."[1]

Clowser was an Ohio State loyalist, a reporter so close to Woody Hayes that, when Clowser was once late for Hayes's weekly press conference, the coach refused to start until the *Cleveland Press* correspondent arrived.

As the Ohio State basketball team won game after game, Clowser accused Indiana's Branch McCrackin in print of being the lone voter in the coaches' anonymous poll not to vote Ohio State first in the land.

Clowser was wrong, but the one-man witch hunt shows that he was, as Cleary called him, "an Ohio State freak." But he got freakiest about Lucas.

The house mother at the fraternity Lucas had joined, Beta Theta Pi, told Clowser that Lucas had laid out his life in such a way as to be known, in order, as a gentleman, a fine student, and a basketball player. Lucas was a point of pride for the entire country, leading the 1960 Olympic team that also boasted future Basketball Hall of Famers West, Robertson, and Walter Bellamy to the gold medal as its top scorer and rebounder and one of its best play-makers.

Basketball was hardly an obsession with him, however. He chose Ohio State from over 500 suitors because it was the only school that stressed academics first. Steinbrenner's best man and the Pipers' investor and former Ohio State All-American Jimmy Hull, helped steer Lucas away from Cincinnati to Ohio State. There, Lucas insisted on an academic, not athletic, scholarship, in case he grew tired of basketball.

He denied many times that he wanted to play pro basketball, saying he did not fancy living out of a suitcase and miss watching the four boys he hoped to father grow up. (He had actually planned his life down to the gender and number of his children. He thought he could plan his life, A to Z, an odd presumption for an indecisive man, it turned out.)

Lucas was also a source of enormous state pride in Ohio, the leader of a team made up entirely of Ohio boys. It was an Ohio state, lower case, team in literal terms with no pipeline to the teeming boroughs of New York, such as the one enjoyed by the University of North Carolina, and no connections to basketball in Washington, D.C., which had taken little Seattle University to great heights in the 1950s.

In addition to alphabetizing anything (a-g-h-i-n-n-t-y) in an instant, Lucas could memorize reams of phone numbers in the encyclopedic Manhattan phone book. The only thing he forgot, his former Ohio State roommate John Havlicek told *Sports Illustrated* magazine's Ray Cave, was a defeat. To that point, Lucas had lost only 13 games in six years.

"I play a defeat over and over," said Havlicek. "With Luke, it's as if a curtain comes down. As if it never happened."[2]

In naming Lucas its Sportsman of the Year in 1961, a year in which Roger Maris hit 61 home runs, beating Babe Ruth's 1927 record, *Sports Illustrated* obviously took into account Lucas's academic record, global popularity, and unquenchable intellectual curiosity.

Cave praised Lucas's willingness to wander the streets of Moscow, his interpreter in tow, on the Pipers' barnstorming trip, making friends and exchanging ideas while older and less worldly teammates like Swartz and Adams hid in their hotel rooms, seeing spies under the bed.

"The average Russian is just like the average American. Or for that matter like the average citizen of any country I know about firsthand," said Lucas. "If you took away the heads of government in Russia, it would be a land a great deal like ours."[3]

Then Lucas held forth on the grand patterns of history.

We are advancing into a different age, but humanity has always been facing the dangers of new ages. They thought no one would survive the plague. They thought the machine gun was the ultimate weapon of war. Now this is the atomic age, but it's just another phase of history. My generation must realize that it soon will have the responsibility of running this country. It must accept this responsibility as a challenge, not fear it. We can't go along with those who would rather be Red than dead.[4]

Frank Gibbons of the *Press* was in thrall to the Lucas mystique as much as Clowser, urging government service on him and saying, "If this isn't a ready made shining symbol of the youth of this country we may never have another."

Incisively, however, Gibbons became the first writer not to buy into Lucas's often stated disinclination to play in the pros. "When he stopped playing basketball, he would stop being a symbol," Gibbons wrote.[5]

After games on the Russian junket, said John McLendon, Lucas often arrived in the locker room a half-hour after the rest of the team, having spent the time with Russian fans, who knew and admired him from his play in Rome the year before. Invariably, Lucas would head to the showers after removing a sweat suit festooned with souvenir badges and pins of all sorts, given him by the worshipful fans.[6]

"The Russian people really loved him. He was a very modest guy. I never saw anybody who could rebound and throw the ball out like him, not even Wes Unseld," said Adams of the "Wide U," a player known for rocketing his passes. "The first time he fired it out to me, it went through my hands into the stands. I wasn't ready for it."[7]

Lucas made it a point after NCAA games to shake hands with rival players who had not sprinted to the locker room after another drubbing by the Buckeyes. He was so squeaky clean that his sweat suit probably smelled of apple pie and cinnamon.

Lucas was really the first Bill Bradley, who came along later in the 1960s. Bradley, also from the Midwest (Missouri), was a driven, obsessive player who took the Ivy League's Princeton Tigers to the 1965 NCAA Final Four and then studied abroad on a Rhodes Scholarship before joining the New York Knicks—with whom he was eventually paired with Lucas and Barnett on the 1972–73 NBA champions.

Bradley, in John McPhee's acclaimed essay, "A Sense of Where You Are," was depicted as a physical marvel with the peripheral vision of an Argus.

For his part, Lucas had 20–10 vision, meaning he could see at 20 feet what those with 20–20 vision saw at 10 feet. The great baseball hitter Ted Williams had such acute vision. So did World War II fighter ace and Cold War test pilot Chuck Yeager.

While peripheral vision might seem to be more an asset than visual acuity in basketball, a sport of passing angles and spatial relationships, perhaps the vision allowed Lucas to read the spin on shots more accurately than others and thus position himself for rebounds more adroitly.

In addition to his visual gift, he made an intensive study of rebounding. Rebounding wasn't simply jumping ability and height with him. He kept a mental "book" on teammates and rivals alike, knew in which direction they were likely to miss from what range and to which part of the court, and adjusted accordingly.

He thought of the basket as a 12-hour clock face and then took the correct rebounding positions—3 o'clock or 9 o'clock to the sides, 6 o'clock for a short shot falling in the lane, and so on.

He was, like Bellamy, a "stretch big" before the term was fashionable. The so-called "Lucas Layup," a jump shot with a towering arc from the top of the foul circle, far enough from the rim to be a college three-pointer today, was his signature shot. Opposing forwards and centers hated to be drawn out of the rebounding pattern to contest that shot, but Lucas's touch left them no choice.

Beyond all that, he came along, untarnished and cerebral, at a time when college basketball had been tainted and nearly ruined by point-shaving scandals.

He and his teammates also filled the rooting vacuum created when the Ohio State Faculty Council voted against sending the Buckeye football team to the Rose Bowl after the 1961 season, even though they were the Big Ten champions.

Finally, Lucas was white. It mattered.

Although the PGA Tour revoked its "Caucasian clause," forthrightly ending its color ban, on November 10, 1961, just as the Pipers' season was beginning, such avowed color-blindness was not the trend in other sports, even basketball.

The dominant players in both the NBA and ABL were black players—Chamberlain, Bill Russell, Baylor, and Robertson in the NBA; Hawkins, Barnett, and Bill Bridges in the ABL. The paying customers were mostly white.

At the NAIA Tournament in Kansas City—always a magnet for scouts to find such small-school players as Barnett, Earl "The Pearl" Monroe, and World B. Free—Cleary, McMahon, future Marquette coach Al McGuire, and former Kansas University star Clyde Lovellette of the St. Louis Hawks met over drinks.

"I would be hard-pressed to name an all-white All-Star team that could compete in the NBA," said Cleary.[8]

An uncomfortable silence followed, as the basketball men doodled names on cocktail napkins, then crossed them out as so much cannon fodder for Wilt Chamberlain and Bill Russell, Robertson or Baylor.

Finally, a perturbed Lovellette said, "Well, you'd start with me at center, wouldn't you?"[9]

After the ABL folded, Cleary was a Midwest scout for the Knicks and wore a championship ring for his efforts from the 1969–70 season.

Ned Irish, the founder of the Knicks, told Cleary, "Do not come back and tell us about another great black player. Your job is to find a white second-round draft choice."

"Everybody wanted one in the late '60s in the NBA," said Cleary. "I was based in Minneapolis and spent much of the year flying to Fargo to scout a kid at the University of North Dakota, Phil Jackson. He was the player I recommended."[10]

Jackson was a substitute and contributor to the Knicks' 1972–73 NBA championship. He became one of the great NBA coaches with the Chicago Bulls and Los Angeles Lakers. The Knicks took Jackson with the fifth pick of the second round of the 1967 draft, number 17 overall.

"As Phil's career progressed, Irish would call me when he was stiff [drunk], which was at every game, calling at 11 o'clock at night," Cleary said.

"Your guy did great," Irish would say.[11]

Imagine how great Lucas might do. Everyone in the NBA could.

The Cincinnati Royals of the NBA drafted Lucas as a territorial pick four years earlier, straight out of high school at Middletown, halfway between Dayton and Cincinnati.

Asked about the Pipers' chances of signing Lucas to the upstart ABL, were he turn to pro, given the aggressiveness of Cincinnati in the more established NBA, Steinbrenner chuckled and said, "Look, Cincinnati tried to get former Ohio State star Larry Siegfried last year. And if you've been to one of our ballgames, you know he's in a Piper uniform."[12]

CHAPTER 13

"A Team Divided"

B ut Lucas was not in Cleveland yet, and any chance of signing him was, the basketball cognoscenti thought, a long shot that would dwarf the ABL's three-pointer with all its bells, lights, and Ruthian evocations of distance.

If the Pipers celebrated New Year's Eve, it probably was with champagne of an unfashionable vintage. It did not appear that a very good year lay ahead.

On New Year's Day 1962, Heaton wrote an advance on the Pipers' upcoming game in Akron against the Chicago Majors, calling the Cleveland club "a team divided."

Acting in his role as team captain, Adams tried to still the troubled waters with a statement that bordered on the obsequious. "We were down, and I appreciated that [Steinbrenner] came in and said what he did," said Adams. "George has worked hard for this team. He's the type of fellow I'd want at the head of a basketball team I owned. He wants a winner, and he'll get it one way or the other."[1]

At least to the beat writers and headline writers, McLendon had already won the debate over basketball tactics.

"Racehorse Pipers Tied for First," the *Press* chortled after a 117–99 victory in Akron over the Majors. The lure of the first pro basketball game in the Rubber City in 20 years proved resistible. An announced crowd of 1,635 watched.

The unnamed freelancer for the *Press*—neither Heaton nor Sudyk ventured the 50 miles south to cover the game—called Adams "One of the top jockeys on Cleveland's racehorse basketball team" and bemoaned the fact that the jockey had gone head over bridle after being "bumped hard under the basket during the second quarter," which forced Adams to leave the game.

Barnett led the way with 30 points. Such a performance was nothing new to McLendon, who reflected on Barnett's Tennessee State career to the *Plain Dealer*'s Bob Dolgan. "He was easily our best man, even though we had Warley and Barnhill," the coach said. "The team knew it and was more interested in getting him the ball than anything else. In fact, I was accused of having a Barnett offense. Well, now he has more of a team perspective, which is necessary in a tougher league."[2]

Down 13 points in the third quarter, the Pipers stormed back to win their fourth game in a row on January 3, beating Chicago again, this time at Public Hall, 114–104.

McLendon was dismayed by the 25 turnovers his team committed and the 0-for-11 start in field goal attempts but said, "When you don't play good basketball, it is a good sign if you can still win."[3]

Some of the same refereeing McMahon had deplored might have helped. The Pipers made 40 of 50 free throws to the Majors' 22 of 24. The victory left the Pipers tied for first with the Rens with 21–17 records and four games to play in the first half of the season.

"The Pipers have found another good big man—and just when they needed him most," wrote Clowser in the *Press,* noting that Dees contributed nine points in the game, had played good defense, and had been on the floor during the fourth quarter comeback.

It was not a judgment that withstood the test of time. On January 6 at Public Hall, in a meeting of David and Goliath, the Pipers, the league's smallest team, were tossed into the quarry, losing to the San Francisco Saints, who, due to the uncertainty about the Jets and rosterchanges, were now the league's tallest team, 103–93. Jim Francis and Kenny Sears, both six foot ten, and Mike Farmer, six foot nine, were all taller than Dees and Romanoff, who were both six eight. The Saints collected 62 rebounds to the Pipers' 48 in a 103–93 Saints victory.

"The Saints were too tall, that's all," Heaton concluded.[4]

In Columbus two nights later, the Pipers were aided by the absence of Farmer and Francis, who had scored 35 in the Saints' win. A stiff neck kept Farmer idle and heavy cold sidelined Francis. Barnett scored 37 points in the 140–107 Pipers victory.

But, to resume the equine metaphor that had become all the rage in Cleveland, Barnett was beaten in a "photo finish" for team scoring honors by Johnny Cox with 39.

"Cox is the best player who can't play basketball that I've ever seen," Adolph Rupp had said years before at a coaching clinic in which he and McLendon appeared. "[Cox] can't run and he can't dribble, but he can help any team plenty."

McLendon said, "It's true that Johnny isn't that talented in many ways, but there's one thing he can do. He can put the ball in the basket."

"You can't teach that to anybody. You've either got it or you don't," McLendon added, in a remark that might dismay the shot technicians who are employed in today's game to diagnose and correct shooting flaws.[5]

Undersized as a six-foot-four, 190-pound forward, Cox gave up approximately 25 pounds to most of the men he defended and rebounded against. He made up for this with a pugnacity that Sudyk tactfully described as being "scrappy [and] rather accurate with his knuckles."

Small, slow, too light—Cox survived on his shooting eye. He was a gunner, or, as such a player is called now, a "volume shooter."

McLendon knew when to use a relaxed hold on the reins with his players. Cox was such a player. "I've never told Cox to hold back on his shots," McLendon said. "The only thing I've asked is that he not take those exceptionally long ones too often."[6]

Barnhill, Cox, and Barnett all served together for a year in the peacetime Army at Fort Knox, Kentucky. When McLendon took the NIBL job with the Pipers, the two former Tennessee State Tigers urged the coach to sign Cox, who had impressed them in games at the base.

Before that, Cox was a great high school player in basketball-mad Kentucky, playing two years in the small coal-mining town of Neon and then being recruited by powerful Hazard High School for his last two years. There, Cox set scoring records that were surpassed only by Kelly "King" Coleman of the Majors.

According to McLendon, Cox walked into Rupp's office before Kentucky recruited him and told him he was going to make the team, even though no one from his part of the state had ever played for the "Baron of the Bluegrass."

Cox became a starter on Kentucky's 1958 NCAA champions. His number 24 jersey hangs in the rafters of Rupp Arena in Lexington, Kentucky. The 1958 Kentucky team was known as the "Fiddlin' Five," because Rupp had quipped that his players were fiddlers when he really needed violinists. In the same vein, Cox had little neon to his game except for his hometown, but he could light up a scoreboard.

In the race to the first half division title, the Rens were proving the truth of Cleary's comment about the distractions, jet lag, and inhospitable resident referees in the state of Hawaii. The Chiefs overcame a 19-point halftime deficit to beat the Rens, 107–105, in a game Hawkins missed with a sprained ankle.

Sudyk noted that the first half playoffs would begin on January 12. But Pittsburgh and the Pipers, neck and neck in the race for the East championship, would not by then have played an equal number of games. Cleveland would have played 42, the Rens 43.

"Somewhere along the line, the Rens played an extra game. ABL games have been rescheduled and some others added, almost at will by the clubs involved," Sudyk wrote, because of the uncertainty surrounding the Jets' franchise.[7]

Eventually, the league decided that, of the Rens' final two games on the West Coast against the Saints, only the first would count in the first half standings, while the second would be their first of the second half.

Preparations for a possible East Division playoff game between Cleveland and Pittsburgh, which would precede the best-of-three playoff series between the winner and Kansas City, had, however, become complicated.

On January 9, Dolgan wrote of the possible pre-playoff playoff game, "The site will be determined in this ridiculous fashion: The scores of tonight's four ABL games will be totaled. If the sum is an odd number, the game will be here in Public Hall. If it comes out even, the game will be in Pittsburgh."[8]

Steinbrenner's snort of disgust could almost be heard in the prose of Dolgan, who reported that the Pipers' owner, convinced that the 5–4 advantage Cleveland had in head-to-head games was a more equitable and sensible way to decide the matter, was protesting the decision.

It did not come to that. Saperstein, abandoning the idea of determining the playoff site based on head-to-head records, also abandoned the arithmetical approach. Instead, he flipped a coin, which would become a reliable Saperstein expedient in a pinch. The result gave the hypothetical game to Pittsburgh.

The Renaissance, however, lost their final game of the first half schedule, 128–119, to San Francisco in a game played in Los Angeles. Hawkins, who had been ruled out of the game, instead played and played valiantly, scoring 47 points, including 18 in a row at one point, all in vain.

The Pipers took advantage. Barnett's 41 points and 15 rebounds led Cleveland to a 141–124 victory over the New York Tapers in a game played in Lorain, Ohio. That secured at least a tie for the East and a playoff game in Pittsburgh.

The Pipers clinched the title outright by beating Kansas City in Chicago the next night, in overtime, 115–110.

The Steers' spot in the playoffs had been assured for days, but their motivation was to beat Cleveland, force both the Pipers and Rens to play the extra playoff game the next night in Pittsburgh, and then trample the exhausted survivor.

It almost worked. The Steers led, 91–79, before Barnett and Roger Taylor led a fourth-quarter rally. Staverman's tip-in in the last 30 seconds tied it, 106–106, and sent the game into overtime. But the Pipers, behind baskets by Warley, Cox, and Barnett, pulled away.

Taylor, with 30 for the Pipers, and the Cleveland scourge Bill Bridges, with as many for Kansas City, were the top scorers. Cox with 20 and Barnett with 19 backed Taylor.

"They outrebounded us," said McLendon. "But we won because we were shooting hot. They have two fellows who really climb those boards—Larry Staverman and Bill Bridges."

"This Bridges is something else," McLendon added. "He's only 6–5, and we haven't figured out how to stop him yet. I had John Cox, Nick

Romanoff, Archie Dees, Ben Warley and Jack Adams on him, and he still scored 30 points."[9]

Neither the *Press* nor the *Plain Dealer* covered the game, which denied posterity Sudyk's whimsical humor, Dolgan's flavorful anecdotes, Clowser's authoritative air, and Heaton's consistently even-handed treatment.

The Pipers finished the first half with a 24–18 record, one game ahead of Pittsburgh. Kansas City won the West Division with a 28–12 record, seven games ahead of San Francisco.

The first half playoffs began two days later in Kansas City. What was to come provided enough color, controversy, bluster, bullying, and humiliation to satisfy any drama critic or crusading sportswriter.

CHAPTER 14

The First Half Playoffs—
"Heads Will Roll!"

Past is often prelude in sports.

In baseball, the concept takes on tactical and technical aspects. The previous at-bat or even the previous pitch often sets up what the batter will encounter in the next time at the plate or on the next offering.

The past can also be a motivational tool. A previous defeat is often the spur for revenge in the teams' next meeting. "Bulletin board" quotes by the opposition are prominently displayed to inflame football players.

In basketball, past becomes measurable—in miles traveled, anyway. Fatigue, mental and physical, is an opponent as real as the opposing team. The modern NBA term for this is a "schedule win."

That, in a nutshell, is why the Pipers lost the first half playoff series to the Steers, two games to one.

Since Steinbrenner's barrage of criticism at the Cagers Club, the Pipers had played nine games, all of them pressure-packed, in six cities in 15 days. They had played in Washington; in Cleveland at Public Hall; in "home" games in Columbus, more than two hours away, and in the seats of adjoining counties (Akron and Lorain); and in Chicago. Their record in the games was 7–2. As a finish, it was impressive.

Except it wasn't the finish. It also was no way to prepare for a series against the league's best team.

The Pipers practiced on January 11 in Kansas City and then played the first playoff game there on the 12th. The series would continue at

Public Hall on the 13th and, if necessary, on the 14th. The winner was guaranteed a spot in the ABL Finals in the spring.

Before the playoffs began, Kansas City fretted about how to support the brilliant Bridges. Bridges had had to do so much because Larry Comley, the Steers' best rebounder among the team's reserves, had been called up to the Army and was not available as the first half of the season drew to a close.

McMahon hoped Bryce Vann and Greg Pruitt could take Comley's place in the rotation. He was half right. Vann would play an important role in the playoff series. Pruitt would provide one of the indelible images of the ABL in a donnybrook in the league's dying days.

Despite the Pipers' fatigue, Fritz Kreisler of the *Kansas City Star* cast Cleveland as the favorite, arguing that the holdovers from the NIBL champions, plus Barnett, were expected to have their way with their opponents in the fledgling league.

That it did not happen, that the Steers became the league's best team by overall record, still did not mean much in basketball, a game of head-to-head matchups. The Pipers went into the playoff series as the only team with a winning record against Kansas City.

The Pipers put Cox on Bridges in the opener, and he did a good job. Cox, however, was not around for the conclusion of a dismal 106–93 Pipers loss.

After a melee under the basket midway through the third quarter, with the Pipers trailing, 74–49, Cox and the Steers' Maury King traded punches and were ejected. The ejection galvanized the Pipers, as they urged their tired bodies to run "with such fury that you almost could see the Steers' knees buckle," according to Kreisler.

Staverman unbuckled them, scoring 25 points to make up for only nine points by Bridges.

Before being ejected, King, who scored 17, held Barnett to 10, barely more than half his 19-point total in the overtime victory two nights earlier.

"In this league, you have to match baskets, and we didn't," said McLendon of the Steers' 45 field goals to the Pipers' 32.[1]

It was an odd admission for a man who predicated much of his offense on getting to the foul line. That was the only part of the Pipers' game that really performed, as the Pipers enjoyed a 27–12 advantage at the foul line.

McMahon proved the aptness of Kreisler's observation that he was the players' friend by constantly breaking off his interview with media members after the game to congratulate first one player and then another in the locker room.

In a 98–87 series-squaring victory at Public Hall the next night, Barnhill, who was playing with his left leg taped from thigh to ankle due to a "gimpy knee," came off the bench to score 13. The Pipers, who had led by 15 at halftime and by 13 in the middle of the third quarter, saw their lead shrink to six points as Bridges (22 points) finally found his touch.

Into the game came Barnett and Barnhill, the "B&B Boys." That was Heaton's riff on the Yankees' "M&M Boys" (Mickey Mantle and Roger Maris) of the previous season's epic home run race. In the last quarter, the "B's" killed the Steers, scoring 16 of the Pipers' first 18 points.

From the Steers' perspective, the second game turned on the play of Dees and Nick Romanoff. Dees, a surprise starter, held Bridges in check and Romanoff, who didn't play at all in the division-clinching game in Chicago, scored six points in the early going to get the Pipers off to a fast start.

Steinbrenner must have been pleased by the 4,276 in attendance. The same night at Philadelphia's Convention Hall, Chamberlain scored 73 points against the Chicago Packers, yet only 3,516 showed up.

But only 2,313 showed up on a Sunday afternoon at Public Hall for the third and final game against the Steers.

The *Press*'s Frank Gibbons addressed the attendance woes in a column earlier in the season. Gibbons said Public Hall, which had not been a sports venue for years, was a problem. Most of the games had been switched there because the Barons had priority at the Arena.

Fans could walk to the Arena, but it was a long hike to the Hall. Shuttle buses were installed for the playoff games at the Hall.

Gibbons said the ABL was as close to the NBA as the American Football League was to the NFL. The Pipers also were "a basketball team of exemplary virtue."

He guessed they had several players who could play in the NBA. Barnett, Barnhill, Cox, Warley, Dees, and Connie Dierking (not yet acquired) actually did.

But artistic success was not enough. "Artists may work best in cold and lonely garrets. But sports teams have got to have people who pay to look over their shoulders. . . . It might help if the Pipers had a player nine feet tall who could pot baskets while blindfolded or standing on his head," Gibbons wrote.[2]

In the third game, Kansas City built a big lead; weathered a flurry by the Pipers, who closed to within six points in the fourth quarter, on the strength of Bridges' work; and pulled away for a 120–104 victory.

Mantis played his best overall game with 23 points and a Steers' record 11 assists. Kreisler said Mantis augmented his usual accurate jumper with "unbelievable drives up the middle."[3]

Tormohlen almost had a triple double with 12 points, 13 rebounds, and nine assists.

Staverman, told to "fire away" by McMahon, rather than "operating a la Jerry Lucas and passing off," hit 10 of his 12 shots for 24 points. Bridges added 22.

McMahon chose to praise Vann's defensive energy as a decisive factor, citing a steal he made at midcourt that became a breakaway layup when the Pipers were only trailing by eight points with six minutes to play. "If that guy could recover half of the balls he slaps, he'd be great," McMahon said.[4]

"After that series, I felt we were invincible," said Cleary. "I couldn't see how we would lose the final playoffs. The Cleveland club just had so many players coming and going that year. Our roster didn't change much. We stayed the same."[5]

Heaton wrote that the Pipers "appeared ragged and weary."[6]

Barnett got only 16 points (or 18, if you count everything he deposited in the basket, as we shall see shortly). Typical of their lack of continuity was the fact that Adams scored 25 of his 30 points in the first half, while Siegfried netted all 26 of his in the second. Two soloists do not make a choir.

Wrote Sudyk: "The Pipers could not have rolled a seven with a pair of loaded dice. They missed nearly a dozen layups. John Barnhill, all alone, slipped and fell under the basket on a fast break and Dick Barnett tipped in a rebound for Kansas City—it was that kind of day."[7]

Such days were unacceptable to Steinbrenner. The furious owner barged into the locker room after the loss. "John McLendon had a real big problem with [outsiders'] transgressions on his locker room," said Barnett.[8]

It had been a bad day by the players and George wanted his hours back. The only feasible way to get even was to take the unsatisfactory performance out of the players' paychecks. "Heads will roll!" Steinbrenner screamed.[9]

CHAPTER 15

The Players Revolt

Surprisingly, Steinbrenner pulled himself together a short time after his tirade.

"We won, and Tormohlen from his Pipers days knew this place, Diane's Bar, on 105th and Lorain," said Cleary. "We had three or four hours to kill, so, since Gene knew Diane, he asked her if she would open it up for us. It was just chili dogs and beer."[1]

Tormohlen, while working for the Cleveland Parks and Recreation department in his NIBL days, had played softball with many of the regulars at the bar. "There was a bowling game, like a pinball machine, in it," Tormohlen said. "In the summer, you could tell the regulars because they all had scars on their shins from bumping up against the machine."[2]

Flushed with their victory, visions of a winning playoff share of about $500 each dancing in their heads, the Steers could have afforded a more lavish victory meal. Diane's Place had its attractions, however. Congratulations from a beaten Steinbrenner might have been rare enough to be priceless.

"George showed up. I'm not sure how he found out about the victory party. I was quite surprised he came. He was very gracious," Cleary said.

"We'll get you next time," Steinbrenner said when he left.[3]

The Steers returned home with Kansas City's first professional sports championship since the Blues won the minor-league American Association championship in 1953. The players found victory had given them a more famous admirer. Former President Harry Truman, who lived in the Kansas City suburb of Independence, Missouri, did not follow any sports closely, but he was proud of the Steers for winning. Truman sent all the players signed copies of his memoirs.

"I still have it," said Cleary. "In mine, he enclosed a photograph with a note."

"Please return the photograph. I'm running out of glossies," the note read.[4]

While the Steers basked in Truman's approval, the beaten Pipers did not receive any of the graciousness Steinbrenner was passing around at Diane's Place.

The players normally were paid on the first and 15th of the month. At 8 A.M. on the 15th, the day after they lost the third playoff game, two of the Pipers called Sudyk at the *Press* building, complaining that they had not been paid. Not only were the checks for their losing share (25 percent) of the playoff gate receipts missing, so were their regular salary checks. They threatened to boycott that night's game in Pittsburgh.

A front-page story on the threatened boycott hit the streets in the first edition at 10 A.M. Steinbrenner's gaskets, always insecurely sealed, blew in a screaming, veins-popping tirade. "Your story is a pack of lies!" he shouted into Sudyk's ear over the telephone. "I will see to it that you never work on a newspaper again! I will blackball you nationally!"

"For a young reporter in his 20s, it was very intimidating," Sudyk said.[5]

Next, Steinbrenner ordered McLendon to tell the players they would not be paid unless they retracted their statements.

The dial on his rotary phone all but smoking, Steinbrenner next called *Cleveland Press* editor Louis Selzer, a legend in Cleveland journalism, demanding that he fire Sudyk. Selzer responded with a classic gesture—increasing Sudyk's pay by $25 per week.[6] Steinbrenner, who always had cash-flow problems because of Henry's intransigence, answered that with his trademark blend of truculence and threat.

"The boys will be paid tomorrow [the 16th]," he said. "Their deposit slips were not put in the bank yesterday [the 15th] and if they don't like it, well, that's just too bad."

Six of the payers were married, three had a single child, another had two children. Because of Steinbrenner, most were bouncing their personal checks quicker than the fancy dribbles of the Globetrotters.[7]

Born to wealth, Steinbrenner acted as if he were the one being asked to make sacrifices. "I'm getting tired of all this turmoil. We have the highest-paid players in the league. They have no gripes coming," he said.

Next, coming off very much as a spoiled rich boy who did not get his way, Steinbrenner petulantly threatened to smash his toys. "The way I feel now, I'd just as soon pay off the whole bunch and call it quits," he said.[8]

McLendon would remain as coach for several more tense days, but the job became untenable with Steinbrenner's threats to fold the team. Steinbrenner knew McLendon's nature, his loyalty to his team. In the end, McLendon fell on his sword to save his players' jobs. Until he did, turmoil was an understated word for the atmosphere surrounding the team.

"What would anyone think if he was told by the boss on pay day that no one would be paid and if you don't like it, too bad," said one player who, prudently, chose to remain anonymous.

"They talk, talk, talk about wanting a winning team, then they pull a stunt like this," said another, also under a cloak of anonymity. "We were to get a bonus and a suit of clothes for winning our division title. Now I wonder if we will get anything."

Physically fatigued and emotionally overwrought, the Pipers team still boarded the bus for the 130-mile trip to Pittsburgh. They unanimously agreed not to play against Pittsburgh on the 17th in Cleveland, a vote that Steinbrenner chose to interpret as an "ultimatum," although the players did not use the word.

"You have to say that the playoff put us in poor shape for the start of the second round [half]," said McLendon, determined to return the focus to basketball. "We have 13 of our next 14 away from home with no rest."[9]

Other ABL teams had been idle since the last day of the first half race. Despite what the coach said, however, the record shows that the Pipers played nine more games in 14 days when the second half race began on January 15. Eight of those games were on the road, in Pittsburgh, Commack (New York), Kansas City again, and Hawaii.

Remarkably, amid all the turmoil, the Pipers and Rens played one of the memorable games of the ABL season. The 110–108 Cleveland victory would have proved that a cohesive team will always beat one man, except the Pipers were united only by opposition to Steinbrenner.

The game came down to a head-to-head duel between Barnett and Hawkins. Hawkins, soaring and swooping, more like a condor than a hawk, given his height and wingspan, scored his ABL record 54 points. Barnett, with his distinctive jump shot, on which he looked like some early practitioner of an obscure form of yoga, scored 40. Skull also scored the last two baskets. The ball was in the air at the buzzer on his game-winner.

The next night, as part of a doubleheader on Long Island, the Pipers, basketball's vagabonds, lost to the Steers, 118–100. Once again, a one-man gang took the Pipers down. Bridges scored 48.

Steinbrenner, whistling a determinedly happy tune before the next game at home, said he expected attendance to improve and that some real rivalries were developing, particularly with Pittsburgh. Only 2,143 showed up at the Arena that night for another defeat, however, 107–97 at the hands of the Rens. Hawkins scored 36 and dominated three defenders—Romanoff ("Nick did the best job on him, but he isn't good enough offensively," said McLendon), Dees ("Usually scores, but couldn't stop Hawkins," said McLendon), and Warley ("Hasn't played well since his injury a month ago," said McLendon).[10]

Bucky Bolyard added 31 points for the Rens.

As for rebounding, the Pipers again could only throw up their hands, and then bring them down, wrapped securely around nothing. Pittsburgh owned the boards, 55–44.

It was the end of a grueling stretch of six games in as many days, counting the playoffs, and it almost was even more. A proposed Pipers game January 18 in Youngstown was canceled because the suspension of play by the Jets had thrown the schedule into such disarray that two other teams for the proposed doubleheader could not be found. San Francisco, it was later revealed, had refused to make the trip because of a feud between the Saints owner and Steinbrenner. Youngstown organizers, who had sold 3,500 tickets, would not proceed without the second game.

The bigger basketball news, however, was Heaton's story, headlined "Piper Deal May Bring NBA Here." In it, Heaton disclosed a "confab" in Cleveland among Steinbrenner, Buffalo Bills owner Ralph Wilson, and Syracuse Nats owner Danny Biasone. Rumors of a Pipers-Nats merger had surfaced before, but Heaton's story was fleshed out with more substance. The merged team would play in the NBA in Cleveland the next season. Wilson would become the majority stockholder of the team.

The story had plausible elements. Wilson had lost a pitched fight for Ernie Davis, the AFL Buffalo Bills' top draft pick, the first black player to win the Heisman Trophy, to Modell's Browns. Davis would die of leukemia before ever playing a down with Cleveland, in one of the city's most wrenching sports' might-have-beens. By rescuing the Pipers, Wilson would look like a generous civic savior, both of the Pipers and of their owner, as Steinbrenner looked here, there, and everywhere for a lifeline in a sea of red ink.

Wilson's insurance company already was involved tangentially in the Cleveland sports scene. He had recently written a $1 million policy on the colt Carry Back.

The possibility of a merger, creating a powerful team that would be hard for the NBA to refuse, resonated with Steinbrenner and would resurface in a changed form after the season.

"We talked over the whole basketball situation. It's an interesting one. George is a real go-getter," said Wilson with a pronounced note of understatement.[11]

Wilson, however, never put in more than his reported $50,000 investment. How much of that was actually deposited in the bank is unclear.

On January 18, despite Saperstein's jolly forecast that the Los Angeles franchise would move to Dallas, Houston, Portland, Oregon, or possibly Cloud Cuckoo Land, where they might play in a Steinbrenner-like stratocumulus arena, the Jets went out of business. With the Los Angeles franchise grounded and stored away in the hangar, the ABL was officially down to seven teams and the scheduling nightmare an uneven number causes.

Saperstein, for whom the Southern California territory was a battleground, made a solemn promise to bring the team back in some guise or other down the California coastline in Long Beach for the next season.

In the dispersal draft that followed, Hal Lear and George Finley of the Jets went to the Pipers. Both were simply bargaining chips in the quest for other players later. "You were nothing but a chess piece," said Adams, describing the endless roster modifications in Cleveland.[12]

In a portent of trouble ahead for the Pipers, the Jets' Bill Spivey, a Piper in the preseason, went to Hawaii in the dispersal draft. The next day, the Pipers traded guard Roger Taylor to New York for six-foot-seven-inch rebounder Ben Keller. The same day the U.S. State Department offered McLendon a two-year job conducting basketball clinics and serving as an ambassador for the sport overseas. He declined it.

The Pipers winged their way to Kansas City, where their other chief rivals waited, convinced that they had Cleveland's number. The number was 44. It was the number of points scored by Bridges in the series' first game, a 115–114 victory by the Steers. The score seemed closer than it really was because of Warley's three-pointer as time ran out.

The next night, the Pipers lost again, 132–120. Bridges scored another 30. Sharpshooter Nick Mantis preyed on the slumping defense for 23, including two three-pointers in the Steers' 40-point finishing kick in the fourth quarter, wiping out Cleveland's slim lead after three periods.

The Pipers had a 1–4 record in the second half. They were heading to Hawaii, paradise under the Pacific moon, for a four-game series. And nobody won often in Hawaii.

Another day—albeit one softened by sun and surf and lazed by palm trees and sand—meant another loss in the fourth quarter. Last-place Hawaii surged past the Pipers, 108–100, on the strength of a 33–15 point swing in the final quarter. Spivey poured in 31 points in the opener. It was his lowest output of the four-game set.

"Spivey had been in the Kentucky gambling scandal, and he resented not getting a chance to play in the NBA. So he took it out on us," theorized Adams.[13]

Although Barnhill told Murry Nelson all the Pipers seemed to do was drive around to sightsee and lie on the beach during their stay in Hawaii, they summoned one night's worth of resolve from somewhere within themselves. Without flu-ridden Archie Dees, with Siegfried ejected for fighting, with Spivey scoring 40 more points, the Pipers still broke their five-game losing streak with a 114–113 victory on January 26.

There were obvious matchup difficulties with Spivey for the Pipers, particularly on Hawaii's home floor. Also, if the referees employed by Hawaii had been X-rayed, the results probably would have shown the whistles they swallowed.

"Spivey would throw that left elbow out like Ron Artest [later named Metta World Peace] and bust you with it," said Tormohlen. "The Chiefs had a referee who lived the whole season in Hawaii and did all their games. The Hawaii club tended to get the close calls. Spivey would throw that left elbow out and then shoot his hook shot. It never was a foul in Hawaii. I saw him and that referee go out together after one game, probably for some chicken fingers."[14]

By the time the four games were over, Spivey had scored 151 points, an average of nearly 38 per game.

The Pipers played the third game meekly, losing 121–114 (40 more for Spivey). Cleveland never threatened after falling behind, 30–18.

The Pipers now were in last place in the East. Another loss (featuring 41 more in the endless Spivey torrent) by a score of 106–94 followed. It was Cleveland's aloha to the islands.

A sullen Pipers team, its collective temper on simmer, tried to brawl its way to a series split in the fourth and last game. Cox and Dave Mills of the Chiefs were ejected after "a skirmish that came close to setting off a riot."[15]

According to Sudyk in a follow-up feature on Cox in the *Cleveland Press,* the Pipers forward and Spivey also traded punches. Following that exchange, "Cox was bopped by an irate Mrs. Spivey after he returned to the bench."

The fact that two key players (Siegfried in the second game, Cox in the fourth) could get themselves ejected during the series when the team was in such a tailspin shows how frustrated were the players.

The Pipers protested the loss in the fourth game, claiming that Spivey had been ejected along with Cox. Referees, averse to being exiled from paradise, allowed Spivey to remain in the game. The Pipers now had lost seven of nine in the second half. Counting the playoffs, they had lost nine of their last 12.

The reason for the resentment and anger that were driving such alternately listless and violent performances would soon become apparent.

Sudyk's late paychecks story of January 16 and Steinbrenner's concern for how cheap it made him look was about to boil over into the papers again. Ironically, the publication of the divisions within the franchise occurred because of Steinbrenner's attempt to control the damage.

When the Pipers boarded their plane for the long flight back to Cleveland from Hawaii, it was their last trip with McLendon as their coach.

CHAPTER 16

Heads Rolled

George Steinbrenner had the contradictory ability to chase victory at all costs, seize it through ruthless means, and lose the respect he sought to gain with it.

He finally was able to throw enough money at enough problems, as the beneficiary of an astronomically rich cable television deal in the mid-1990s with the New York Yankees allied with personal wealth, to see success on the field outstrip his destructive acts off it.

In a sports world coarsened by many factors, including big money, talk radio, social media, the entitlement culture, and the decline, fall, death, and cremation of sportsmanship, his reputation improved significantly with a string of Yankees' World Series victories. In a ranking of top owners by deportment and judgment, he wasn't the firstest, but in a ranking of owners by their financial resources, he sure had the mostest.

That was not the case with the Pipers when he owned them, of course. For two weeks, Steinbrenner had been fuming about Sudyk's story of a possible player revolt. It had put him in a very poor light, particularly in view of the unfortunate fact that it was true.

On January 29, 1962, the *Press*'s sports editor, Bob August, received a message from Adams, the Pipers' captain, which was signed by all of the 10 players who were on the Hawaii trip.

It wasn't a statement. These were articles of surrender. The letter appeared on the left side of the first page of the *Press* sports section. On the near right side was McLendon's response. In boldface italic type was the headline: "A Statement . . . and a Charge of Coercion." The statement asserted that there was never a no-pay, no-play "ultimatum" (quotation marks in the original) or any resentment toward "Mr. Steinbrenner," as the white-flag letter called him throughout. The players would have played for a whole month for him "without" pay (quotation marks in the original) if he had asked them to for a logical reason. The letter said there was no rancor on the bus ride to Pittsburgh. The Steers, who were taking part in a doubleheader there, shared the bus with the Pipers, and it was just a big gabfest all the way. There could hardly have been a more craven attempt to clean up Steinbrenner's image.

"We feel that this thing was enlarged by someone's imagination into a real unjustified slur against Mr. Steinbrenner," the surrender agreement read.[1]

Just to clear up that incorrect perception, the message ended with a hymn of praise for Steinbrenner: "We would like it clearly understood that Mr. Steinbrenner has our unquestioned support. . . . We admire his drive and determination to win this championship. . . . We feel we have let him down by not coming to you sooner with a true picture in this matter. . . . Somewhere your reporter got some unreliable information and we hope all this can be set straight so we can get down to the business of trying to win that championship."[2]

The only even implied criticism was the part about gladly playing for a month, while the lights flickered and went dark and the furnace grew cold in players' houses due to unpaid bills, provided only that the otherwise praiseworthy human dynamo in charge had given them a "logical reason."

McLendon's rebuttal to the letter was powerful for its very lack of showy histrionics. John McLendon was a pioneer, a forward-thinking man, who embraced new concepts of training the body and who had had a lifetime's lessons in holding his tongue. He would not bow to the whims of an unreasonable man, though. McLendon had the strength to let go of the job he loved because it saved the jobs of those he loved even more.

"On the basis of the statements made by Pipers President George Steinbrenner, I feel that I will have to ask immediately for a settlement in regard to my contract," said McLendon in a story that ran on the right side of the front page of the *Press*'s sports section.[3]

McLendon added that the players' statement was obtained without his knowledge after he had destroyed an earlier version. The coach said the players were coerced into signing it. McLendon said it was Steinbrenner who issued an ultimatum.

Sudyk said, "McLendon walked over to the Press building [after the team's return from Hawaii] and told me he was resigning in protest."[4]

According to McLendon, Steinbrenner told him: "Either you or Jack Adams get a statement from those players which reinstates me before my family and friends or I will fold the club and all of them will be out on the street and they won't be able to collect on their contracts by the way we have it fixed. Now I am not kidding, you get them to give their denial of the remarks I made or I will get them."[5]

With nothing more to fear from Steinbrenner after he had been traded to New York, Taylor had no reason to bow and scrape before him. Taylor confirmed McLendon's version of the events. "We were told in a group that George wanted us to deny what was in the Press story or that he would fold the club and see to it that no one was paid for the rest of the year," Taylor said.[6]

"I felt on my own personal principle standards I could not allow such an act to be culminated," McLendon said. "I am and have been able to withstand personal attacks but I cannot stand by and see a good group of young athletes intimidated. . . . Furthermore, I cannot be a party to an act which puts a player of mine in an untenable position. This position on my part destroys all their respect for me and confidence in me."[7]

McLendon said, other than the implication of an ultimatum being made by the players, to Steinbrenner, "The Press story represented accurately the situation as it existed."

In an additional story, McLendon said he went public because "when the president's [Steinbrenner's] actions affect the thinking and performance of the team I must speak out. I don't appreciate the sneaking behind my back with the statement and attempting to divide the loyalty of the players."[8]

Heaton followed up the story the next day with a newsier top, the trade of Adams to New York for the six-foot-nine Dierking, who helped shore up the rebounding deficiency. Remarkably, the headline on the story read: "McLendon Stays as Pipers Coach; Adams Traded."

Heaton was 50 percent right. Adams had indeed been traded.

"We had flown 10 to 11 hours back from Hawaii. I was exhausted from the trip, when I heard my name being paged at the Cleveland airport," Adams said.

"I've decided to fire McLendon. I want you to take over," barked Steinbrenner.

"I found out later that Siegfried had talked to Steinbrenner about me, that he thought I could be a good coach. But I was very fond of John McLendon. And I knew George wanted a big name, anyway. I couldn't do it," Adams said.

"Then you're traded," Steinbrenner said.

"I had to get right on a plane to Pittsburgh and play for the New York Tapers that night," said Adams.[9]

McLendon then drove to Akron and spent the evening with Sweeny, the Clevelander who first and most truly believed in him.

"Sharman, Ex-Celt, New Piper Coach" was the headline on Heaton's story the next morning.

The *Plain Dealer* columnists, Cobbledick and Jimmy Doyle, said nothing. No such reticence was felt by Frank Gibbons at the *Press*.

"Owner Steinbrenner really has nobody except himself to blame," wrote Gibbons. "If, for a valid reason, he found himself in a position where he was forced to postpone pay day, he should have explained it to the players, or had Coach John McLendon do it. Anything less than this smacks of serfdom, and that went out with armored uniforms and the mailed fist."[10]

Gibbons said he was willing to believe no organized ultimatum was issued, but he added that even George Steinbrenner had to pay the Pipers. "Had pay day been postponed longer than it was without explanation, I'm certain the team wouldn't have shown up some night. Would you?" wrote Gibbons.

McLendon "acted honorably with the proper loyalty" in a "trying situation," Gibbons said. "He felt unwanted as coach of the Pipers, but he wanted to do a good job right to the finish. . . ."

"George merely forgot that the Pipers are people, not the puppets McLendon says they were made today," Gibbons concluded. "All George has succeeded in doing is getting rid of a coach who is one of the most respected in basketball."[11]

"No way those two guys, McLendon and Steinbrenner could co-exist," said the Rens' Joe Gordon. "That was a marriage made in hell."[12]

Hamilton spoke for the players who so admired McLendon when he said, "McLendon did everything in the world to make it last. Steinbrenner didn't like him from the start, didn't respect him, and didn't pay him. It was unbelievable."

The charge is new that Steinbrenner stiffed McLendon too.

"Steinbrenner paid him like he paid the players, which was once he got ready to," said Hamilton.[13]

In future years with the Yankees, Steinbrenner—who became known, autocratically, as "The Boss"—fired and rehired employees many times.

One of the *five* firings of Yankees' PR man Harvey Greene by The Boss reflects Steinbrenner as he first wielded his combustible, almost comical powers after he had the money to back up the bluster.

Assigned to chaperone the volatile manager Billy Martin in Arlington, Texas, Greene begged off because the Yankees had a day game after a night contest, and Martin was not an early-to-bed kind of guy. Greene trusted television analyst Mickey Mantle, a man with his own epic reputation for carousing, to watch over Martin. "I realize that was putting the fox in charge of the hen house," said Greene.

The PR man returned to the team hotel at 2 A.M. after updating the team statistics, there to find a bloody, dazed Martin lying in the hotel manager's office.

Martin, with the Mick in tow, had headed to a nearby "gentleman's club" called "Lace" after the game. There, in between the strippers' pole dances, the skipper wound up in the men's room, standing next to a heckling Rangers fan at a urinal.

"You're talking like a pretty big man if that's all you got," said Martin, with a sidelong glance as the heckler relieved himself.

On such occasions, Martin often threw the first punch. In this case, to his regret, he did not. Jumped from behind and struck on the head with a blunt object, Battlin' Billy got much the worse of it.

Meanwhile, back at the ranch, the Yankees' beat writers had been awakened by a fire alarm at the team hotel that went off after a small blaze in the sauna. The awakened writers streamed from their beds in time to watch Martin's dazed, battered arrival. They now were staking out Martin, who had been half-carried into the manager's office where he was recuperating behind a locked door.[14]

"Damn it, Greene! You're fired!" shouted Steinbrenner, when the PR man, his face white with fear, rushed onto the scene.

"I was the first man ever fired for not going to a strip joint," said Greene.[15]

Such firing and rehiring of Steinbrenner's staff in sports began with the Pipers. Steinbrenner tried to patch things up, as he did with Greene and Martin several times.

In McLendon's case, Steinbrenner gave him a figurehead vice president's job and sent him around town to talk to youth groups.

The next month, on February 23, before the Pipers beat the Tapers at the Arena, the Cleveland Browns' off-season basketball team played the Pittsburgh Steelers' team. Such games were common then, before players became too prohibitively expensive to risk their health and well-being in them.

Jim Brown was the leading scorer as the Browns won the game, 71–56. A Steeler player, Red Mack, played while wearing a felt hat, "a la Goose Tatum," wrote Heaton.

The "coach" of the Browns team that night, appointed to lead the shabby circus by Steinbrenner, was John McLendon.

It had to be hard for McLendon to be part of such tomfoolery as the circus attraction before a real game, played by the very players he had coached, in front of the fans who had cheered for him and them. But, as ever, John McLendon found reserves of personal strength and finished with a victory in a caricature of the game to which he had devoted his life.

Steinbrenner quickly completed negotiations to bring Bill Sharman, who was still subject to a personal services contract with Vito Guarino, a part owner of the defunct Jets, to Cleveland as the Pipers' new coach. Sharman would stay at least for the remainder of the season and maybe, for the glorious, Jerry Lucas–ensured future of which George dreamed. Guarino would have to be persuaded to release Sharman from the contract, but what was Steinbrenner if not a master of persuasion?

The radio that brought victory tidings, connecting young Doug Bates to his secret garden, had fallen silent after McLendon moved North, where opportunity for black men lay. But McLendon was the same man in the football players' game as he had been on those loud nights of triumph at Kean's Little Garden.

In an era before equality under the law was extended to all Americans regardless of color, no one's personal dignity was as irreproachable and unwavering as that of Southern black gentlemen, of whom John McLendon was an unblemished, utterly incorruptible example.

CHAPTER 17

Bill Sharman, the Meticulous, Generous, Violent Basketball Visionary

B ill Sharman played for the Washington Capitols, a team that folded in the NBA; coached two teams, the Los Angeles Jets and the Cleveland Pipers, that folded in the ABL, itself a league that folded; and coached another team, the Los Angeles Stars, that relocated to Utah in yet another league, the ABA, that folded, as did the Stars. (The oxymoronic Utah Jazz of today are the relocated New Orleans Jazz.)

William Walton Sharman's career, illustrious as it was, still was bedeviled by the rickety financial underpinnings of pro basketball before Larry Bird, Magic Johnson, Michael Jordan, and David Stern delivered it from financial distress.

Sharman also liked to say that he never appeared in a Major League Baseball game but was still kicked out of one.

A late-season call-up with the Brooklyn Dodgers in 1951 when the Dodgers blew a huge lead and lost the pennant to the New York Giants, Sharman and other bench players were ordered to leave the dugout after heckling plate umpire Frank Dascoli for a bad call in late September.

Sharman indeed never appeared in a big league game. He could not have been kicked out of the game against the Giants, though, because he never entered it. In fact, one of the banished players, Wayne Terwilliger, was called out of the clubhouse to pinch-hit in it.

If Sharman's version of the baseball story was not strictly true, the story of his basketball career was a far better tale, anyway.

He was one of the biggest winners in basketball history, with four championships as part of the Boston Celtics' backcourt with Bob Cousy, and coaching championships in the ABL, the ABA (the relocated Utah Stars), and the NBA (the 1971–72 Los Angeles Lakers, winners of a record 33 straight games), and then five more as a Lakers executive.

He was one of the first guards to shoot better than 40 percent in a season, a significant feat because many of the guards' shots, due to their smaller size, are from distance, rather than near the rim.

Sharman was a fitness fanatic before it became fashionable. Whether it was early morning jogs as his wife paced him in the family car, stretching exercises in the locker room before games, or avoidance of red meat and tobacco, he was a man ahead of his time.

A mechanical player, he never tried to do more than his capabilities permitted. He ran defenders into the ground, then hit shots from the well-practiced spots where he was most effective, releasing the ball quickly after Cousy found him with precise, if sometimes ornate, passes.

Sharman was also one of the best free throw shooters ever. Eight times an All-Star, named one of the NBA's 50 greatest players on the golden anniversary of the league in 1997, Sharman was one of only three men to be inducted into the Basketball Hall of Fame as both a player and coach, along with John Wooden and Lenny Wilkens.

He also had an eye for talent. Based on a couple of college games at Southern California against Washington State, Sharman recommended to Red Auerbach that the Celtics sign two-sport standout Gene Conley, who was also a pitcher for the Boston Red Sox.

With the Pipers, Sharman was not only Steinbrenner's requisite big-name coach, he was also the athlete George had never been.

Perhaps Steinbrenner treated Sharman differently than McLendon, not because of race, but because of the box office potential he brought and the fact that the new coach had the athletic background Henry would have respected. (Still, just to be safe, Sharman told Golenbock that he locked the door to the locker room at halftime to prevent Steinbrenner's intrusions.)

"With the great career Sharman had with the Celtics, he commanded the respect of all of those guys, the players and Steinbrenner too," said the Rens' Gordon.[1]

On the court with the Celtics, Cousy got most of the attention for his ball-handling wizardry. To columnist Sean Kirst of Syracuse.com, Sharman said, "When I first started playing, 1950, for about three years we had a basketball that had stitches in it, and it was a terrible ball to try and dribble. Bob Cousy, my roommate, he had to play with that ball, and the things he did with it were just remarkable."[2]

So was what Sharman did as the shooting guard with that ball. Shooting with a Frankenstein's monster of a ball seamed with stitches, playing on hardboards laid on a skating rink in Baltimore, playing in the South with temporary rims when he was with the Capitols, Sharman still was one of the best marksmen in the NBA. During his first five years, his free throw shooting was 86 percent. As Kirst said, it would have been even higher with better floors, better lighting, better backgrounds, and a better ball.

When he discussed the poor conditions, Sharman could just as easily have been talking about the high school gyms in the towns along the Lake Erie shoreline where the Pipers played, and the lighting that gave the raspberry to Thomas Edison in some of them, and the cramped floor at the Olympic with the Jets, and the hyper-Darwinism of the environmental adaptations needed to compete in pro basketball in that era.

Sharman was so competitive that he was a player-coach with the Jets and, although he restricted himself to coaching only in Cleveland, he first indicated after his lone half-season with the Pipers that he wished to continue as a player too.

The competitiveness had a combative aspect. When Sharman was in his 11th and final season in 1960–61, Jerry West, then a rookie, hit seven straight jump shots over him. In its salute to the league's 50 greatest players, with both West and Sharman qualifying, NBA.com noted, "On the seventh, Sharman took a swing at West. The punch didn't connect, but the message did. West viewed Sharman a little differently on his next trip down the court."

"Bill was tough," West recalled in Sharman's obituary in the *Los Angeles Times*. "I'll tell you this, you did not drive by him. He got into more fights than Mike Tyson. You respected him as a player."

Said Gene Shue, a five-time All-Star in Sharman's era, in a telephone interview: "Bill Sharman was just a vicious player. I don't know whether it was my defense, whether I was too close to him when I was guarding him or what. He was a guy who was always coming off screens, but invariably—invariably—when he went up for his jump shot I would get clipped in the jaw with his elbow. Not on the side of the jaw, right at the point of the chin. It happened more than once, so I remembered it."[3]

"Bill was a master at running off the screens," Shue continued. "In those days, there was no protection if you were a guard playing another guard. They had [Jim] Loscutoff, or big, strong guys like that, who would just knock you down. Playing Bob Cousy was much easier than playing Bill Sharman because of the way Bill played and just knowing how to use screens, and when he went up for the shot he'd always make it."

Later Sharman told Shue, "Gene, you were the one who played me better than anyone."

"That was a huge compliment," Shue said.[4]

Cousy said Sharman's temper was so explosive that sometimes, on the court, he went into a "killer mode."[5]

It is sobering to realize how violent all the major sports were then. Although players are much bigger and stronger today, severe penalties are mandatory for fighting in the NBA. That is because of the enormous size of the players, because basketball is the only one of the four major team sports in which players do not wear pads or helmets, and because the league still shivers when it thinks of the frightening brawl that sprawled into the stands in Auburn Hills, Michigan, between the Detroit Pistons and the Indiana Pacers in 2004.

Off the court, Sharman was a man ahead of his time too. Color-blind in an era of racial prejudice, he became a friend of Earl Lloyd, the first black player in the NBA, when both were with the Washington Capitols.

"Remember, Washington was in the South in the back-of-the-bus days," Lloyd told Kirst, his biographer, in the book *Moonfixer*. "Here's a guy [Sharman], when he found out I didn't have an automobile and was riding the bus to camp, he told me he would pick me up every day on 14th Street and Columbia Road in Washington. And he did. . . . In all our conversations, race never came up. Never. . . . If he heard anything from anyone else about giving me those rides, he never said a word, and I know what it must have meant when everyone else saw the two of us arriving together."[6]

Sharman said part of his strength, as in the real estate business in which he dabbled, was location, location, location. He had been the Pacific Coast Conference's Most Valuable Player in his final two seasons at USC.

"I think maybe it's being from California, mainly . . . my parents, they were never prejudiced out here, and I don't think the prejudice out here was quite as strong as it was in the East," said Sharman.[7]

Californians are often stereotyped as laidback individuals with inordinate interest in how the surf is running and who say "dude" a lot. Sharman was not like that.

In addition to the violent streak, he was meticulously, obsessively prepared. He was a big believer in details. The little things made the difference, he thought. Accordingly, he was one of the first coaches to see the value in film study.

Sharman and John Wooden coauthored an instructional book on shooting. Presumably unmentioned in the manual was the fact that Sharman shot three-for-20—and Cousy two-for-20, for a five-for-40 asphyxiation job by the starting backcourt—in the double-overtime seventh game of the 1957 Finals. The Celtics somehow still defeated St. Louis for their first championship.

Part of Sharman's legacy today is that he introduced the unpopular but ultimately effective light morning player practice on game days known as the "shoot-around." Convincing Wilt Chamberlain, a noted insomniac, to get up early enough to participate in it was one of Sharman's earliest and biggest challenges on the Lakers' championship team.

In a blog on ESPN.com, basketball writer Charley Rosen said the shoot-around began during the 1955–56 season, when Sharman would go to a nearby high school gym to shoot on the day of a game. "That night he felt much less lethargic than he usually did after sleeping or fidgeting all day," Rosen wrote.

Eventually, other Celtics joined him, and Sharman narrowed his personal drill into an obsessive requirement that he make five shots in a row from his favorite shooting spots before leaving. With the Los Angeles Jets of the ABL, Sharman made the shoot-around part of the team's routine, over the resistance of his players.

As a cure for bed head, it worked. But Sharman felt it gave them much more—positive visual cues when the ball fell through the net, with such positive reinforcement leading to ever greater numbers of shots going in. Sharman claimed his already good foul shooting improved to a superb 92 percent once he started the shoot-around routine. Most NBA teams still use the routine.

He was a rarity, an Old School player who did not cherish the good old days. He welcomed new ideas, even radical ones. He said he would never have coached in the ABA had the league not legalized the three-pointer.

He favored all sorts of experimentation to make basketball more popular, including a bizarre idea for a baseball style doubleheader, featuring the same two ABL teams playing two 30-minute-long games. The idea was tried only once in the second year of the league's existence and proved extremely unpopular with fans in postgame polling.

Sharman might have won several more championships as a coach had he not seriously damaged his vocal cords during the Lakers' championship season, when, suffering from laryngitis, he shouted instructions over crowd noise in a tortured rasp.

"I've been around a lot of coaches but none like him," West told the *Los Angeles Times*. "He's a different type. A remarkable guy. He doesn't miss a thing. He has the ability to get the most out of people. He always sees a bright spot even when things are darkest."

Sharman, who had movie-star good looks in his youth, had worked his way through USC as a Hollywood movie extra. Late in the Pipers season, he told Sudyk he saw himself the night before on television in a Tarzan movie, carrying a spear. Better pay, $250 a day, came when he was shot down on camera in movie Westerns.

"I don't want to brag, but my death scenes were quite dramatic," Sharman said.[8]

Back from the cinematic dead, he was the perfect coach for the Pipers, whom he was about to resurrect.

CHAPTER 18

Sharman Takes Over

Because Steinbrenner was so overbearing and McLendon so long-suffering, because the sociology of the pioneering, veteran black coach and the bombastic, neophyte white owner was so compelling, most books that deal with the Pipers effectively stop covering the season with McLendon's resignation.

They include a reluctant addendum that the team did rally to win the championship under Sharman's tutelage. Given their 2–7 record at the time of the coaching change, it really was quite an achievement.

Were McLendon and Steinbrenner simply too different, with too many of each man's sensibilities jarred and expectations disappointed, for each to fulfill the other with a championship?

Steinbrenner, of course, treated his handpicked, big-name coach considerably better than he had McLendon. Indeed, at the Silver Anniversary NBA All-Star Game in 1997, held in Cleveland, Sharman said, "He'd take us all out to dinner after games. But when we lost, he would be pretty upset."

Sharman loved meatloaf. It was not as if Steinbrenner had to splurge on white tablecloths and a French chef.[1]

When asked if McLendon had been the right coach in the wrong circumstances, Cleary said, "I think he was the right coach, but I don't know if he was given the right personnel. George made him get rid of Ronnie Hamilton [the point guard who was an NIBL Piper and Tennessee

State mainstay]. Now Hamilton didn't score much, but in John's system, Hamilton made it go. Hamilton was left-handed. He couldn't comb his hair with his right hand. But he was the real brains of the Tennessee State teams."[2]

Steinbrenner's insistence on adding size was clearly correct, however. "There is no real outstanding big boy," Sharman said after putting the Pipers through their first practice under his direction.[3]

Although the process of acquiring more size had begun while McLendon was coach, is it possible that he was too slow to modify his belief system to the realities of play in an improved league?

Off the court, the sale of 80 percent of the stock in the team to the Buffalo Bills' Ralph Wilson was announced—but announcing something, particularly by Steinbrenner, wasn't the same as doing it.

The *Press* raised anew the chimera of the often rumored but never completed merger with the Syracuse Nationals, saying entry to the NBA through such a deal was the goal of the Wilson ownership. In any case, a dazzling series of lineup moves by Sharman bandaged the team's wounds. The biggest change was a seismic one for Barnett, who had signed with Cleveland mostly to reunite with his beloved college coach, but also because he wanted to play forward and not guard, as he had done in Syracuse. Sharman moved Barnett back to the backcourt, where his six-four height gave the Pipers a rare size advantage.

This was a bigger change that it first seems. The screens come in different places for guards and forwards on both the offensive and defensive ends of the floor; cutting obviously is different; and a forward brings his elbows and size to bear, while a guard brings his range and quickness.

Sharman also made Cox, Darrow, and Dierking starters. This displaced Barnhill, who had started since he was a sophomore at Tennessee State. "I've been starting basketball games for a long time," Barnhill said. "I don't think I'll ever get used to being on the bench when the whistle blows to start the game."[4]

While depth was a team strength and the substitutes were capable, the new starting combination clicked. Sudyk called the moves "worthy of a checker champ."[5]

With only three days to prepare for his first game, Sharman chose to emphasize the positive. The more wide-open Pipers game appealed to Sharman, whose Jets played at a controlled tempo. Now he wanted to play faster.

"This is good basketball. The league has fine personnel. The only difference is the 15 or so superstars in the NBA, but we can catch up in a couple of years," Sharman said.[6]

Fifteen or so superstars, however, is not a small thing for a league that had only one in Hawkins, especially in a game in which, with only five players on the floor at one time, a single superstar can have a disproportionate impact.

There were others in the ABL who were very good players, such as Bill Bridges, or who served as the final piece that made a jagged puzzle a glorious mosaic, such as Barnett with the Knicks. But the bottom line is that the ABL was down three starting fives in superstars without the financial resources to lure away any of the NBA's resident ones.

Sharman's first game, a 120–104 victory over Chicago at Public Hall, proved typical of the improvisations forced by the ABL's hectic travel schedule and the winter weather in the Midwest. Attendance (2,338) was also typical.

The Pipers were supposed to play the New York Tapers in the nightcap of a doubleheader, but the Tapers and San Francisco Saints, both coming from the West Coast, were delayed in Chicago. The Saints, embroiled in a feud between their own and Steinbrenner, were perhaps held up by that as much as the weather.

The Majors, the fourth dance partner in the quadrille, faced Cleveland instead. Ben Warley, thinking the Pipers were playing the second game, arrived late, but Dees filled in ably with 16 points. Barnett, playing at his old guard spot, scored 31 points and made 15 of 21 shots. Cox led the scoring with 36.

The scheduled doubleheader took place the next afternoon. The Tapers won, 112–109, to the satisfaction of the three ex-Pipers—Swartz, the second-leading scorer in the ABL, Taylor, and Adams. Swartz got the biggest measure of revenge with 31 points.

Swartz's rebound basket broke the last tie at 108, a basket made easier by the loss of Pipers center Ben Keller, who had a tooth knocked out and suffered a gashed lip early in a rebounding melee.

While Sharman bemoaned the lack of rebounding, it was the outside shooting of the six-foot-eight-inch baseball-basketball player Gene Conley, the same Conley who had caught Sharman's eye at Washington State, which stands out today as a foreshadowing of the way the game has changed.

"Gene Conley's three three-pointers killed us," said Sharman. "Who figures that big guy to be shooting and hitting that far out?"[7]

Sharman died in 2013. He lived to see seven-foot Dallas Mavericks star Dirk Nowitsky win the three-point contest at the NBA All-Star Game and seven-foot-three Zydrunas Ilgauskas pop in threes for the Cleveland Cavaliers.

The Pipers lost to the towering Saints, 126–123, the next night in Sandusky. Tactically, the absence of Cox, who had played against the Tapers with the flu, was decisive.

Attendance was slightly better in Sandusky, 63 miles to the west, with 1,750, than it had been at the Public Hall game, which drew 1,523.

The sparse turnouts for the now last-place Pipers, who had lost nine of 12 games in the second half of the season, were becoming a bigger and bigger story. In Lebovitz's "Ask Hal, the Referee" column on March 1, he replied to a reader's question about which sport—pro basketball, minor-league hockey, or the sham that was pro wrestling—drew the most fans. Lebovitz offered this chart:

Wrestling (14 Arena dates)	221,687
Barons (38 dates)	193,851
Pipers (17 dates)	35,000

The averages were 15,385 for wrestling (floor seating increased attendance); 5,101, Barons; and 2,059, Pipers.

The comparison was imperfect. Only eight Pipers games had been played at the Arena when Lebovitz compiled the attendance figures, due to schedule conflicts with the Barons. Only 13 regular season games would be played there in all. Public Hall near the lakefront was not conveniently located and had drawbacks as a sports facility. It is likely that Lebovitz included Public Hall figures for the Pipers.

Still, the point was unmistakable. The Pipers were dying at the box office.

Back in the friendly, but increasingly vacant, confines of Public Hall, the Pipers ripped San Francisco in their next game, 144–115, before 1,738. In many ways, those fans should have been good messengers, spreading the word of the allure of ABL basketball to wrestling fans in a town that loved it.

The Saints' Jack Allain was ejected for a flagrant foul, one made with intent to injure. Three technical fouls were assessed. The Saints made 42 of 55 free throws. The Pipers sank a preposterous 68 of 84 foul shots. The game ended before the start of baseball season.

Sharman lauded Darrow: "Little Jim is the sparkplug I've been looking for. He's a good shot, smart and a good playmaker."[8]

This had to gall Steinbrenner, who had placed so many hopes on Siegfried as an attendance magnet, a result that would require a starting role for the former Buckeye. But if the owner said anything, it remained private. Such was Sharman's spell over Steinbrenner.

Warley fought through the foul-shot quagmire in the Saints game for 30 points and 12 rebounds. "Warley is as tough as a spike and about as wide," assessed Sudyk.

Warley himself said, "This is my best game as a pro and the first time I've really felt good since I was injured last December."[9]

In a 129–118 victory over San Francisco in Pittsburgh, Barnett erupted for 43 points. He might have been a reluctant guard, but he was a very good one.

The Rens fell, 125–114, at Public Hall for the Pipers' third victory in a row and fourth in the six games Sharman had been their coach. Romanoff's physical defense limited Hawkins to 13 of his 36 points in the second half with nothing from the field until the game was out of reach.

Romanoff's layup with 55 seconds to play was the difference in a 105–103 rematch in Pittsburgh. Hawkins got only 24 against the rugged tandem of Romanoff and Dierking.

The next game was on February 12. With Valentine's Day looming, when a young man's thoughts turn to love, those of the Pipers turned to another formal, futile protest of a loss to Hawaii.

Dierking and Romanoff were the focal points of the Hawaii game, since they were charged with containing Spivey, who had gone on a rampage in the islands against a demoralized Pipers team that was missing its paychecks. Spivey got only 22, but the Chiefs still won a wild 137–136 victory in double overtime.

Govoner Vaughn, one of Saperstein's ex-Globetrotters who shuttled between deliberate farce with the basketball clowns and the unintentional variety in the ABL, tied the game at the end of the first overtime in the last second at 127 and won it in the final second of the second extra period with a layup.

The Pipers simply gave the game away, losing a 101–88 lead at home at the Arena with eight minutes to play in the fourth quarter.

In the final 15 seconds of the fourth quarter with the score tied, Siegfried called a timeout the Pipers did not have and the resultant technical foul and free throw forced the overtime. Cox had a chance to win it, but could only split a pair of foul shots in the final second of the regulation game. The Pipers afterward claimed referees improperly applied the bonus free throw rule and the timeouts rule in the overtimes.

Sudyk, however, was not sanguine about the chances of the two-pronged protest. It was announced earlier in the day that the Pipers lost the protest of their loss in the last game McLendon had coached—ironically, against the Chiefs in Hawaii.

"League Commissioner Abe Saperstein, who flicks protests into the waste basket like the ashes from his cigar, has not allowed a protest all season," Sudyk observed.[10]

Even a black-and-white violation, such as with the misapplied rules, was not enough to convince the commissioner with the Silly Putty spine to do the right thing in the case of the double-overtime loss. Even more galling, a discrepancy in the official scorer's book—unthinkable at home—cost the Pipers a precious point.

Adding to the unreality was the fact that Hawaii coach Red Rocha had announced his intention to protest the game while it was underway. Of course, he withdrew it when his team won.

Attendance was announced as 6,090, many of them youngsters admitted for free. They brought with them the capacity to reach annoyingly high vocal registers when they screamed, which was, groused Sudyk, almost constantly.

On Valentine's Day in New Castle, Pennsylvania, a suburb of Pittsburgh, the Pipers beat the Chiefs, 115–103. Barnett led all scorers with 33 points but it was the "D and D Boys," Darrow and Dierking who supplied the critical points. Dierking scored 11 of his 16 and Darrow eight of his 12 in the third period after Hawaii had tied the score at 68.

The three-game series with Hawaii concluded in Pittsburgh a night later, a 112–108 victory achieved despite 44 points from Spivey. The difference was that, at halftime, Sharman ordered a full-court press, reasoning that, although Spivey was unstoppable when he got the ball in the paint, the ball handlers who delivered it to him could be advantageously harassed and impeded beforehand.

The Pipers, who had begun the week in last place, flew to Chicago for a February 17 game against the Majors in first place in the East Division with a 9–10 record. The Majors, leaders at the start of the week, were now last.

"All four teams in our division are so equal that the club with the occasional hot hand and the one that wins the most close ones will take the title,"[11] said Sharman, who soon would pick the Tapers, with Swartz and Roger Kaiser, the second and third leading scorers in the ABL at the time, as the team to beat.

Neither a hot hand nor the ability to make the plays that decide the close games was in evidence in Chicago. Outscored, 33–16, in the final quarter, the Pipers lost, 113–106. The loss put the Pipers third on the standings seesaw, with both New York and Pittsburgh passing them.

They were heading for an unscheduled five-day break in the constant procession of games. While the players probably thought it was much needed after the emotional and physical toll the second half of the split season had taken on them, it would not be a tranquil time of buffing and polishing plays.

On February 18, the other ABL owners went public with a threat to expel the Pipers.

CHAPTER 19

To the Brink of Expulsion

Scheduling games was such a problem in pro basketball, with arena availability concerns—caused by different tenants' games, trade shows, the Ice Capades, religious revival meetings, circus bookings, and other events—that even after the age of computers, the machines at first proved unequal to the task.

The NBA schedule was instead pieced together by an aging Philadelphia basketball fixture and former owner of the SPHA's (South Philadelphia Hebrew Association) team, Eddie Gottlieb, aka "Gotty," a man with raccoon eyes ringed by dark circles and shoulders bowed by the schedule burden. He kept the schedule in his pocket at all times so he could jot down a sudden brainstorm. Somehow, he would deliver the schedule on time.

Imagine how difficult it was in the ABL after Los Angeles dropped out in midstream. The crazy-quilt schedule got crazier and more bedraggled, particularly given the impositions placed on it by the imperious and increasingly impecunious Steinbrenner. Basically, Steinbrenner decided to take his ball club and go home, or at least close to it, declining to visit San Francisco and other far-flung (Hawaii) and relatively near-flung (Kansas City) sites in the shrunken West Division.

Sudyk reported that the Saints' failure to meet the Pipers at Public Hall on February 4 in Sharman's second game as head coach was due to Saints owner George McKeon's personal pique as much as travel problems.

The Saints also had declined to participate in the scheduled Valentine's Day doubleheader in New Castle, Pennsylvania.

The no-shows were in retaliation for the Pipers' "refusal to meet them on the coast at a previous date," Sudyk said.[1] If San Francisco wouldn't play in the East, neither would Cleveland in the West. "For this reason, we will definitely not go to San Francisco under any circumstances. But we will agree to go to Kansas City if we must," Steinbrenner said.[2]

The dispute broke out at an ABL meeting, which had been convened in Chicago to try to complete the season schedule. Only Sharman was there to represent the Pipers. Flieger was sick, and Steinbrenner skipped the meeting because of a "previous commitment" but still felt free to bellow criticism from Cleveland.

"Steinbrenner should have attended the meeting himself," said Saperstein, who belatedly recognized an insult when he had been given one.[3]

The clear cost-cutting motive behind the curtailed travel induced Saperstein, along with the other ABL club owners, to wonder why Steinbrenner was still the loud guy with the megaphone, making crazy demands in Cleveland, when Ralph Wilson was the announced new majority owner of the Pipers.

"I know nothing about it," Saperstein said of the sale of the Pipers. "There had also been reports that Cleveland, because of its alleged refusal to play road games, might not be in the league next season."[4]

This was typical of Saperstein. As a commissioner, he was on the road with the Globetrotters too often to keep pace with the news. "Abe had so many balls in the air, including the little side deal with the Globetrotters. He was always calling in from Beijing or some place," said Cleary. "As a commissioner, he was a joke. As a promoter, he was great. And he was a good guy. But he should have just put some guy in his office in Chicago and called him the commissioner."[5]

Said Wilson of the ownership question, when contacted by the Cleveland papers, "Steinbrenner is in complete charge of the franchise."[6]

In the bill of particulars that was released, the ABL charged that the Pipers canceled games without league approval, scheduled doubleheaders in undersized arenas, were tardy with the payment of the league's 5 percent of gate receipts, failed to submit a financial report after the first half playoffs, failed to notify the league of the sale of the team to Wilson, made "indiscriminate" remarks about leaving the league, and were guilty of "actions detrimental to the league."[7]

The failure to report the gate of the playoffs was a serious matter and a familiar refrain because it involved money Steinbrenner frequently did not have. The Steers, after winning the playoffs, were supposed to receive 35 percent of the gate receipts while the Pipers took home 25 percent.

Steinbrenner had stiffed his players at home and when they were behind the Iron Curtain, in the NIBL and the ABL, and now he was balking at meeting his team's financial obligations to the league. The other owners voted to give the Pipers six days to answer the charges and pledge allegiance to the shot-torn and tattered ABL flag.

Taking note of the chaos, NBA commissioner Maurice Podoloff said, "There is not the slightest chance that Cleveland will join us next season." His words would prove to be good as Steinbrenner's word.[8]

Two days later, John Glenn orbited the earth in the space capsule Friendship 7, becoming the first American to do so.

In the more gravity-bound sphere of basketball, Ohio State's unbeaten team would make its first television appearance of the 1961–62 season on the same weekend as the Pipers' expulsion vote. If Jerry Lucas noticed the franchise was barely afloat, it did not seem to perturb him. The fact that such a powerhouse team as Ohio State had played games that were only heard on radio and read about in newspapers until so late in the season showed how high the hurdles were for an upstart league like the ABL in getting a network contract.

With good reason, the Pipers discounted the seriousness of the expected expulsion threat. "The league was already down to seven teams," said Cleary, meaning the ABL needed reinforcements, not exiles.[9]

No one but an irate McKeon wanted to cast out Cleveland, which clearly was one of the stronger teams. McKeon, as loose a cannon as Steinbrenner, albeit of smaller bore, even claimed the day before the expulsion question was resolved that the Pipers had already been thrown out, a charge both Saperstein and Steinbrenner denied.

Steinbrenner did show up at Saperstein's behest before the vote to defend his stewardship of the Pipers franchise. Typically, he had tried to show up Saperstein again with a letter detailing his rebuttal of the various charges. "The whole matter has been blown out of proportion by the San Francisco people. They have gone to great lengths to push us out of the league," said Steinbrenner. "Club owners were upset that we wanted to jump to the NBA. We would be happy to remain right where we are."[10] The latter was patently false. But it was also behavior that would become typical in struggling leagues.

In *Dr. J*, Julius Erving said he was shocked to learn that the New York Nets and Denver Nuggets, the ABA's most successful franchises, had applied to join the NBA while still playing in the ABA. "I didn't even know you could do that," said Erving.[11]

Unwittingly, they were only following the Pipers' lead. In the Pipers' case, the result of the expulsion vote was a foregone conclusion, a 5–1 vote in favor of reinstatement. McKeon was the lone "yea" vote.

"We are happy to have kept the Pipers," said Saperstein. "It can be one of the best franchises."[12]

At the same time, Wilson resurfaced to confirm his purchase of majority control of the Pipers, claiming $150,000 was "very near the actual purchase price."[13] There would later be questions about the finality of those arrangements in the dying days of the Pipers' short, stormy life.

The ABL expulsion meeting ended with plans to expand for the next season, which were indicative of the state of denial in which Saperstein lived, encouraging contradictory rumors of a team headed to the Southwest (Dallas) or maybe it was the Northwest (Portland). Actually, expansion, given the fragile state of the entire ABL, was, as would be said today, so over.

But castles in the air, even for supposedly hardheaded businessmen, present endless opportunities for sprucing up imaginary battlements and dusting off tables in the mead halls of the mind. It became a great irony that Steinbrenner's plans to leave the ABL eventually depended on financial aid from McKeon. Perhaps professional sports create strange bedfellows.

Or, in this case, mutually untrustworthy ones.

CHAPTER 20

"We Still Have a Chance"

In the middle of the expulsion controversy, Dick Barnett almost drove the Pipers' franchise into a ditch. His 1962 Dodge convertible skidded in falling snow on Liberty Boulevard on February 22 and crashed into a ravine alongside Doan Brook in the East Side suburb of Cleveland Heights. Since Barnett was the team's best player, the whole franchise winced when his car slammed to a stop.

Barnett suffered severe lacerations over both eyes, which required 50 stitches at Mt. Sinai Hospital. Sharman had built his team around Barnett, who was averaging 26 points per game since belatedly joining the Pipers.

"I'll have to juggle the lineup in case Dick isn't ready," Sharman said of Barnett's plans to try to play in a protective face mask. "I hope he'll be all right, but he won't be at his best."[1]

Barnett could not play on February 23 at the Arena against the Tapers.

The same well wishes that the coach extended to the six-foot-four guard before the game almost could have gone to six-nine Connie Dierking.

In another anarchical ABL game, the Pipers won, 138–121. Barnhill scored 27 points in relief of Barnett, but it was lost in Dierking's impersonation of a volcano with legs.

Five technical fouls were called. Dierking was ejected for his sixth personal foul and then tacked on two technical fouls for blowing his stack about the last personal. The Tapers converted the tantrum into seven points, on the original basket and foul shot, the two technicals (all those points by Warren Spraggin), and also a basket after retaining possession.

Dierking cursed former NIBL referee John Morrow, offering to punch him in the nose as he tried to charge the arbiter. It was a good thing Dierking was restrained. Morrow was a former Golden Gloves champion in Chicago.

Deemed worthy of a second story in the *Plain Dealer* was Jim Brown's 30 points leading the Browns' basketball team to victory against the Steelers. The football players' preliminary game, the one in which the Browns were coached by McLendon, helped draw 3,417 fans.

McLendon, carrying the empty title of Pipers vice president, spoke the next day at the Cleveland Heights High School booster club. The topic was the trip to the Soviet Union with Lucas, not McLendon's fractured relationship with Steinbrenner.

On February 25, the Pipers squeaked past Kansas City, 111–109, on the strength of Cox's best game as a Piper.

Peter Gunn, a private-eye TV show, had gone off the air in 1961 after a four-year run. "Johnny Gun" for one night took its place, with Cox scoring 41 points, including the game-winning layup in the final seconds.

Barnett scored six points in the first half, playing in a cumbersome face mask, and then discarded it and chipped in two more field goals in the fourth quarter. He also threw the pass that led to Cox's game winner.

Sharman continued the discussion of Cox's physical limitations, saying of the six-foot-four 190-pounder, "Coxie is just a couple of inches and about 15 pounds from being one of best basketball players anywhere."

There is a psychological tool called "Pygmalion therapy," based on the George Bernard Shaw play *Pygmalion.* The play was itself based on a Greek myth of a sculptor named Pygmalion, whose statue of a woman turned into his flesh-and-blood future wife through his love for it and the sympathetic intervention of Aphrodite, the love goddess. The Broadway musical *My Fair Lady,* featuring Henry Higgins as the Pygmalion character, was in turn based on Shaw's play. The therapeutic approach requires positive reinforcement. Pygmalion therapy is the belief that a player can be transformed by supportive teammates and coaches. *You are what you are told you are.*

Against the Steers, Keller blocked Tormohlen's attempt to send the game into overtime on the last play.

After the game, Sharman went all Professor Henry Higgins on overload about Keller. "Ben looked like big Bill Russell then," gushed Sharman.[2] Perhaps on the lift of the pure hyperbole of Sharman's comments, the Pipers embarked on a road trip that spanned the distance from New York to the reluctantly revisited San Francisco, with a stopover in Chicago to play the Majors. The trip was broken only by a neutral court game in Canton, 75 miles from Cleveland.

Things did not go well, either in reaching the initial destination or in the results after finally hacking through the wilderness to get there.

In his Connie Hawkins biography, David Wolf said Commack Arena, the itinerant Tapers' new home, could be found only with the "aid of an Indian guide."[3] No latter-day Sacajawea was on hand, though.

The Pipers took a late flight to New York, then set out in rental cars that got separated, scattered, and so thoroughly lost that the players straggled in just in time for the game.

Five more technical fouls were called, as Swartz and Barnhill nearly came to blows, but the Pipers' elbows were sharper than their eyes in a 101–90 loss. "We weren't loose. It was our worst game of the year," Sharman said.[4]

Matters did not improve overnight. The Pipers came into Commack as the most accurate team in the ABL, shooting 44 percent from the field. The team that couldn't drive straight to Commack couldn't shoot straight once it got there, though. The Pipers left Commack with two losses, the second a drab 102–86 exercise. In the pair of games, they shot an aggregate 35.6 percent.

Although fast break basketball created easy baskets, Sharman felt the team did not run well on the road and planned to slow down the pace as the Pipers headed to Chicago.

The Pipers scored more than they had on Long Island, 111 points, but the Majors scored even more, 115, on March 3.

Rallying from an 11-point deficit in the fourth quarter, the Pipers faded after taking a 97–96 lead in the last six minutes. Both teams had six players with 10 or more points. Barnett's 24 led the Pipers, who were without Archie Dees.

Dees was sidelined with a sprained ankle suffered during "a rugged two-hour scrimmage" in Cleveland the day before the game. Such a prolonged, hard scrimmage seems foolhardy, given the demands of the Pipers' trip. The Chicago game was the Pipers' third straight loss and left them third in the East with an 11–14 record.

"This is the first time in the last six years that any team I've been with has lost three in a row," said Sharman. "We're not a big team, and I'm afraid the wear and tear of such a long schedule is beginning to tell."[5]

The ABL schedule, however, like Humpty Dumpty's words in Lewis Carroll's *Through the Looking Glass,* meant just what each squabbling team chose it to mean.

The Pipers were openly trying to duck their upcoming series in San Francisco. Steinbrenner attempted to switch opponents with Hawaii, which was slated to play Chicago in a series in Florida.

Such a switch would have saved airfare for both teams and allowed the Pipers a chance to make up ground against a division rival, but nothing came of it.

To Canton trudged the Pipers, short-handed and road-weary, their losing streak a burden to their hard-driving coach, with archrival Kansas City the opponent on March 5.

Every game counts the same in the standings, but some games have added importance. Players call them "message" games. The Steers, with easily the best overall winning percentage in the league, had the chance to let the Pipers know they had met their match. The Steers missed their chance, however.

Warley scored 18 of his 23 points in the first half in a much-needed 104–92 Pipers' victory. Only 1,396 braved a blizzard that veiled Canton in white two hours before tip-off. If the conditions reminded Barnett of his close call in the ditch of Doan Brook, he did not act like it, scoring a game-high 28 points.

Next, the Pipers headed West to San Francisco, where the troubled Saints, losers of six straight games, with the ABL's tallest line up and one of its testiest owners in McKeon, posed troubling matchup and manhood problems.

Sudyk advanced the games by advising the Pipers "to spend some time on the manly art of self-defense against the pugnacious Saints," describing the games against the "misnamed Saints" as "a three-sport competition: boxing, wrestling, with a little basketball squeezed in here and there."

He cast the Saints as forerunners of the Detroit Pistons' "Bad Boys" of the 1990s, writing that the Saints' frequent prolonged losing streaks could be attributed to the fact that "they have not learned to dribble and shoot with clenched fists."[6]

By the time the Pipers arrived in the Bay area, they were already, literally, behind the eight ball. Only eight players made the trip.

Wolf in *Foul!* asserts that eight-man traveling squads were an ABL rule, designed to hold down costs. That was true only in its second season, though. Ten-man Piper teams were listed in box scores often in the away games in 1961–62.

The attrition was due to the injury to Dees and the refusal of Dierking to get on the plane because he had a fear of flying. How he had lasted so long in pro basketball is a secret that cannot be solved now because Dierking died in 2013.

Substitute Rossie Johnson also stayed behind, a measure likely imposed by Steinbrenner to cut costs, no matter the price his team had to pay on the court.

"I'm gonna pack my sneakers in case I'm needed," Sharman joked, sourly. "If we pick up any injuries or foul out a few, I may have to play."[7]

Sharman told Sudyk that he hoped to remain with the Pipers the next season, but a clearer understanding on the demands of operating costs versus competitiveness would first have to be reached.

In the series opener in San Francisco, the Pipers' fourth loss in five games, 103–101, left them with a 12–15 record. Mike Farmer, one of the Saints' big men at six foot seven, scored 32 points. Guard Whitey Bell's jump shot with five seconds to play made the difference.

The entire series with San Francisco turned into a seesaw of exchanged two-point victories. In the middle game of the three-game set, the Pipers prevailed, 100–98, behind Barnett's 33 points. Sharman hailed his team's competitive spirit, saying, "Keller [who scored 14 points] cut his hand badly while dunking the ball in a pre-game drill, but was able to play with a bandaged hand."[8]

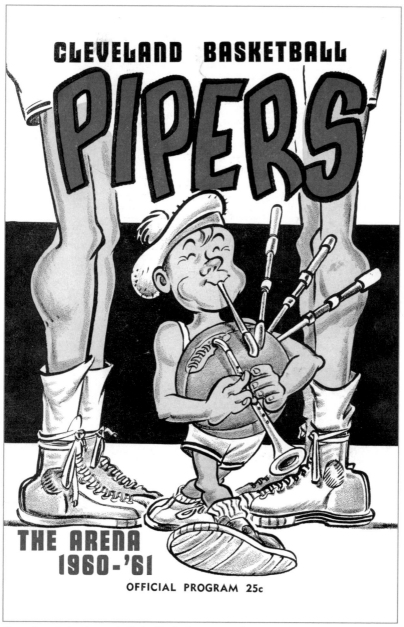

Short, but obviously musically inclined, the unnamed mascot of the Pipers was created by the *Cleveland Press*'s staff cartoonist Lou Darvas. Here, the bagpiper adorns the cover of a game program in the team's NIBL era.

CLEVELAND PIPERS 1960-61 SEASON

Back row: Tormohlen, Allain, Sharrar, Warley

Center: Whaley, Barnhill, Hamilton, McCoy, Taylor

Front: McCollum, Swartz, McLendon, Adams, Akers

The official team photo of the 1960–61 Pipers commemorates a team that won the triple crown of amateur basketball championships—the NIBL regular season and playoff titles and the AAU championship. The Pipers were the first Ohio team to win the AAU championship.

Jack Adams, a hard-driving forward and Pipers captain, coached the team when coach
John McLendon was late to an ABL game in Pittsburgh because of a flat tire.

Jack Adams, shown warming up, was offered the job of Pipers coach when George Steinbrenner was about to fire John McLendon. Adams refused to take it and was traded within minutes.

Roger Taylor, after he was traded to New York, confirmed that Steinbrenner threatened to fold the team if the Pipers players boycotted a game.

Gene "Bumper" Tormohlen, known for taking charges, takes aim at the free throw line after himself getting fouled.

The Pipers' Grady McCollum was traded at halftime of a game to the opposing Hawaii team for $500. John McLendon overruled Steinbrenner's orders that McCollum suit up and play for Hawaii in the second half.

Grady McCollum joined several Pipers teammates in an exhibition game against Jerry Lucas's Fabulous Buckeyes after the 1961–62 collegiate and ABL seasons. The victory by Lucas and his teammates convinced the former Ohio State star he could play professional basketball.

Gene Tormohlen shoots a sweeping hook shot—a shot rarely seen today, but one many big men had in their arsenal a half century ago.

Ron Hamilton, the point guard of John McLendon's Tennessee State's NAIA champions, also directed the offense for his old college coach's team in the NIBL.

Ron Hamilton, the "quarterback" of the Pipers' NIBL team, said Steinbrenner never respected John McLendon.

"Deadeye" Dan Swartz was traded after he complained about paychecks during the AAU Tournament and on the Russia trip. Swartz sprayed George Steinbrenner with tobacco juice when told of the trade.

John "Rabbit" Barnhill, one of the smallest men on the floor, came off the bench for Bill Sharman after starting with the Pipers for John McLendon, his college coach. Barnhill's offensive rebound and assist in the final minutes clinched the final game for the ABL playoffs.

John McLendon (center) is flanked by Dan Kean, brother of legendary Tennessee State athletic director Henry Kean, and Howard Gentry, for whom the school's current athletic complex is named.

Adrian Smith, a Piper opponent at Akron in the NIBL days, overcame grinding poverty to play at Kentucky and become the unlikely Most Valuable Player of the 1966 NBA All-Star Game.

Jerry West, one of basketball's greatest players, heavily criticized the Los Angeles Lakers' trade of former Piper Dick Barnett. West put Barnett second on his list of the most underrated players in NBA history.

With Cox ailing and Keller hurt, Johnson boarded a plane for the third and last game, to be played across the Bay in Oakland.

The agonizing, 106–104 defeat might have disheartened a lesser team. Farmer and Bell were again the Pipers' nemeses—Farmer tipping in Jim Francis's miss to tie at the fourth-quarter buzzer and Bell providing overtime jumpers that won it.

Regaining the ball with seven seconds to play in overtime, the Pipers played for the win, not another overtime period. Darrow's three-pointer at the buzzer popped in and out of the basket.

As his team flew home, Sharman stayed behind in Los Angeles for the next two days to spend time with his family, a perk in such a tense divisional race that Steinbrenner would never have allowed McLendon.

In telephone interviews with both Cleveland newspapers, the coach replayed the tight San Francisco series in a defiant way, conceding nothing. "We still have a chance," he said. "Both losses were decided on a missed rebound in the last seconds. Connie helps in that way."[9]

At least momentarily chastened by his penny-pinching, Steinbrenner said, "The spirit is good on the team. We can catch the leaders in this stretch of home games."[10]

Seven of the Pipers' last 10 games were in northeast Ohio, six of them in Cleveland. It would all come down to the last home stand of the season.

CHAPTER 21

Cochampions

The finish of the marathon season, perversely, was a sprint. The Pipers played their last 10 games in just 13 days. As demanding as the schedule was, it also had competitive clarity.

The Pipers faced Chicago and Pittsburgh, the East Division co-leaders, who were 2½ games ahead of Cleveland's 13–16 record, a total of seven times in the 10 games—three of them against the Majors, four against the Rens.

It began with another trip, this of 60 miles from Cleveland to the northeast corner of Ohio in Ashtabula. Before a crowd announced at 1,300, the Pipers defeated the Majors, 110–101. Barnett scored 35 and Cox 25, but the encouraging news was the return of the ground-hugging Dierking, who showed no signs of acrophobia on the court, scoring 19 points and grabbing 18 rebounds.

Cox retrieved 14 misses, as the Pipers held a 58–51 rebounding advantage. Siegfried, who was credited with a good defensive job on Chicago's Herschell Turner, played with a broken middle finger on his left hand, suffered in another practice the day before the game.

The rematch the next night at Public Hall was a shootout inside a melee, wrapped in a thriller. In describing the Pipers' 124–122 victory, Sudyk used boxing and gangland motifs before finally getting around to a passing reference to the spectacular two-man scoring duel.

The pugilism: "Chicago sandman (knockout artist) Kelly Coleman aimed a couple of swings at referee Jim Gaffney"; "Ex-Globetrotter

Sweetwater Clifton, in dark trunks and weighing 200 and Piper Ben Warley, squared off with several swings before referees could halt the one-rounder."

The "Scarface" stuff: "Our side and the Windy City boys engaged in the toughest gang war since Al Capone and Jimmy Valentine muzzled each other during prohibition"; all this aided and abetted by the *Press*'s headline writer: "Pipers Survive Cage Gang War."[1]

Then, at long last, basketball, for it was a game to be remembered: Chicago's Tony Jackson set an ABL record with 12 three-pointers on his way to 53 points. Barnett scored 41 in response, including the winning basket.

The Pipers were the best defensive team in the ABL—but at times, particularly against Connie Hawkins, but also in this game against Jackson—they seemed powerless against a player on a hot streak.

As violent as the game was in the early 1960s, it is a surprise no one decided to see how well Jackson could shoot from a recumbent position on the hardwood floor, while his defender headed to a neutral corner.

A last-minute traveling call on Coleman caused the flare-up between Coleman and Gaffney, who lost his whistle while ducking haymakers. "Gaffney is a homer all the way. He was thrown out of the NBA for incompetence. Officiating like this is ridiculous," said Chicago coach Andy Phillip.[2]

The change of possession on the traveling call set up Barnett's jumper from the wing with 20 seconds to play.

It was a big surprise when the Pipers beat Kansas City, 116–101, in the second game of a doubleheader at Public Hall on March 16. It was a surprise because the schedule in the *Plain Dealer* that morning said they were playing Pittsburgh. Heaton dourly wrote, "The league schedule, changeable as the weather along Lake Erie, was switched at the last minute by Abe Saperstein, commissioner and owner of the Chicago Majors."[3] McMahon received a telegram telling him of the change while the first game of the doubleheader, between the Rens and the New York Tapers, whom Kansas City had been slated to play, was already in progress.

In that game, the Tapers did the Pipers a favor, beating the Rens, 103–101, primarily by making all 37 of their free throws. In the Pipers-Steers game, Barnett scored 38 and Tormohlen, another ex-Piper who enjoyed the chance to make Steinbrenner squirm, scored 37 in defeat.

The explanation for the change in opponents was that it was made to "balance the schedule." Heaton wasn't buying it. "It was one more incident in an operation that has been confused from the start," he wrote. By the time he filed for the *Plain Dealer*'s final edition, even the gentlemanly Heaton had had it. "It was one more incident in an operation that has been bush league from the start," he revised.[4]

The victory over the Steers, "who are far ahead in the Western corral [division]," wrote Heaton, left the Pipers, despite a decidedly mediocre 16–16 record, only one-half game out of the lead in the Eastern paddock.[5]

The Pipers took over first place by percentage points after a St. Patrick's Day victory over Hawaii at Public Hall, 107–100. It was their fourth-straight victory. A creditable job on Spivey, the tallest player in the league and one of its most accurate shooters at 51 percent, was the reason why. The Chiefs' pivot man scored only 18 points. Barnett with 35 points hit half of his 28 shots, slightly improving his 49 percent shooting mark on the season. He was the only guard in the ABL top five in the statistical category. Cox added 30 points.

The game was again marred by rhubarbs with the referees. One of the ABL's regular referees did not make the game to team with Gaffney, himself an interesting selection, given the remarks Phillip made about homerism.

Gaffney was joined by George Struthers, "a well-regarded man from Dayton," according to Heaton. The esteem was shared neither by the Chiefs nor Pipers, however. The entire first half and part of the third quarter was a long harangue between aggrieved players and Strothers. "Some of the early disturbances were caused by Strothers' unfamiliarity with the unusual ABL rules," Heaton reported.[6]

Playing their fifth game in six days, the Pipers' depth and Chicago's unrelieved fouling led to a 111–102 victory at Public Hall. Barnett scored only 13 points as he coped with a sprained ankle. Darrow reinjured a bruised heel. Dees had been out for three weeks with his own bad ankle. Siegfried with 15 and Barnhill with 23 took up the slack.

Although the Pipers absorbed a 71–49 beating on the boards, they won the game by making 39 of 55 free throws to the Majors' 22 of 30. No less than five Chicago players fouled out and, although Jackson did score 31 points to lead his team, he made only four threes as the Pipers extended their defense.

The next day, the Pipers announced their intention to select Lucas as a territorial pick in the upcoming ABL draft. They took Ohio State's John Havlicek with the second of their two allowed territorial picks.

The Pipers had exclusive rights in the territorial draft to players from Ohio, Indiana, and Tennessee. Heaton wrote that "The Pipers are grabbing a ticket on the long shot with Lucas, who has been adamant in his determination not to play professional basketball. Steinbrenner is a first-rate salesman, however, and claims he has a chance to land the big fellow."[7]

A tag-team defense of Romanoff and Dierking against the Rens' Hawkins was in store the next night. Romanoff was a player the Pipers did not expect to have. He was supposed to have been traded to Hawaii soon after Sharman arrived. But after Keller suffered his gashed mouth against the Tapers on February 4, Romanoff raced from the stands, where he had been watching as a spectator, to the locker room to don a Pipers' uniform.

Now Romanoff, with his wheat germ, his protein pills, his Michael Phelpsian consumption of health foods each day, his appetite for contact against Hawkins, and his general good play, had clearly retained his roster spot.

Hawkins scored only 18 points, proving the timeless efficacy of mugging skilled players, as the Pipers easily won, 124–102.

"The key to the title will be written on the backboards," Sharman said, in a confused comment that was not an endorsement of graffiti. "If we get our share of the rebounds, we ought to do pretty well otherwise."[8]

In the final minutes of the Pittsburgh game, hecklers urged Neil Johnston, the Rens coach, to bring back the Steelers, whose basketball team beat that of the Browns, 61–59, in the preliminary game. The Browns must have missed McLendon's coaching.

With six straight wins, the Pipers were in first place with a 19–16 record as they finally left Cleveland for two games in Pittsburgh, the first against the Tapers in a doubleheader, the second against the Rens.

But nothing ever was easy for the Pipers. The Tapers survived a Pipers' rally from a 98–91 deficit in the final three and a half minutes to win on Ron Zagar's 24-foot jump shot from just inside the three-point arc at the buzzer, 100–98. Cox's two three-pointers had begun the failed comeback. The loss in the March 23 doubleheader in Pittsburgh dropped the team one-half game behind Chicago, which defeated the Rens in the second game.

The ABL announced individual player honors on the same day. Out-stripping the twenty-first-century prodigy LeBron James, Hawkins, who did not turn 20 until midsummer in 1962, was named the ABL's Most Valuable Player in a vote of league players. James was "only" Rookie of the Year in his first season.

Joining the Hawk on the first team were Barnett, the Steers' Bridges and Staverman, and the Tapers' Swartz. Cox made the second team, along with the Majors' Turner and Jackson, the Chiefs' Spivey, the Saints' Ken Sears, and the Steers' Nick Mantis. Six players were named because Mantis and Jackson tied for the fifth spot.

The same day Saperstein announced a new playoff plan. The first half champion Steers were automatically in the Finals, where they would meet the survivor of an elimination tournament involving the other six teams.

The Pipers, who won their division in the first half, would receive nothing more than an opening night bye in the elimination tournament should they win the second half division title.

Predictably, Steinbrenner was displeased.

Predictably, Steinbrenner filed a protest.

Predictably, Saperstein rejected it.

The Pipers remained in Pittsburgh to play the Rens the next day. The final three games, all against the Rens, ended their long series with Pittsburgh, which had begun so long ago with McLendon the coach and Steinbrenner instituting a curfew after the opening-game defeat.

Cleveland lost the first of the final three, this time by a score of 135–124.

Barnett with 12 and Keller with 11 combined for 23 straight points in the fourth quarter to cut all but three points off an 18-point Rens lead. Hawkins' 38 points topped Barnett's 35.

The final home game, played before a turnout of less than 1,000 at the Arena on March 24, 1962, was an up-and-down the floor, hell's a-poppin' 136–126 shootout win over the Rens. Hawkins scored 42, Cox 41, Pittsburgh's Walt Mangum 28, Barnett 25, and Dierking 23.

Two threes by Barnhill broke a 119–119 tie and tipped the game the Pipers' way.

A victory the next day in Rochester, New York, against the Rens would clinch a second half tie with the Majors.

"Chicago is finished with their season. Just as a matter of pride, I want to win it in the worst way," said Sharman.[9]

Barnhill scored 11 of his 13 in the final quarter, as the Pipers pulled away for a 114–106 victory. Barnett scored 26 overall, and Dierking essentially countered Hawkins, scoring 29, one fewer than the league MVP.

The Pipers finished the second half with a 21–18 record. They were 19–11 under Sharman, a .633 clip that was second only to Kansas City's 26–13, .667 record.

The same day, at the draft in Chicago, the Pipers' choices reflected all of Steinbrenner's fascination with Ohio State. After formally selecting Lucas and Havlicek, the pair's Buckeye teammate Mel Nowell went fifth. Purdue's Terry Dischinger was the Pipers' third-round pick. Hubie White, a Villanova guard, went in the fourth round.

ABL teams weren't bashful. They coveted rich prizes.

"We'll get some of them and maybe Lucas," said a confident Steinbrenner of his team's selections.[10]

The playoffs were beginning Thursday with a doubleheader in Pittsburgh. A single loss in any game until the ABL Finals would end the Pipers' season.

Jerry Lucas's last season at Ohio State had already ended in another disappointing loss to Cincinnati in the national championship game. The Pipers' only chance to live beyond the dwindling days on the ABL's calendar was somehow, against all odds, to sign him.

CHAPTER 22

The Buckeyes' March Sadness

Jerry Lucas played varsity basketball at Ohio State for only three years because freshmen were ineligible in his era, but his precocious skills and those of his teammates were obvious from the moment they stepped on the floor. The Buckeyes were national champions in 1960 with all four of their victories by double-figure margins in the NCAA Tournament.

They were perceived to be invincible. Indeed, they remained just that until Cincinnati's Bearcats beat them, 70–65, in overtime in the 1961 national championship game. That was the game that left Siegfried with such distaste for all things Cincinnati that he might not have liked the city's famous Skyline chili. (To be fair, because the sweet stuff contains cinnamon, it is something of an acquired taste.)

The Buckeyes' excuse for the loss was that the archaic third-place game, an insulting contest neither semifinal loser wanted to play, which remained a Final Four fixture until the 1980s. (The term "Final Four" had not been coined yet. In 1975, *Plain Dealer* reporter Ed Chay was the first to use it for the NCAA Tournament semifinals.)

The third-place game in 1961 between St. Joseph's of Pennsylvania and Utah lasted four overtimes before St. Joseph's prevailed, 127–120. The nervous energy expended in the waiting drained the defending-champion Buckeyes of their vim. Havlicek said he remembered walking down the tunnel of Kansas City's Municipal Auditorium again and again to the court to check the scoreboard to see if the eternal game was any closer to its conclusion.

The excuse rankled the Bearcats, who had to wait too. Ohio State's No. 1 ranking, despite the loss in the national final, from the first day of the ensuing 1961–62 season on, bothered them too.

There is no such creature as a Bearcat in nature, but it was not a myth to Ohio State. With ursine/feline strength and claws, the Bearcats proved as real as a recurring nightmare, beating the Buckeyes again in the 1962 national final, 71–59.

All season, Steinbrenner followed Lucas's team with the zealotry of the most avid fan. Jimmy Hull, his close friend, had been a star on the 1939 team and had been providing updates too.

Such was the excitement in Hull's era that *Columbus Dispatch* columnist Paul Hornung said, "crowds of 1,800 were hanging from the rafters of the old Coliseum."[1]

By contrast, Hornung said attendance was more like "700 and 500 cash customers" for the two Pipers games played in Columbus at the same Fairgrounds Coliseum.

The Pipers weren't a draw, but Lucas was, and his team's almost unbroken success fed Steinbrenner's dreams of what could happen on the court and, equally as important, at the box office with the Ohio State superstar.

In their previous season, Lucas's Buckeyes played four regular-season games that they won by five or fewer points and then squeaked past Louisville by a single point at Freedom Hall on the Cardinals' home court in the NCAA Tournament's Mideast Regional.

The Buckeyes had no such scares in Lucas's senior season, winning by double digits every time out until Wisconsin crushed them, 86–67.

The competitive disparity of the Buckeyes' season denied them the need to execute in the clutch or to maintain their poise when behind late in games. By contrast, the Bearcats were battle hardened. They lost to Missouri Valley Conference rivals Wichita State and Bradley and had to survive a playoff game against Bradley just to get into the NCAA Tournament to defend their title.

The term "March Madness" as a national work-place distraction and office-pool fascination hadn't been coined yet, but Ohio State became familiar with the other side of the month, March sadness. March became, lion or lamb, whether they had been warned about its Ides or not, a month of shock and sorrow for the team.

"I always believe in miracles, but I don't have much hope of beating Ohio State," said Badgers coach John Erickson after beating Ohio State on March 3, 1962.[2]

Wisconsin had not come remotely close in its previous games with Lucas's team, but the Badgers made shots in the upset and the Buckeyes did not. "They shot very well and, well, I don't know when we ever shot any worse. Not lately, for sure," said Ohio State coach Fred Taylor.[3]

"They took it like the champions they have been and still are," wrote *Columbus Dispatch* beat man Dick Otte. "After Taylor removed his regulars, they moved over to the Wisconsin bench to congratulate Erickson even before the game ended and pandemonium broke loose."

"We'll simply have to take our lump and bounce back," said Taylor. "This isn't the end of the world by a long shot."[4]

By the time they reached the championship game, however, the Buckeyes were taking it with a limp. A *Columbus Dispatch* photograph showed Lucas taking an ungainly fall—"one of the most-noted spills in sports history," read the caption—in the second half of an easy national semifinals victory over Wake Forest, a team that included future basketball television analyst named Billy Packer.

An adjoining *Dispatch* photo showed a solemn Lucas, sitting on a bench in the locker room, an ice bag on his left knee, as Havlicek put a consoling arm over Lucas's shoulder. "A slight sprain," Lucas called it, saying of the championship rematch the next night against Cincinnati, "I'll play."[5]

Guard/forward Tom Thacker made his only field goal of the game in the last three seconds for a 72–70 Cincinnati victory in the other semifinal over John Wooden's first Final Four team at UCLA. No one had expected Thacker to take the shot, but the better shooters were tightly guarded. A poor shooter, Thacker was open for a reason.

In the championship game, Thacker played like Lucas while Lucas did not.

Otte wrote, "Lucas played the entire 40 minutes with no noticeable slowing of his natural gait."[6] But he made just five of 17 shots against the Bearcats, after leading the nation in field goal percentage for three straight years. Lucas managed only 11 points, just two above his career low as a Buckeye.

"This is a real great satisfaction to me and the boys," said Bearcats coach Ed Jucker. "Everybody thought it was a fluke when we beat Ohio State last year for the title. We had a point to prove—and we proved it."[7]

Thacker scored 21 points in the championship game. Said Jucker, "Thacker played like five men out there."[8]

Clearly, Lucas was not himself, and, just as clearly, Cincinnati's Paul Hogue was determined to prove his strong play against Lucas the year before was no fluke. Hogue led all scorers with 22, double the total of Lucas.

"I wasn't wearing the bandage, but Lucas said it didn't hurt him," said Taylor.[9]

Sitting on the same bench on which he had rested the injured leg after the Wake Forest game, Lucas denied the injury bothered him. "No, it didn't. Not a bit. It had no effect on me," he said.

"Paul Hogue is much improved over last year, about 300 percent, and as strong as any tall man we've faced all year," said Taylor.[10]

Havlicek's comments about how easily Lucas forgot losses aside, Lucas would later only tersely call Hogue "improved," declining to get into percentages, while praising Purdue's Terry Dischinger as the best opponent he faced.

From a distance of over a half century, Lucas looks churlish with those comments, but Steinbrenner probably only saw in him a kindred spirit. Lucas hated to lose as much as Steinbrenner did.

CHAPTER 23

The Sudden-Death Tournament

The only break the Pipers got in the elimination tournament was their opening round bye.

The series of five sudden-death games began March 29 in Pittsburgh with a doubleheader—Hawaii versus New York and San Francisco versus Pittsburgh.

The latter game, whose winner the Pipers would play, was a pick-your-poison proposition for the Pipers. If the opponents were the Rens, Hawkins was overpowering, averaging 33 points per game against Cleveland, so there was always the chance he could win one game single-handedly. But the Pipers still had a convincing 10–6 (.625) record against the Renaissance Men. If the opponents were the Saints, the "li'l Pipers," as Sudyk called them, would have to face the tallest team in the ABL and one that did not often ignore the chance to punish opponents with its physical and pugnacious style. The Pipers held a 6–4 (.600) advantage against the Saints.

Not only was San Francisco slightly more effective against the Pipers than Pittsburgh, but the Saints' biggest strength was rebounding, and that was precisely the Pipers' biggest weakness. That is the very definition of a bad matchup.

Hawkins was second (to Bridges of the Steers) in the ABL in rebounding with 1,038. Alarmingly, at least for the Rens' chances, the second-best rebounder on the team was Walt Mangham with 594, a gap almost bigger than the ground between the Allegheny and Monongahela rivers, before they meet in Pittsburgh to form the Ohio.

By comparison, Bridges' 1,059 rebounds were only 251 more than Tormohlen's 808.

Hawkins was a one-man show, dominating the box score. But he was young, thin, and inexperienced. One defensive focus can be easier to maintain than several points of emphasis, not that you could particularly tell it by the Pipers' work against the Hawk.

San Francisco was not only taller, but the Saints were much more balanced on the boards. Jim Francis led the team with 760 rebounds, with John Berberich next with 541, then Mike Farmer with 480, and Ken Sears with 471.

The Saints' total rebounds were more impressive because, due to the collapse of the Los Angeles franchise, they played only 76 games. Kansas City played 79. The Pipers, Rens, and Tapers all played 81, although the Pipers also had the three games of the first half playoff with the Steers on their bodies' log. Hawaii played 82 games. The Chicago Majors played 83.

On a per game basis, the Saints led the ABL in rebounding with an average of 53.6. Kansas City was next with 52.9. With an even 50 per game, the Pipers finished third, as they had been early in the season when the *Cleveland Press*'s Lou Darvas drew his "WOWIE!" cartoon.

For the Pipers, a possible meeting with San Francisco was not exactly like Achilles being forced to compete in a heel-and-toe walking contest. But it was close enough for worry. This matchup of course is exactly what happened. The Saints ended the Rens' season with a 107–103 overtime victory.

In the other sudden-death game, the Tapers beat another one-man team, Hawaii and Spivey, again in overtime, 125–116.

On March 30 at the Arena, the Pipers and Saints began their quarter-final game with their shooting as cold as the ice underneath the court, according to Heaton, who put attendance at 1,500. Sudyk termed the turnout "spare, about 1,000."

The Pipers won a tense struggle, 117–112. Barnhill scored eight of his 13 fourth-quarter points in the last two minutes. This enabled the quicker Pipers to survive the loss of Dierking, who contributed 23 points while battling a sore shoulder and knee before fouling out. Warley, who scored only eight before fouling out, played and tried unsuccessfully to cope with a heavy bandage because of a back injury.

Cox, who backed Dierking with 22 points, aggravated an ankle sprain, suffered the day before the game in—yet again—practice. Barnett managed 18. The surprise was Archie Dees, who chipped in 20 points in relief of the other injured and eventually disqualified big men.

The Saints made it interesting with four three-pointers, the equal of the Pipers' quartet. Barnhill meshed one, Cox three. Saints guard Whitey Bell made two of the 25-footers and the rugged Farmer, another big man with range, also made a pair.

Sharman said the Pipers' 56–48 rebounding difference told the story. "If we do as well in our next game, we may be in the title series," he said. "That column tells the story," he added, pointing to the rebounds column of the box score.[1]

Unfortunately, neither the *Plain Dealer* nor the *Press* ran anything in the box score but field goals, free throws, and total points, with an underline noting, in the manner of a footnote, the three-point totals.

The *Kansas City Star,* as was the case in most ABL matters, was more thorough. The *Star* listed rebounds, which are so indicative of desire and can have such a demoralizing effect on opponents. An offensive rebound is a new lease on life, forcing the opponents to play defense for as long as another 30 seconds. A defensive rebound begins the withering counterattack of a fast break.

The next game would be against the Tapers, another unpleasant surprise for the Pipers. Dan Swartz, the ABL's top free throw shooter at 90.5 percent, led a 115–108 victory over Chicago in the other half of the Arena doubleheader, making 21 of 22 free throws.

(A great free throw shooter is not necessarily a great basketball player, but it is worth noting that Swartz's percentage at the line edged the NBA's best, Dolph Schayes of Syracuse, who made 89.7 percent. The other members of the ABL's top five—the Tapers' Roger Kaiser and Roger Taylor, Staverman and Farmer—were all better than the Knicks' Willie Nauls, who at 84.2 percent, was the established league's second-best.)

Although Tony Jackson led the Majors with 27 points, he was blanked on the arc. It was a defensive performance by the Tapers that Sharman, after his team withstood a bombardment of a dozen triples by Jackson in just one game, must have envied.

The Tapers were the vagabonds of a hobo league. They had moved from Washington during the season to Long Island and would relocate to Philadelphia for the truncated 1962–63 season. Still, they were a very tough matchup.

Taylor and Swartz, unfailingly called "Deadeye Dan" by Heaton were both former Pipers. They had a point or 20 to prove to Steinbrenner, especially the volatile Swartz, whose parting, readers might recall, included a great gusher of tobacco juice and cud, aimed at Steinbrenner.

The Tapers managed only a 31–50 overall record, worse than every club except Hawaii, which was 29–53. But the Tapers played much better in the second half after their trades with Cleveland with a 17–22 record. More importantly, the Pipers were only 5–8 (.385) against the Tapers overall, with just one victory in five games in the second half race.

That record, in part, led Sharman to call the Tapers the team to beat. None of the grim omens mattered.

The Pipers flew to Kansas City for the ABL semifinals versus New York as a wounded club. Siegfried stayed behind, receiving treatment to unknot the spasms in his back. It got worse when Swartz KO'd Darrow, one of the smallest players in the league, with a right cross in the third quarter, leaving him concussed, if not tobacco splattered, and leading to Swartz's ejection.

None of the injuries, none of the attrition mattered, either.

Barnett scored 24, Dierking 20. The Pipers raced to a 20-point halftime lead and routed the Tapers, 107–84, at Municipal Auditorium.

Darrow was ruled out of the first game of the Finals, beginning the next afternoon. Siegfried was declared out for the championship series opener too. That meant the Pipers had no reserves at guard. Barnhill and Barnett would have to play every minute of the first game of the Finals. And that did matter.

The Pipers played 91 games in their lone year of existence, four more than the second busiest team, the Steers. They had already played in a pitched playoff series that went the maximum number of games against Kansas City.

Going to the ABL Finals, they had played seven games in 11 days in four cities. Two of the games were win-or-go-home affairs. They would play three more elimination games in the Finals.

Steinbrenner only cared about the destination. But the journey was an epic in itself. It needed only clashing rocks, whirlpools, and a witch who turned men into swine—a plausible explanation for Swartz's behavior, at any rate—to be an odyssey.

CHAPTER 24

Champions

While the Pipers played "Survivor," the Kansas City Steers rested and practiced for a week before the best-of-five Finals began. McMahon put them through a particularly punishing workout at Kansas City's National College.

"It got rough out there, and that's the way I like it," McMahon said. "It shows they're ready to play."[1]

Not so ready was reserve Charlie Henke. A photograph in the *Star* the next day showed him with a blackened right eye. "Rebounding Casualty," read the caption, more proof of the counter-productiveness of extremely physical practices.

Kreisler made good use of his access to practice, noting that the Steers worked on rebounding position, the better for Goliath to keep the li'l Davids away from the rock, fast break defense, outlet passes for their own fast break, and a subtle re-tooling of play options due to the pressure other teams were putting on Bridges and Tormohlen.

Good news for the Steers was delivered in the form of guard Nick Mantis's probable return to play after sitting out the last two games of the regular season with a blood clot in his right arm. The six-foot-two Mantis, at 37.1 percent, was the ABL's deadliest three-point shooter.

The Steers held a light drill on the eve of the Finals after the East-West College All-Star game at Municipal Auditorium. That evening, the Pipers beat the Tapers on the same floor, thus earning the right, in their reduced state, to face the rested and refreshed Steers the next day. The Steers had the league's best record and would have finished 10 games ahead of the Pipers if they had been in the East.

The Finals began on April 1. April Fool's Day. It would have been a marvelous prank if the Pipers had won.

Against all odds, trailing by 19 points in the third quarter, they roared back, driven by the launching-pad arms of Cox and Barnhill. In the 126–115 opening game loss, the Pipers made 10 threes, nine by the Cox and Barnhill combination, with a barrage of five creating havoc in the final quarter.

In only a minute and a half of the fourth quarter, Cox hit three threes before you could say "rat-a-tat-tat," and Barnett added one of his convulsive jumpers. A collapsing defense on Bridges created steals by the Pipers' guards.

The lead of Kansas City shrank to 102–100 before Tormohlen's three brought the crowd of 3,246 to their feet and ended the run.

A flurry of Barnhill's high-arching shots got Cleveland as close as 116–111 with 4:13 to play, but the Herd, as Kreisler liked to dub the Steers, began working the 30-second clock. The Pipers did not have enough stamina left to play such extended defensive minutes.

"They drive you nuts," McMahon said of the rash of three-pointers to his mentor, Alex Hannum, who had coached McMahon with the St. Louis Hawks.

"They make you bring your defense out and open up the middle," Hannum said. "They make you change your whole philosophy."[2]

The Pipers made 10 of 22 threes as they tried to rally, while the Steers made half of the four they tried.

Effectively without a bench, Sharman used Barnett and Barnhill for the whole game, and Cox missed only two minutes. Bridges strangely went all the way for the Steers, who led comfortably for much of the game, and Mantis played all but five minutes.

"I don't want to alibi, but it can make a difference late in a game," Sharman said, when asked about the Pipers three-games-in-three-nights schedule. "Not as much on offense as on defense because that extra step can mean a lot."[3]

In Kreisler's story a puzzling note sounded, which would turn into a full-blown controversy, with Steinbrenner at his overbearing worst, Abe Saperstein at his ineffectual worst, and the ABL at its chaotic nadir.

"Further playoff plans were announced, with the third and (if necessary) fourth games to be played [April 5] and [April 7]," wrote Kreisler of the Cleveland dates. "The date and site of the fifth game (if necessary) has not yet been determined. If Kansas City gets the game, it will not be played in the [Municipal] Auditorium because of scheduling conflicts."[4]

Most leagues aspiring to a modicum of professionalism would have had their showcase event's dates firmed up *before* it began.

The Pipers enjoyed a day without a game on April 2, and spirits further improved with the arrival of Siegfried and the probable return to the lineup of Darrow.

Cox's five threes in the opener occupied the Steers' tactical thinking, particularly since he complemented the outside game with a hook shot inside.

At times, it seemed that the Steers were going to need a cut man as much as a coach, Wilfong showed up at practice with eight stitches under his left eye after colliding with Tormohlen in the first game.

There was no fondness between the teams. Steinbrenner was considered a rogue owner, but more old grudges festered between players.

Tormohlen said of his opposite number, Warley, "You didn't drive down the lane on him. He was real skinny, but tough. He played six years in the NBA. When I was with Kansas City, he knocked me down on a layup. I'm not going to talk real nice about a guy who left the arena with three of my teeth in his pocket."[5]

The second game began on a somber note. Benny "Kid" Paret died early that morning of injuries suffered in a savage beating by Emile Griffith 10 days earlier in their boxing match at Madison Square Garden.

A huge 64–45 rebounding advantage reinforced all Sharman's worries in the Steers' 118–82 rout. Tormohlen scored nine points in a third-quarter flurry to sap the spirit of the Pipers' comeback.

Tormohlen, Staverman, and Bridges all had a double-double in points and rebounds, but Bridges' 26 and 10 were not as overpowering as his 36 and 15 had been in the opener.

The defensive job Maury King did on Barnett, sending the Pipers' scoring leader to the bench in the first half with only one basket, was matched by his job in limiting Barnett's replacement, Barnhill, to two points in the second half.

"It's too late to change anything. We're just going to have to get better individual performances," Sharman said. "When we got behind, we lost our poise."[6]

"Don't let that score fool you. That's a good ball club. They can be tough at home, especially with that crowd behind them," cautioned McMahon.[7]

But the crowd only turned out for the minstrel shows of the Globetrotters. As the series moved to Cleveland, the Globetrotters were the featured opening act, amid a three-ring circus display of pregame acrobatics, variety acts, the ubiquitous Calloway, and other attractions.

The basketball clowns were the headliners in a pregame lollapalooza of vaudeville acts, offering, said Sudyk, "as much variety as Ed Sullivan's 'Your Show of Shows,' with a Mr. and Mrs. Punching act, Max Patkin, the baseball clown, a table tennis match between world champions, cycling and juggling, and Cab Calloway, who has been on the road longer than a bald tire, will emcee."[8]

The game was supposed to start at 8:15 at the Arena. It didn't come close. The game didn't begin until 11 P.M., and it was watched by fewer than half of the 7,624 who saw the Globetrotters in the opener. Those who stayed, however, were loud.

Before the game, the Steers announced their customary addition to the injury list, noting that George Patterson suffered a cut below his right eye in practice but would be available for the game.

The Steers and Pipers also agreed to carry 11 players instead of 10 for the remainder of the series, a move that was more beneficial to the Steers than Cleveland, as it turned out. Larry Comley, a key figure in the first half championship for Kansas City, was home on leave from the Army. The Pipers agreed to let the Steers add him to the active list, in return for their adding Siegfried to their roster.

Comley played a big role, scoring 25 points in the third game. Siegfried did not get into the third game or any others in the Finals.

Barnett single-handedly kept the Pipers in the do-or-die game, scoring 24 of his 36 points in the second half and making King's "glove-like" defense in the second game, as the *Kansas City Star*'s Dick Mackey had called it, look like a mitten that wasn't fittin'.

The Pipers rallied from 11 points behind in the fourth quarter to win it on a shot fans would see forever on ESPN had it happened today—Barnett's 20-foot hook shot from the corner against King, which snapped the net cords with two seconds to play in a 116–114 thriller.

"A hook shot Bob Ripley wouldn't believe," Sudyk wrote, referring to the creator of the popular Ripley's Believe It or Not newspaper feature.[9]

After Kansas City's last shot, a miss by Tormohlen that rolled tantalizingly off the rim with one minute to play, the Pipers had the ball for almost the entirety of the final minute. Barnett dribbled the 30-second clock down and then missed for the 12th time in two dozen tries with a hook. In the rebounding melee, the ball rolled out of bounds, and the Pipers kept control.

Barnett's second hook of the extended possession came after he tried to draw a foul by cutting inside. At splashdown, the shot brought about 100 fans out of their seats in a stampede to the court to backslap Barnett and celebrate.

"The crowd really responded when we began to close in on the Steers in that last quarter. You'd be surprised at how much of a lift that can give a team," said Sharman.[10]

The phlegmatic Barnett, "who fills the basket with the outward enthusiasm of a man in the dentist's waiting room" in Sudyk's words, admitted the winning shot brushed the edges of improbability and luck.[11] "I guess I'll have to admit that wasn't one of my normal shots," Barnett assessed. "But heck, I could do it again—in 10 tries."[12]

"It was classic Barnett. He threw his body back as far as he could and hit that shot," Cleary said.[13]

Fall back to Game Four, baby.

"I'll give him that same shot tomorrow," said McMahon. "It took that wild, left-handed hook shot to beat us. There wasn't anything [Maury] King could do. There isn't a man who could stop it."[14]

Dierking added 30 points with 22 rebounds, as the Pipers won the third-game rebounding scrum, 57–53. Keller had another 10 boards. Cox added 25 points. He also made the only three-pointer of the game for the Pipers to erase the 11-point deficit and pull into a tie at 101.

Bridges' 34 points and 17 rebounds were wasted for the Steers. His tendency to take root, develop growth rings, and flower in the lane, cost the Steers dearly. Mantis drilled a three-pointer late in the game that was negated by a three-second lane violation on Bridges.

"Bill has played marvelous ball against us," said Sharman, looking at the big picture. "He's been very consistent and hasn't shown any real weakness. The Steers are so strong that they push us around. They're not a dirty ball club, just powerful."[15]

McMahon was unhappy with the Steers' execution, singling out Staverman, who made only four of 12 shots. "I've never seen Staverman so out of it. At halftime, we talked about setting some picks so he could get the offensive feel of the game. We didn't set one in the second half," McMahon said. "I can't call every play from the bench like [the Browns'] Paul Brown."[16]

The Steers' coach also lamented the open looks Barnett had enjoyed before his spectacular game-winner, which he blamed on the failure of the Steers' big men to switch out on him. "The one thing I've preached all year is give a good shooter an open shot and he's going to hit 65–70 percent," he complained. "You've got to switch off and get on him. Make him pass the ball. Never the open shot."[17]

Modern-day statistical analysis has determined that the shooting percentage on contested shots, compared to open ones, goes down 20 percent, almost without fail, no matter who shoots, given average ability.

Heading for the elevator to his room back at the Steers' hotel, McMahon said, "I hope Winnie [Wilfong] has some sleeping pills. I'm going to need them."[18]

The fourth game was to be held in Cleveland on April 7. If there were to be a fifth game, it would be played—where exactly? The site was still being argued over.

"These kids have a great heart and just won't quit no matter what the score. We're not the biggest nor the strongest in the league, but we're here playing for the title," said Sharman before playing Game Four, which would be the last game of the year in Cleveland—unless the schedule changed again.[19]

The Pipers thought the fifth game was to be played in Cleveland, the Steers in Kansas City. But the Ice Capades were booked into Municipal Auditorium for April 8.

Cleary announced the fifth game, if necessary, would be held at Kansas City's little Rockhurst College in Mason-Halpin Fieldhouse. This enraged Steinbrenner, who thought Saperstein had promised otherwise. Saperstein had to decide soon, but "his lips remain sealed on his perennial cigar," Sudyk wrote.[20]

In the fourth game, the Pipers were depending on the six-foot-nine Dierking to give some resistance to Bridges. Instead, while Keller grabbed 18 rebounds to Bridges' 22, Dierking delivered the game-winning shot on a hook from the lane with one second to play. "Two buzzer-beaters," said Cleary. "What can you do?"[21]

Bridges made only five of 17 shots, leaving Staverman (seven of 13) and Tormohlen (eight of 16) the only players on the cold-shooting Steers to make half or more of their shots. Despite the 35 percent shooting and a 52–43 deficit on the boards, Kansas City pulled even at 98 with 23 seconds to play on two Tormohlen free throws.

The Pipers worked carefully for the last shot, with Cox turning down an outside shot at the last instant after spotting Dierking cutting across the lane near the free throw line. "Cox didn't give up the ball very often, but he did to Dierking, who just let it fly," said Cleary.[22]

The reaction to the thrilling end of the last professional basketball game to be played by a Cleveland team in the city for eight years was the same as at the end of the third game. It was bedlam in the stands as the 4,115 fans at the Arena roared.

It was rivaled afterward by the clamor, controversy, and chaos of the unraveling playoff plans, which Saperstein seemed to be improvising on a minute-by-minute basis.

Given new life by back-to-back buzzer beaters, Steinbrenner, incredibly, was willing to snuff any chance for the championship, ruin the culmination of the season, and thwart the dreams of his players because he did not get his way.

It is difficult to think the Pipers had much of a case for playing host to the fifth game since there had been no official announcement at the league meetings or afterward that the concluding trio of Finals games would be played in the East Division city. That, however, is what Steinbrenner contended. Moreover, given the presence of Hawaii and San Francisco in the sudden-death tournament, there was no guarantee that an East team would even make the championship series.

While Steinbrenner was correct to be upset by the coin flip that would have given Pittsburgh home court advantage for an East Division playoff game in the first half race, because the Pipers had the lead in the season series, he was wrong to claim home court in the Finals. The Steers had the best record in all respects—first half, second half, and overall.

It smelled of another cost consideration, as Steinbrenner tried to avoid another trip to Kansas City by his team because it had turned into a financial hemorrhage.

Next, Saperstein decided the final game would be played in St. Louis—after a one-week delay, which was necessary to set up a Globetrotters game as the preliminary attraction. As long and drawn out as are the current NBA playoffs, this proposed delay was unconscionably long and calls into question the efficacy of Saperstein as both commissioner and promoter. Almost everyone would have completely forgotten about the ABL during the one-week layoff.

Backing off from that preposterous idea, Saperstein next said the fifth game would be played in Cleveland on Tuesday, April 10. Somewhere in this hectic flurry of indecisiveness, the Steers were offered a cochampionship with the Pipers. The Steers indignantly declined.[23]

This was followed by another flip-flop, as the gale force of the Steers' protests caused Saperstein to spin like a weathervane when the wind changes.

Back the game went, he blustered, to Rockhurst College at 8:15 Sunday April 8. The late notice, by telegram on April 7, of that decision, claimed the Pipers, made it impossible to arrange transportation on short notice in an era when all teams traveled on commercial planes.

The Steers, however, had reserved 15 seats for the Pipers on the same flight they were boarding to Kansas City after the fourth game. At the conclusion of the Saturday game, Cleary found the seats had been canceled. He reserved them again, but they went unclaimed.

Amid all this waffling, Steinbrenner next said the Pipers would for-
feit. "That suits me fine," said the fiery McMahon, when informed of
Steinbrenner's comments. "You can bet we'll be there. And you can bet
we won't be showing up in St. Louis next week. We'll be ready to play
in Kansas City. It's our home game. I think it should be up to us where
to play it. We came [to Cleveland] for two games in the first half and
beat them. We had the best record in the league. I think it's about time
we had the home court for a change."[24]

Sharman said after the fourth game, "It's not my decision. I'll do
what they tell me to do."[25]

"We're not going," said Flieger.[26]

The only team at Rockhurst College on Sunday April 8 was Kansas
City. The Steers held a light workout. The Pipers did not show up. The
game was not forfeited.

In yet another message to the teams, Saperstein telegraphed,
"Completely surprised controversy developed for final playoff game
with vacillations, erroneous statements etc. Finalized effort with usual
sporting gesture—tossing up coin. Result controversial game must be
played previously designated college gym in Kansas City no later than
Monday night, April 9."

Steinbrenner said the decision to toss a coin to decide such an important matter was "typical of the indecision and disorganization of the
ABL."[27] Joe Gordon, the Rens PR man and future general manager, said
conditions made it tough for anyone to be ABL commissioner, especially
a man as pliable as Saperstein.

"Circumstances were such that you also had to consider the ownership you had in sports at that time," Gordon said. "They were all kinds of
strong-minded people. Steinbrenner was, the Littmans [the Rens' owners]
were. They were extremely successful in so many different areas of business. It's not as common now, but in those days, those owners thought
they had all the answers. It wasn't just in the ABL. You couldn't tell them
anything. Under the circumstances, it was mission impossible."[28]

The owners knew they had a soft touch in Saperstein. "The Littmans
asked for special considerations, and he would agree to it," said Gordon.
"He was doing everything he possibly could to have that league survive.
Whoever had his ear last got the answer he wanted."[29]

"It's so different today," Gordon added, drawing on his experience with the Steelers. "In all the leagues there is such a strong structure at the league level that it's hard for some owners to screw up—contrary to what has happened in Cleveland."[30]

Steinbrenner left playing the game up to a vote of the players. Citing "the good of the league" and saying enough embarrassment had been caused, the Pipers voted to play, boarding a 10:30 P.M. flight Sunday that was due to land in Kansas City at 2:30 in the morning the day of the championship game.

"It's too bad we have to play in some dinky college gym," said Steinbrenner.[31]

All the Pipers except Dierking boarded the plane. The hero of the fourth game had not overcome his fear of flying and was reported to be driving to Cincinnati to catch an overnight train to Kansas City. "If he doesn't make it to the court on time," Sudyk wrote, "Cleveland's stock will drop lower than anything in Kansas City's stockyard."[32]

After all this wrangling. Kreisler had had enough of Steinbrenner, Saperstein, and the ABL. "A.B.L. Labels Itself As a B-U-S-H League" read the headline on his story.

"In one Lost Weekend of wrangling, the American Basketball League has stripped itself of major league status," he wrote. "After that relatively short and confusing time, the new league can hardly expect to escape the also short and painful label B-U-S-H."[33]

Citing the "charges, counter-charges and bickering" over the decisive fifth game, Kreisler wrote, "Decisions were reached and proclaimed. Few, if any, were backed up." He pointedly scorned the idea of a week's wait for another Globetrotter doubleheader across the state in St. Louis. "Any replay of the travesty that occurred in Cleveland last week (when the A.B.L. playoff game followed the Globetrotters and did not start until 11 o'clock) is hard to be accepted as anything major league. It seems any major league event should be scheduled before most people are asleep."[34]

Kreisler liked covering the league and wrote enthusiastically about it, but he did not pull any punches about the last great fiasco of the season. "The Cleveland team's open disregarding of Commissioner Saperstein's decision to hold the game here Sunday is flagrant in itself. It is especially so when you consider it was committed by a team that faced expulsion from the league earlier because of other irregularities. . . . We think both the players and the fans deserve better than the instability the A.B.L. has shown over the weekend. . . . A M-A-J-O-R league would see to that."[35]

The winner of Game Five would be awarded the C. W. "Bud" Hoeber trophy, it had been announced during the hectic Finals. Hoeber, who had died on July 9, 1961, had been the co-owner of the Steers. In the event, nothing more was heard of him or the trophy.

"The boys are fighting mad about the situation," said Sharman, "and I only hope that the confusion of the last 24 hours doesn't upset them too much on the court."[36]

It didn't.

Surrounded by the controversies that had probably been encoded in their principal owner's DNA and that certainly were mostly his fault— with their acrophobic big man riding the rails; with the whole long, exhausting, exasperating season almost forfeited on account of the owner's unreasonableness; with very few friends around in the climactic game—the Pipers nevertheless were ready.

On the evening of April 9, 1962, four Rockhurst College freshmen held signs that read, "Welcome Pipers to our 'dinky gym'" and "Welcome 'pros' you fit right in."

The Four Aristocrats played "Everything's Up to Date in Kansas City" and the Steers' song, "Hey, Look Me Over." Readers may recall this was the same ditty during which a baton twirler was winged by her own implement after losing it in the lights of Public Hall. The result was much the same, metaphorically anyway, for the Steers.

"Mason-Halpin Field House would have made a good fort," said Fritz Kreisler. "It had concrete stands. It's not used at all now except maybe for women's games at Rockhurst. There was no extra room at all in that place, just barely enough for the benches for the players."[37]

Its listed seating capacity was 1,500. Kansas Citians thronged to it in such numbers that attendance was estimated at 3,000, double the capacity. So impressed was Ken Kreuger—the surviving owner, who had kept the franchise afloat although he lived in St. Louis—that he gave everyone at the game two tickets to a contest for the next season.

"All the fans paid," said Cleary. "Basketball was good in Kansas City."[38]

So rare is a Cleveland championship that fans today probably would expect it to be accompanied by an event worthy of the Rapture or at least a downtown parade. Nothing so apocalyptic occurred. "Everybody had packed to go home immediately after the game," Cleary said. So there wouldn't have been a parade in Kansas City either.[39]

"Cleveland didn't have anybody in the stands other than the guys on their bench. My recollection is that Steinbrenner did not come to the game. I'm sure John McLendon was there," Cleary said.[40]

Both teams were, to some extent, strangers in a strange land. Said Cleary, "The gym was a problem for both teams. We never played or practiced there. The floor was a little smaller than usual. But we were just off. I don't know how we hung around [on the scoreboard]."[41]

The Pipers, booed throughout the game, scored 106 points. The Steers, cheered thunderously whenever they showed the faintest sign of climbing back into contention, scored 102.

It was really not that close. Barnett scored 26 points on 10 for 23 shooting. The Pipers held a 12–3 lead in points behind the arc, with three of the triples by Cox and the other by Barnhill. Only Mantis had a bonus-point field goal for the Steers. In the series, the Pipers made 22 three-pointers, the Steers only 12.

The Pipers collected 54 rebounds, with 14 by Dierking and 10 by Keller, to 44 for the Steers. Dierking, proving how immense the trade for him really was, also scored 20 points.

Other than Staverman, who kept the Steers in it with drives and intermediate jump shots and tallied 26 points, Kansas City settled for jump shots and often missed.

Cleveland led at the half, but only by 49–46. On the way to the tiny locker room at halftime, Sharman stopped Cleary. "Hey, when this game ends, I've got a 10 o'clock flight to LA, and it's the only one I can catch. Can you have someone take me to the airport? I'll pay the guy," Sharman said. Cleary grabbed an intern and told him he was to be Sharman's chauffeur.[42]

Although Kansas City took a brief 65–60 lead in the third quarter, Cleveland led, 79–77, at its end. In the quarter, the Pipers lost Darrow, who reinjured strained ankle ligaments.

The last tie was at 83, and it was broken when Cox rifled in a three.

Bridges, who scored 24 of his 31 in the second half by sniping from the outside, also got 13 rebounds in the game. He and Barnett matched baskets for almost half of the fourth quarter before the Pipers pulled ahead, 100–92.

With one last effort of will as much as ability, Bridges scored six straight points to cut the lead to 101–98 with 2:15 to play. "Kill a little time. Get a good shot. No three-pointers [for the Steers]," Sharman shouted above the din in the Pipers' huddle.[43]

The Pipers used up most of the 30-second clock before Barnett missed.

Barnhill again defied the expectations of what a relative mite could do in a game of giants, outjumping everyone for the rebound and then locating an open Cox in the corner for the three-pointer that doubled the lead and effectively put the game away.

Providing exactly the spark Sharman wanted from him off the bench, Barnhill finished with 14 points. At the final buzzer, a grateful teammate seized Barnhill and lifted him gingerly in a bear hug. Several Pipers clapped their hands in glee as they headed for the locker. One did a few steps of the Twist as the Four Aristocrats broke into the Notre Dame fight song. Kansas City fans booed raucously. Of all the Steers, only Staverman shook hands with the victors as they left the court.

A snippet of film exists that is the only video evidence that the Pipers ever played. In it, the players romped joyously into the cramped locker room. Barnett grabbed a thematically appropriate plumbing pipe near the ceiling as he stood on a bench, steadying himself with one hand, while pouring champagne in a foaming torrent over a teammate's head.

A pleasant story arose about the aftermath of the championship game, in which the Pipers handed the championship Bud Hoeber trophy, not to Sharman, but to McLendon, who was there to support his beloved former charges.

But Sharman wouldn't have been present anyway. He was urging his young driver to step on it on his way to the Kansas City airport as soon as the game ended.

As for the trophy, Cleary said, "I'm sure there was something, but I never saw it."[44]

There certainly was no trophy presentation. Barnett said there was no pay, either—except for himself. Barnett told Wolf, "I got $17 for the five games. But I never told anyone about it because I didn't want my teammates to feel bad."

Neither the *Plain Dealer* nor the *Press* saw fit to staff the final game. The headline on the Associated Press story in the *Plain Dealer* was "Pipers Top Steers, Win ABL Crown."

The headline on the "jump" of the story from the first page of sports was, erroneously, about a baseball game—"Nats beat Tigers." The only daily newspaper in Cleveland bungled the record.

For almost everyone, Pipers and Steers, front office and players, reimbursed or stiffed, the chaotic season was over. "Staverman was the only one who stuck around," said Cleary. "He pitched batting practice for the Athletics."[45]

Baseball was beginning with its connotations of a greening world and warming weather.

Whether the Pipers would stick around after a season in which attendance averaged barely 2,000 per game depended on Steinbrenner's ability to reinvent them as a team the NBA had to have. That effort would begin with Lucas. "We could play in a church league with Lucas and pack the house," Steinbrenner said.[46]

CHAPTER 25

A Contract That Overshadowed Wilt's

The Pipers' signing of Jerry Lucas was an astonishing triumph, which even at the time, bore the seeds of an appalling defeat. It was based on Steinbrenner's shrewdness and vision, but it was doomed by his deceptions and history of financial struggles. It was a necessity for leaving the crumbling ABL, joining the NBA, and bringing throngs of fans through the "Jerry-built gate," as the *Plain Dealer*'s Jimmy Doyle punned of the Pipers' prospective attendance boom.

So high were the stakes for admittance to basketball's major league, however, that paychecks were expected to be punctual, irregularities at the banks rectified, and sweeping promises reinforced by the one thing on which Henry Steinbrenner was not going to release his grip—the family fortune.

Signing Lucas made George Steinbrenner the wonder of the basketball world. It got him to the last stride before the final hurdle. In order to clear it, George came close to forming a "super team" with the best players from the Steers and the Pipers, plus Lucas. He almost beat bigger odds than anything Henry ever encountered either in the hurdles of his youth or the shipping storms and treacherous shoals of his maturity.

But so shaky were the underpinnings of the deal that, when it shattered, it left George Steinbrenner $250,000 in debt and the Pipers and their investors with over half that in losses. It revealed Steinbrenner to be just what the Cincinnati Royals had charged he was—a man whose word you could bank on, as long as you put up the money.

The collapse of the Pipe dream left the ABL unable to prolong a wounded second season past New Year's Eve in 1962. It made Lucas the equivalent of a free agent, but it also called into question his truthfulness and the business acumen of his Columbus adviser, Joe Hardy, in agreeing to the deal in the first place.

Cleary had long harbored at least a few doubts about Lucas, whose class rank, said Ohio State coach Fred Taylor, was in the top 4 percent of the School of Commerce. "Studies were easy for Lucas because he had what amounted to a photographic memory," Cleary said. "And there's a lot of memory work involved in college."[1]

The negotiations with Steinbrenner eventually left Lucas with his own sense of moral rectitude intact, although others felt it had been compromised. His deal with Steinbrenner gave him little else. "I never saw any of that money," he said.[2]

Steinbrenner began laying the groundwork for the deal at the same ABL meetings late in the regular season in which indecisiveness about the Finals playoff format led to such controversy. At the meetings, Steinbrenner, the openly mutinous owner of a team that faced expulsion after trying to break away on its own terms, dictated the schedule and travel arrangements for the next season. Even by the loose standards of the ABL, he would seem to have been a strange leader to follow. But such was the personal magnetism of Steinbrenner that again he pulled it off.

"George was the type of guy that you had confidence in him because he was so self-confident in himself," said the Rens' Gordon. "When he did or said something, in his mind he was 100 percent right."[3]

Steinbrenner wanted a schedule reduction to 65 games. This clearly was an inducement to Lucas, who had been troubled by his knees, even before a sprain limited him severely in Ohio State's second straight national championship game loss to Cincinnati.

The next ABL season would begin on Thanksgiving Day in 1962 or in early December. Lucas was slated to be in school, working on his degree, until December. The schedule would also consist mostly of games within the division to contain travel costs.

Speaking at the Central YMCA banquet in Cleveland on April 10, Lucas said of Cincinnati's three-year $100,000 offer, which included a new car, "I told the Royals I wasn't interested in their offer. It wasn't interesting to me in any fashion. I haven't changed my mind about pro basketball. I still don't want to play it."[4]

"You won't get this boy with money," Steinbrenner said dismissively of the Cincinnati sales pitch.[5]

Details of what the Pipers were planning to pique Lucas's interest quickly leaked to the press. It reportedly included about $100,000 in salary for three seasons, which Steinbrenner refuted, saying, "I'm not even thinking in terms of three years." That was true, but the reports were otherwise accurate. The Pipers offered options to buy lucrative stocks, provide an executive job with a company that could position Lucas for a business career after basketball and pay for his education.[6]

"Lucas's contract is the most attractive offer I have ever seen," Sharman told Sudyk. "It overshadows any contract held by Wilt Chamberlain, the best-paid performer in pro basketball."[7]

On April 11, a victory salute to the champion Pipers was held at the Hickory Grill in downtown Cleveland. Barnett received the biggest ovation. During the festivities, Steinbrenner said he had locked up a basketball lease with the Arena. He also said he was "leaning to the ABL" as a future home for his team, despite the persistent rumors of a merger with Syracuse. But Syracuse was now several exits back down the highway to basketball heaven that the NBA represented to Steinbrenner. He was heading there like a human calliope, pealing with empty promises, steam-driven by his own hot air.

For his part, Lucas had dropped out of college in order to pay the bills married life had brought. He had arranged roughly 50 speaking engagements around the state, for $50 to $100 per speech. Lucas's determination to speak to high school players in an attempt try to teach them his own values had already cost him $15,000. Saperstein had offered the money to play with the U.S. All-Stars on a tour against the Globetrotters.

Lucas instead formed a barnstorming team from his teammates at Ohio State, including Havlicek, Mel Nowell, Bob Knight, and Joe Roberts, who played a 10-game schedule against semipro teams in the state. The "Fabulous Buckeyes" opened by overwhelming a Newark, Ohio, team, 121–49.

Lucas's schedule of semipro games and his travel to Cleveland, Canton, Bucyrus, and other towns to give speeches were proof that neither he nor his wife, Treva, was born to wealthy parents. They needed the money.

Increasingly, it was apparent that Lucas wasn't all that unshakable in his refusal to play pro basketball. He met with Mark McCormack, who represented professional golfers Arnold Palmer and Gary Player and would found International Management Group, the Cleveland-based sports marketing conglomerate that would become a global force in player representation. Afterward, Lucas denied any agreement with the agent, sticking to his mantra that he didn't know what he was going to do.

Sudyk concluded on April 6, 1962, "Despite all his public statements, Jerry Lucas, three-time All-America from Ohio State, will play professional basketball." Included in the story was the possibility that Lucas's signing with the Pipers, which Sudyk rated as no better than an "outside chance," could lead to an NBA invitation and to the Buffalo Bills' Ralph Wilson finalizing his purchase of the team at last.

Characteristically vague, Steinbrenner would say only that "Ralph's share of stock is different, but nothing's definite."

So strong was the interest in all things Lucas that Lebovitz in his "Ask Hal" feature in the *Plain Dealer* fielded a question about why Lucas wore plain white socks at Ohio State although his teammates wore socks with two vertical scarlet stripes. The stripes were actually a baseball-style stirrup, which, Lebovitz said, made Lucas's arch feel uncomfortable. The socks were elasticized and were also objectionable because of the "tension" they put on in his lower legs with their snug fit. "Would you say he's lessened his sox appeal?" Lebovitz asked.[8]

In the meantime, the Fabulous Buckeyes were playing up to their name. In a game against the Akron Tramonte Black Label team, which was bolstered by three Pipers—Cox, Barnhill, and Warley as well as former Piper Grady McCollum, he of the halftime trade to Hawaii—the Fabulous Buckeyes won, 79–73. Lucas, although reportedly 20 pounds underweight, scored 37 points. The four ABL players combined for 42.

That game and victory in an invitational tournament in Charlestown,

West Virginia, helped prove to Lucas that the pros were no tougher for him to master than numbers in a telephone book were to memorize.

Cobbledick said in the April 21 *Plain Dealer* that no decision was expected from Lucas for at least six weeks. It took only three and a half. On April 30, Lucas met with the Pipers, after which a confident Steinbrenner said, "It's like no other contract which has been presented to an athlete. Jerry is very impressed, and we are very impressed with him."[9] After lunch at the Union Club, Steinbrenner made his formal offer at the Cleveland Athletic Club.

In what today would be called his "q score," meaning the familiarity a target audience has with a celebrity or product, Lucas ranked very high. Strangers greeted him warmly on the streets of downtown Cleveland and urged him to sign with the Pipers. In touring the Cleveland waterfront, Lucas amazed Steinbrenner by chatting with a Japanese sailor in the seaman's native tongue.

After a tour of prospective apartments in the West Side suburb of Rocky River, Lucas and his wife headed back to Columbus. Steinbrenner said Lucas had been the Most Valuable Player of the West Virginia semipro tournament. "He seems to be getting excited about basketball again," said Steinbrenner.[10]

On May 12, Lucas said he would reveal his plans by the end of the week.

On May 14, he played golf with Royals' executives.

On May 15, he signed with the Pipers.

Exactly what kind of a contract with what riders and stipulations would be a matter of controversy, but it seems clear that the first agreement was with the Pipers and Steinbrenner, with the understanding that the team would play in the ABL.

By signing a name as big as Jerry Lucas, Steinbrenner foreshadowed the American Football League's New York Jets signing of Joe Namath on January 2, 1965.

The problem was that Steinbrenner's coup occurred in the neglected backwater of pro basketball, not in pro football, a telegenic sport that was growing quickly in popularity with the presence of a TV set in almost every American home.

Lucas gave the story of his signing to *Sports Illustrated* because he had become close to the magazine's writers, who had virtually lived with him for the Sportsman of the Year story. LeBron James, 52 years in the future, revealed his return to the Cleveland Cavaliers on the SI.com website to a writer at the magazine, Lee Jenkins, with whom he had grown close.

Steinbrenner had begun his pitch by talking about education, Lucas revealed in the story. George was well aware that such emphasis was how Ohio State beat out 150 other schools for Lucas's services.

The Pipers promised a 70-game schedule, according to the *Sports Illustrated* story. Apparently, like the 76-to-83-game schedule played by ABL teams in the league's first year, the revised schedule—of maybe 65 games, as Steinbrenner wanted, or maybe 70, as the magazine said—was expanding or contracting as the situation warranted.

The aim was that the season would not begin until Lucas finished school in December. The contract was for two years, not three, giving Lucas more leeway to plan for whatever the future held. The stock and investment portfolio alone "virtually assured me an income for years," said Lucas.

All in all, the investments were worth $40,000 and Lucas's salary was to be $10,000 per year. The $60,000 "adds up to far less than the Cincinnati offer," Lucas said. "But to me it is much more in long-range terms."[11]

Lucas said he felt the Pipers would draw better with him on the team. (How could they not?) He also said Steinbrenner had showed him the books, and that the team lost $170,000 on the season.

The Pipers were also pursuing Havlicek. There was even a parenthetical insert in the story by *Sports Illustrated* editors: "(Teammate and fellow All-America John Havlicek will probably join Lucas at Cleveland. –ED)."[12] This was either an early instance of the infamous "Sports Illustrated jinx" or another in a long list of might-have-beens for Cleveland sports fans.

Addressing his responsibility as what would decades later be termed a "role model," Lucas said he had conflicting ideas to the very end about playing professionally. He had been told many times over the last six weeks by parents he didn't even know that they wanted their boys to grow up to be like him.

"On the one hand, I felt I should not [turn pro], because you can set an example for children by showing them there are many more important things than money," said Lucas. "On the other hand, I have come to realize how quickly I would be out of the public eye if I did not continue my athletic career, and how I would consequently be less able to achieve many of the things with youth and youth organizations that I hope to."[13]

This was the same argument the *Press*'s Gibbons had advanced earlier.

Many of these quotes appeared verbatim—the Fabulous Buckeye's memory was at work again!—in Cleveland newspaper stories after the Pipers' own press conference at the Pick Hotel.

"Sports Illustrated offered [Lucas] a sizable sum of money," wrote Heaton, meaning for the exclusive story of his decision, "but in a truly Lucas gesture, he told them to use the money to send magazine subscriptions to orphanages. That's the type of fellow the Pipers will have going for them in the title defense next winter."[14]

The payment, according to *Columbus Dispatch* sports columnist Paul Hornung, was $500. Hornung, setting the cynical tone for his column, called the gesture "noble—and a pretty good deal for SI."[15]

The coverage of Steinbrenner in Cleveland was effusive. The stormy team president announced he would soon be stepping down as president. Years later, the nicest thing a *Plain Dealer* profile of him could say was that his image "took a pasting" as Pipers' president. But it was peaches and cream after the Lucas signing.

"It seemed to be a publicity stunt," Heaton wrote in a "Pinch-Hitting" column for the vacationing Cobbledick. "Those who scoffed at the Pipers' audacity forgot one thing. George Steinbrenner is a master salesman and he has been selling young men for a long time."[16]

Heaton then referred to the "Bay Village squire" and his recruiting successes in the Cleveland area for Purdue, where Steinbrenner had been an assistant football coach.

Heaton ended the column triumphantly by saying that with Lucas "Cleveland has the two top college personalities of last season. Ernie Davis is already in the Browns' fold, with Art Modell, another young salesman, beating the Buffalo Bills."[17]

Two athletic celebrities of similar magnitude would not be in Cleveland at the same time again until 2014, with the return of James and the Browns' drafting of Johnny Manziel.

"Signing of Lucas Is Job Well Done," read the headline on Gibbons's column in the *Press*.[18]

"Almost as interesting as Lucas in this modern success story is Steinbrenner, the embattled president of the Pipers," wrote Gibbons. "He admits he is stepping down ('There's a new man coming in as president—someone who will present a better public image than I've been') immediately following his greatest victory."[19]

The same recruiting success Heaton praised in regard to Purdue had saved Steinbrenner with the Pipers. "Steinbrenner has done a multitude of things wrong in the operation of the Pipers, but this one he did exactly right. Lucas is getting him off the hook, even if he may not be able to take the ABL off one," Gibbons wrote.

The next day, the *Press* ran a wire service about Cincinnati reaction that was the first smudge of cloud on the Pipers' sunny day. "It was sort of like Pearl Harbor," said the angry Cincinnati Royals general manager, Pepper Wilson, who remembered well the round of golf with Lucas the day before he signed in Cleveland.

"Jerry was smiling and gracious on the golf course, but at the same time we were being bombed someplace else. That All-American boy image is a little tarnished, I'd say," said Wilson. "Apparently, with this thing all cut and dried, Lucas accepted and kept a date with the Royals officials yesterday [May 14] and at no time indicated he had made a choice or said he was going to Cleveland."[20]

By now, Lucas's contradictions and indecisiveness were interpreted by southern Ohio and even Columbus critics as hypocrisy and duplicity. "Lucas was a very political guy," said Cleary. "He told you what you wanted to hear."[21]

In a letter to *Plain Dealer* columnist Jimmy Doyle, a reader said, "As a former Ohio State student who lost money on the NCAA tourney favorites, I wonder if it was coincidental that Jerry Lucas didn't commit himself to the ABL until he knew the University of Cincinnati's Paul Hogue was under contract to play in the other cage league?"[22]

In reply, Lucas damned his rival with faint praise, saying only, "Hogue is improved," in a story about his top college opponents. Of Purdue's

Terry Dischinger, Lucas said, "He can do everything on the basketball floor. In addition, he's modest and unselfish, the kind of fellow I would want for a friend."

Lucas's decision to break the news in a national magazine such as *Sports Illustrated,* on the ground that he "wanted everyone to know the reason I turned pro," left Hornung simmering with anger.[23] In a column with the headline "Lucas Goes into Minors, Not in a Major League Way," the columnist noted that both Ohio State running back Hopalong Cassady in signing with the Detroit Lions and golfer Jack Nicklaus's in his decision to turn pro first told the Columbus reporters who had covered them for so long.

Yet Lucas denied to Otte just before the May 14 deadline for the *Dispatch*'s last edition that he had made up his mind. "Ah, well. Who needs friends? They love you at the bank," wrote Hornung.[24]

Nor did Hornung think much of the ABL after attending one of the Pipers' games in Columbus. "I managed to stick through one half and a long wait while then-coach John McLendon marked off the three-point goal circle and the wider foul lane with adhesive tape on the Coliseum floor," wrote Hornung. "After watching Ohio State's Fabulous Buckeyes, what happened at the Coliseum lacked interest."[25]

In his view, Lucas's barnstorming, pick-up team was a better entertainment value.

Hornung turned to the what-ifs that would follow Lucas's decision. "It's a shame we'll never know whether Big Luke was good enough to play major league pro basketball," he wrote. "The ABL, of which the Pipers are champions, is made up of players in the twilights of their careers, lesser-known collegians and holdovers from the defunct National Industrial Basketball League."[26]

Hornung sneered at Steinbrenner's outburst of "We're saved!" after Lucas signed, recounting an interview the sports columnist had with the owner three days before Lucas's announcement. "We might move the club," Hornung quoted Steinbrenner as saying. "Without Lucas, there's no hope for us. With him, we could really go. We're putting all our eggs in one basket."

Sarcastically, Hornung forecast great things for Lucas: "In the ABL, he should lead in everything, including Most Bank Deposits."[27]

Admitting that Lucas made Columbus fans "richer" for having seen him play and calling him a "hallowed figure," Hornung said, "But, if you're going to go, go first-class."[28]

Clowser, whose coverage of Lucas had been glowing for three years, reacted as an Ohio State true believer. He wrote a few days later, "All I can say is that Lucas now knows he has some fair-weather friends who should be ashamed for their attacks on him. It was disgusting to see the bitterness with which certain columnists in other Ohio cities greeted Jerry's decision to play here."[29]

Using words like "shocking" and "knifing" to describe the criticism and "sensitive" and "temperate" for Lucas, Clowser called Lucas a "sterling youngster, whose every action has brought great credit to his university, state and nation."

Citing the "tremendous value to American university life exemplified in a youth like Lucas," Clowser ended the column by writing, "I can only hope that, now that we have been fortunate enough to have him join the Cleveland sports scene, we can be worthy of him."[30]

The Royals' enmity to Lucas and the Pipers would have fateful consequences very quickly. At the time of his signing with the Pipers, however, Clevelanders were ecstatic.

Heaton had the fever too. His *Plain Dealer* copy radiated optimism. "Havlicek to Join Pipers and Luke," read the headline on his May 17 story, seemingly confirming the *Sports Illustrated* editorial insert.

What's more, Sharman might be coming back to coach, Heaton said. After all, what could go wrong?

Into the NBA

Eight weeks after Lucas agreed to the Pipers' terms, on July 10, 1962, the NBA invited the team to join the league. The vote was seven to two. Seven votes were the minimum needed for acceptance. The NBA had been looking for a 10th team to even the size of the East and West divisions and to end the necessity for at least one team to be idle every night.

The invitation was perceived to be the direct result of signing Lucas. He was the main factor, of course, but, as will be seen, there was more to it.

"Lucas is the most talked about basketball player since Wilt Chamberlain," wrote the *New York Times*'s Arthur Daley in his "Sports of the Times" column, which the *Plain Dealer* ran. "If the big fellow had not been Cleveland property, the NBA would not have given Cleveland a brusque hello."[1]

Daley likened the NBA's acceptance of an entire franchise on the strength of one player to the Boston Red Sox and their purchase of the Louisville Cardinals for their farm system, solely because Harold Peter Henry "Pee Wee" Reese was a promising shortstop there and the Boston incumbent, Joe Cronin, "became too big to move out of his own capacious shadow."[2]

The analogy seemed faulty because Reese never played for the Red Sox, but became a Hall of Fame shortstop with the Brooklyn Dodgers. It would prove even more fitting in the long run, however, because Lucas never played for the Pipers and became a Basketball Hall of Famer elsewhere.

Daley's judgment about both Lucas's appeal and Steinbrenner's resourcefulness seemed spot-on. "The NBA admitted the Pipers merely to get a sure-fire gate attraction," Daley wrote. "The hard-boiled pros paid [Lucas] the tribute supreme." Daley then referred to the survival instincts of the young whippersnapper, that Steinbrenner fellow. "Not only did [Steinbrenner] leap off a sinking ship before it plunged out of sight with the immediate folding of the ABL, but he also landed on the firm footing that the NBA supplies," Daley wrote.[3]

As with Mark Twain, the reports of the ABL's death were exaggerated.

Certainly, however, Saperstein's league was in need of intensive care. That did not mean the ABL was finished, however, although Steinbrenner and the NBA treated its glum prognosis—without its champion team, without Lucas as savior—as a certificate of death.

Reports surfaced of a probable NBA invitation to the Pipers on July 7, three days before the team and the NBA became engaged.

In *Abe Saperstein and the American Basketball League,* Murry Nelson wrote of the maneuvering for an NBA franchise: "George Steinbrenner claimed that at an ABL owners' meeting the previous week, he had been given a free hand to negotiate with Podoloff."[4]

But Heaton's *Plain Dealer* story explicitly states that the free hand was supposed to be Saperstein's. Wrote Heaton: "George Steinbrenner, President of the Pipers who holds Lucas' contract as a trump card in any amalgamation of the conferences, disclaimed any knowledge of a switch [to the NBA]. He did say that Abe Saperstein, commissioner of the ABL and owner of the Chicago Majors, received 'carte blanche' at a meeting in Chicago last weekend to negotiate with Podoloff."[5]

According to Cleary, the truth is that Steinbrenner had cut Saperstein out of the loop entirely and had met secretly with Podoloff on the NBA commissioner's yacht on the Connecticut River, pitching to him a proposal for a merger of the Pipers and the ABL runner-up, the Kansas City Steers.

"George did the hard work, sweet talking Podoloff," said Cleary.[6]

Cleary had by then returned to Cleveland as the Pipers' "player personnel director and head of promotions," according to a story in the *Press,* although he was really offered the general manager's job.[7]

After Cleary's position was announced, Flieger never again spoke to him, even after the ABL was dead, even when they would run into each other in the social setting of Art Modell's loge at Browns games.

Joe Gordon, also fearful of losing his job with the Rens because of the ABL's instability, spent three weeks in Cleveland after the season. He met daily with Cleary and Steinbrenner at the Arena, spent evenings with Steinbrenner at the Theatrical Grill, and never quite received the job as a combination PR man and business manager for which he had interviewed. This shortfall in following through was a pattern with many of Steinbrenner's promises.

For Cleary, rejoining the Pipers wasn't much of a gamble. In the wake of the NBA invitation, the ABL might soon be down to five teams or even four if the San Francisco Saints and Chicago Majors merged, as was rumored, with NBA teams. Almost no one would come to the games after the latest convulsion with the Pipers' defection. The league might amount to four or five blocks of all-but-condemned buildings where dead-end teams played in almost complete obscurity.

Cleary also could always take an NAIA or NCAA job back in Kansas City if Steinbrenner's venture failed.

The July 7 *Plain Dealer* story, with the NBA's vote on the Pipers only a few days away, included the kind of false assurances that had taken Steinbrenner and his team to the doorstep of legitimacy in the established league. Said Steinbrenner of the NBA, "We'd love to have a franchise if we could get it, but we won't let the rest of the ABL down if the owners want to continue."[8] This last comment was completely dishonest, a vow of fealty that became chaff under the flail of Steinbrenner's ambition.

Although Podoloff never divulged what happened in the private meetings, nor did he keep a diary, it makes sense that it was during those private, one-on-one meetings that Steinbrenner tried to make his team even more attractive with the possibility of a Pipers-Steers merger.

Such a would-be "super team" would not rival the Miami Heat of LeBron James, Dwyane Wade, and Chris Bosh, but it still would bring together the best of the rest from pro basketball outside the NBA, plus, of course,

Lucas. It would be an irresistible lure to Podoloff, whose own league was struggling at the gate too, just not as catastrophically as the ABL.

Steinbrenner had a championship team with the Pipers, but, just as with the Yankees, when he had the money to fund a dynasty, he wanted more championships. That would show the stubborn old man who had always one-upped him.

A possible inspiration for the Kansas City–Cleveland merger was Lucas's inability to cast the same spell over Havlicek as Steinbrenner had done in convincing Lucas to pay no attention to the player mutiny, expulsion vote, near-forfeiture of the championship, and late paychecks.

On June 5, Lucas arose early in the morning and drove to Cleveland from Columbus for a meeting with Steinbrenner. They failed to get Havlicek's signature on the dotted line. Instead, Havlicek, a former high school quarterback, turned down no-cut contracts from both the Pipers and the Boston Celtics and, on June 14, signed a much less financially secure contract with the Browns as a novice wide receiver. A quarterback in high school, he said he had always wanted to give football a try.

Havlicek would not make the team, but, after being cut in August, would sign with the Celtics instead of what by then was the ghost of Steinbrenner's dream team. In addition to being a response to Havlicek's rebuff, the merger plan reveals Steinbrenner's competitive philosophy. He wanted a team that would beat other teams and beat them and beat them until being beaten was what they expected and accepted.[9] George knew that "good" is the enemy of "great." He was never a complacent man. Reaching for the lion's share of the ABL's best players was just part of a pattern.

Steinbrenner signed Siegfried, but then he wanted Lucas. His honeyed promises lured Barnett away from Syracuse Nationals officials, but then he wanted the best of the rest of the Nats in a merger. He had an NBA team, but then he wanted an NBA champion.

Talk of possible NBA/ABL mergers was in the air everywhere at the time. With the Pipers' defection crippling the ABL, the Warriors and Saints were reported to be likely to merge in San Francisco and so were the Majors and the Chicago NBA team, now renamed the Zephyrs.

Said Cleary of the clandestine plan to gut the ABL and make the Pipers not only desirable at the gate but formidable on the court: "George went to Podoloff and got a franchise. We had a schedule. Cleveland was to open against the Knicks at Madison Square Garden. The team would be half the Kansas City team and half the Pipers."[10]

Sudyk confirmed the plan in general, although he was unsure of which players were involved since he had moved on to the Indians' beat at the *Press*. "I had more than one assignment. I had to miss some games. But I was aware of it," said Sudyk. "Kansas City's players were part of the merger agreement." By the time Sudyk heard inklings of the merger, it was already being strangled in the cradle by the financial chaos on the shores of Lake Erie. "It was part of the whole collapse [of the franchise] and the crazy things that kept happening," said Sudyk.[11]

Some of the details do not hold up, though. The Knicks-Pipers opener has been often cited in biographies of Steinbrenner, but the schedule listing it has never been found.

On July 20, the *Press* ran a story saying the Pipers would open at home on October 18 against the Cincinnati Royals, not in Madison Square Garden against the Knicks.

"Pipers president George Steinbrenner has insisted upon the Cincinnati opener," wrote Sudyk of the clash with Lucas's jilted suitors. The story added that nine of the home games would be played in Pittsburgh because of problems in availability at the Arena. So another Steinbrenner boast, albeit a small one, about all games being played at Cleveland Arena, proved empty.

Another obstacle to the merger was that NBA teams had previously drafted such ABL players as Barnett, Warley, Bridges, Cox, and Tormohlen. But Podoloff, who seemed as susceptible to Steinbrenner's charm as anyone, had removed that obstacle, according to Cleary. "Podoloff had waived the drafting teams' rights to those players," Cleary said. "We could start with 12 players from the ABL. Whoever we selected, they were free and clear and Lucas, too. We'd have been a hell of a team."[12]

Steers in the merged team would have been Bridges, Staverman, Mantis, Maury King, and Tormohlen. "Maybe Win Wilfong too," said Cleary.[13]

The list of coveted Pipers started with Barnett and included Barnhill, Warley, and Cox, plus the return of Dan Swartz from the Tapers.

On July 13, the Pipers announced they had selected Chicago's Herschell Turner, a second-team All-ABL player, and Pittsburgh's Phil Rollins from a pool of ABL players.

Sensing the death of the ABL, NBA teams, according to Nelson, began raiding the ABL in the summer of 1962, just as the ABL had wooed unhappy NBA players in the previous season. But of the four Steers Nelson said the St. Louis Hawks had signed (Bridges, Staverman, Tormohlen, Mantis), all but Mantis played the ABL's second season out to the bitter end on New Year's Eve.

Steinbrenner's dreams would not linger that long. Soon his personal life would begin falling apart too. His marriage, always a stormy one with loud public fights between husband and wife, was breaking apart under the stress. On July 8, Joan (pronounced "Jo-anne") Steinbrenner filed for divorce from the Pipers' president. Although they would reconcile within a few weeks, it is easy to understand why her husband—fighting the unbeatable foe in his own father, needing investors to reach the star that was tantalizingly near, a sports Willie Loman, riding on a smile and the moonshine of empty promises—had neglected his home life.

Joan Steinbrenner listed her husband's assets as a home in Bay Village, appraised at $38,500, a salary of $22,000 and 25 percent interest in the television and movie rights to a book, *The Sheppard Murder Case,* about a Bay View doctor Sam Sheppard.

She also obtained an injunction preventing her husband from disposing of the bank accounts and stocks they jointly held in seven different companies. Golenbock claims that a desperate Steinbrenner nevertheless illegally sold stocks through friendly bankers that were jointly held or were solely in his wife's name.

On the same day that his wife filed for divorce, Steinbrenner, Lucas, and McKeon were spotted together in a third-base box seat at an Indians game.

The only investor who was available to Steinbrenner in the broken ABL was McKeon, who had cast the lone vote to expel Steinbrenner's team.

"We're friends now," said Steinbrenner of McKeon at the ballpark. "We got to know each other better at the league meetings."[14] But McKeon, who had folded the Saints in order to become a 50 percent owner of the Pipers, turned out to be a false friend. Two hundred shares of Pipers stock at $1,000 per share would be sold to the public, Steinbrenner also announced with an optimism that was only tangentially connected to reality.

An investor with deep pockets was needed because the price for entering the NBA was steep—$250,000 as an entry fee, a sizable portion of it serving as indemnification to Cincinnati in return for the Pipers' invasion of the Ohio market, plus a $100,000 performance bond. Steinbrenner said $25,000 of that had already been paid.

As for Lucas, the almost flat-broke Steinbrenner admitted an 80-game NBA schedule wasn't quite what the cornerstone of the franchise had expected and a new contract would have be signed. Lucas, predictably, could not make up his mind. Steinbrenner grandly said, "He can name what he wants. It will be OK with me. It's true we haven't come to an exact agreement, but everything will be worked out."[15]

Eventually, Lucas's hesitancy would be revealed as just more disingenuousness. His adviser, Joe Hardy, revealed Lucas had known all along that the Pipers were trying to get into the NBA and that he would play the full NBA schedule, putting off his graduation until the spring of 1963.

In a tart understatement, Sudyk wrote, "This is a sharp departure from previous statements made by the three-time Ohio State All-American."[16]

Still, in mid-July of 1962, such a bright new day had dawned in Cleveland pro basketball that even Cobbledick was moved to conclude a column about the NBA version of the Pipers by writing, "I wish 'em well."[17] Wishes, unfortunately, were the only currency Steinbrenner had to spend.

CHAPTER 27

Out of the NBA

Within three weeks of the July 10 NBA invitation, Steinbrenner's dreams—his newest imaginary castle, just like that first pleasure dome he had promised to Siegfried—fell to earth.

The first indication of trouble was a long-distance shot the very next day from Saperstein, who was in Madrid, Spain. Saperstein said he had conferred with Podoloff in New York before beginning the European trip. "It was my impression nothing would be effected until I returned," the rotund impresario said.

Saperstein said he would wait "until I am in possession of all the pertinent facts which can determine where legal action is warranted in what very well could be a case of piracy on the part of the NBA."[1] If people in basketball knew anything about Saperstein, it was that he did not forget or forgive a slight.

Contacted a few days later in California, Sharman told the *Press* he was excited about the team. "On paper, there is every reason to believe the Pipers could finish third in the Eastern Division [behind Boston and Cincinnati] and reach the playoffs," he said.

Paper folds, though. Paper can be reduced to ash and smoke at the touch of a match.

Sharman said he had business interests on the West Coast and had been approached about a college coaching offer. "I'm very anxious to get back to Cleveland, however," he said. "Although I want to coach, I would even consider playing again."[2] A college job without the turmoil that came with Steinbrenner and that kept his four children in school in California, rather than uprooting the family, proved more than attractive to Sharman. On July 16, Sharman accepted a job at Los Angeles State.

Significantly, said Nelson, in a private letter to Saperstein, Sharman, who would himself eventually be paid in full, said he had been contacted by several of his former Pipers players with a familiar complaint. They still had not been paid for their second-place finish in the first half playoffs.

Gamely, Steinbrenner announced that McMahon, Johnny Dee of the NIBL Denver Truckers, Pittsburgh's Neil Johnston, and Ohio State freshman coach Frank Truitt, a Lucas favorite, were the finalists for the vacant coaching job.

On July 19, Tom Grace, the executive vice president of the Royals, said the Pipers weren't in the NBA yet and might never get in because they were drowning financially. The Pipers, he charged, had not made required payments on the 10th or 17th of July. They would also miss a third payment on the 24th. "So far, the Pipers haven't met any of their agreements. They haven't even shown a semblance of meeting them," Grace said.[3]

"The Royals just don't have all the facts," Steinbrenner said. "NBA Commissioner Maurice Podoloff and I are in complete accord on the matter of payoffs. The Pipers cannot issue legal payment checks until the official disbanding of the American Basketball League."[4]

Being George Steinbrenner, he could not resist adopting a dismissive attitude: "It's just sour grapes on the part of Mr. Grace because he lost Lucas to us. It's absolutely not true that we will not be in the NBA."

Even so, they would not be playing Cincinnati on October 18 in Cleveland. Pepper Wilson, the Royals' executive, said Gottlieb, the man in charge of the NBA schedule, had turned down the Pipers' request for the game.

On July 25, McMahon signed with Chicago in the NBA, saying he chose the Zephyrs over the Pipers because "I like the Chicago club's background better."[5]

"He got that from me," Cleary said, meaning the war stories he had told McMahon about his treatment by Steinbrenner when Cleary and the coach worked together with the Steers.[6]

On July 26, with the July 30 vote by the NBA owners to approve Pipers' entry looming, Saperstein, citing "an enthusiastic and harmonious two-day meeting of the surviving ABL clubs" in Chicago, threatened to fire all guns. "It came to my attention that the NBA has scheduled a meeting of its board next week to welcome the Cleveland club into its fold," he said. "If it is done, they will also be welcoming a lawsuit."[7]

NBA owners knew how implacable was Saperstein. While the NFL had won an antitrust suit filed against it by the AFL, it had cost $350,000 in legal fees. Without anything approaching the NFL's national television contract, NBA owners did not have the stomach or the funds for such a fight.

With the ABL's intent to soldier on came a serious legal entanglement too. The Steers' players and the others the Pipers had claimed all had ABL contracts. Like Lucas's contract, those agreements would have to be voided and new ones signed with the NBA.

Podoloff had wasted his influence on the Pipers' admission vote. He now could not fulfill the promise he purportedly made to Steinbrenner to sever the ties of ABL players to NBA teams after the Pipers turned out to be nothing but empty promises.

Steinbrenner's NBA chances were dead then and there, although he would not acknowledge it, tried to carpet the rocky road with money he did not have, and sought to bulldoze barriers that had become too sturdy to budge.

On July 27, McKeon withdrew his support for the petition to enter the NBA.

McKeon said he pulled out because of loyalty to the ABL. "I changed my mind when the ABL decided to operate another season," he said. "I can't get into the NBA. I'm going to stay out of pro basketball for a year."[8]

"At the moment, the Pipers franchise consists of a pile of unpaid bills," wrote Lebovitz, who, with Heaton now covering the Browns, had taken over Pipers coverage in the *Plain Dealer.*[9]

"We don't belong in the NBA if we don't meet our commitments," said Steinbrenner, who then turned his anger on his partner of convenience. "[McKeon] voided his agreement with us," fumed Steinbrenner. "He already put up $33,000, and he was supposed to put up $150,000."[10]

The same day, the Royals' Grace said he would sue his own league if Podoloff tried to ramrod the Pipers into the NBA over his objections.[11]

Incredibly, so great was Steinbrenner's personal magnetism that Lenny Littman, the Rens' owner, said, as Steinbrenner searched anywhere and everywhere for investors, "Everybody in the league likes George. If the deal could be worked out so he could get off the hook financially, we'd go along accordingly. The ABL goal is to become part of the NBA. Cleveland and Pittsburgh both deserve franchises. Meanwhile, the Rens will stay with the ABL."[12]

On July 28, scheming that would shame the court of a medieval king broke out over the Pipers.

Howard Marks, a prominent young Cleveland advertising executive, emerged as the head of a syndicate of Cleveland businessmen who were hoping to intercede and save the Pipers.

Steinbrenner himself disclosed Marks's identity, saying of the new group, "They did not want to save the franchise for the city but to steal it from us. This group did not want to make a go of basketball but to wait like vultures until we collapsed and then pick up the franchise for nothing for their own personal gain." Steinbrenner added, "We have a plan that would make the entire ABL a part of our admission into the NBA. After all the NBA doesn't want to become entangled in a [law] suit."[13]

This probably referred to the attempted merger with the Steers, to allowing disenfranchised ABL owners a chance to buy Pipers stock, and to a dispersal draft of the remaining ABL players among the nine NBA teams.

His blood up, Steinbrenner said he had been betrayed by Marks's syndicate. "All the time we were hoping to get backing from the group, they were double-dealing us," said Steinbrenner, charging that the syndicate had approached the NBA without telling him.

"Without Jerry Lucas, the franchise is not worth a thing, and they or any other group does not have Lucas," Steinbrenner said. Then came the last defiance: "I can tell you right now we are not going to collapse."[14]

Marks's version of the story was different. "We were fully prepared to help him, providing a sensible business deal could be made. His price was outlandish," said Marks. "Since we were miles apart, I decided to end negotiations, hoping after he thought it over he would come back with a more realistic figure."[15]

The Dick Schaap biography of Steinbrenner—in which the Pipers' years were researched by Sudyk and the *Press*'s Brent Larkin, later the *Plain Dealer*'s op-ed page editor—claims that Steinbrenner asked for $750,000. The next day he came back, hat in hand, and asked for $5,000. Marks said no both times.[16]

Steinbrenner was done, and he had to know it. So did Podoloff, whose stupidity in accepting the Pipers without a background check, had been a constant theme of Grace.

The Knicks (who hoped to get Lucas), the Royals (who hoped to get Lucas), and the Lakers (who played in Hollywood, the home of make-believe, and knew a box-office turkey when they heard one gobble) were all definitely voting "no" on the Pipers' admission to the league. Still, on the eve of the meetings to decide the Pipers' fate, Podoloff said, "I do not believe that legal action against us or the Pipers will affect Cleveland's acceptance." Asked by Pat Harmon, sports editor of the *Cincinnati Post* and *Times-Star* about the purpose of the meeting minutes before it began, Podoloff said, "It was to hear a new financial plan of the Pipers which will be satisfactory."[17]

No such remarkable and ingenious plan existed.

Asked by Harmon, who covered the conference in New York at the Roosevelt Hotel, how he felt about the Pipers moments before the July 30 meeting, Podoloff said only, "I'm unhappy. I'll say no more."[18]

Harmon peeked through the four-by-five-inch window of the meeting room where the Pipers' fate was sealed. "The meeting," said Harmon—after exchanging waves with Chicago general manager Frank Lane and overhearing several remarks—"wasn't as secret as [Podoloff] intended."[19]

The Pipers were so broke that they couldn't even pay their players, much less the quarter of a million dollars needed for NBA entry. A photograph was shown, displaying a check for $3,155 to a Pipers player that a bank had rejected because of insufficient funds in the team's account.

"I made a mistake once. I won't do it again. I voted for Cleveland the first time around, but I'm afraid it was not what I was looking for," said St. Louis owner Ben Kerner. "I had an idea that a 10-team league would be a good thing, but this man let us down."[20] This man, of course, was Steinbrenner who, at the meeting ran one last audacious bluff, based on the promises of his newest and last partner, Marks.

Steinbrenner made a last volley of promises—an air castle to shame anything built on solid ground, snake oil to beautify the clumsiest proposal, a tongue wagging like a magic wand waving over a failed trick. From first to last, Steinbrenner fought against a shortage of money, credibility, and truth, using weapons of threat, coercion and ridicule.

But, finally, he was beaten.

At the urging of the Royals' Grace, NBA counsel George Gallantz drew up a statement that read, "The Pipers have been held in default on the agreement with the NBA. The NBA will operate with the same nine teams as last season."[21] It was a complete repudiation of Podoloff, who retired after the 1962–63 season.

"I felt if we had a check to present from the syndicate, rather than their word, the vote would have been different," said Steinbrenner.[22]

"I didn't think it was ever going to work, his idea of drafting Jerry Lucas and never paying anybody off," said Ron Hamilton, McLendon's point guard at Tennessee State and in the NIBL version of the Pipers. "But a lot of people believed him, not just Lucas. And they all wound up with nothing."[23]

Gordon Cobbledick sensed higher interest than ever in the Pipers now that, like a recklessly driven race car, they had become a flaming wreck in the last turn.

"We find basketball an unseasonable topic of conversation wherever Clevelanders gather," he wrote, "and it seems to me that the only conclusion possible is that next to winning a baseball pennant or a football championship, the surest way to get yourself and your team talked about is to foul things up beyond recognition."[24]

The more aggressive *Press* took a full swing in an editorial written by the sports editor, Bob August. Headlined "The Sorry State of the Pipers," it said:

If the future of professional basketball in Cleveland—and the interest in it—hasn't been wrecked by now, it has moved perilously close to it.

Instead of a pro basketball season involving the top teams and the best players, Cleveland may have none.

This sorry spectacle can be traced directly to one man, George Steinbrenner, owner of the Pipers.

Steinbrenner, who seems congenitally unsuited to be in the sporting world, has been more of a hindrance than a help to the ball team from the time of the first whistle.

He has engaged in unsportsmanlike conduct, in and out of the gymnasium.

Steinbrenner has hurt the whole range of professional sports in this sports-minded town.

He should get out of pro basketball and stay out.[25]

CHAPTER 28

Endgame

Default reduced Steinbrenner to the state he most despised—that of a loser.

Failure made him guilty of the worst sin that could be committed by a Kinsman or Pipers employee. Defeat was the zero-tolerance error, the one for which he pilloried employees for the Pipers and the Yankees and almost everyone else whose human frailty kept George from getting his way.

Steinbrenner fought back with the only thing he could count on anymore: Lucas. As mesmerized by Steinbrenner as ever, the most sought-after basketball player in the land told friends that "all things being equal," he would stay with Cleveland.

"Steinbrenner has been maligned unfairly," said Joe Hardy, Lucas's adviser and spokesman. "He was the victim of the promises of others, and instead of blaming them or calling names, he kept quiet and continues to battle to keep the Cleveland franchise alive. I'm in his corner."[1]

Both Lucas's ABL contract and the NBA contract he had signed upon the Pipers being invited into that league were void. He was what the NBA and all pro sports feared most, a young superstar and a free agent, unfettered by contractual obligations, able to sign with the highest bidder. Accordingly, Podoloff visited Lucas in Columbus on August 1, offering money for a rookie that seemed to have come off a Monopoly board—$10,000 to begin with, then escalating crazily to $50,000, and on to $60,000, all in vain.

The offers flooded in because, as Sudyk reported, the money for Lucas's contract, the one that would dwarf that of Wilt Chamberlain, had never been put in escrow. Thus, the Pipers had already defaulted on the contract terms. Lucas's continuing loyalty to Steinbrenner seems in retrospect to have been as much refusal to admit he had been duped as anything else.[2]

On August 4, Saperstein said, "The ABL will continue, and Cleveland will have a team in the league. Cleveland and the league will continue with or without Lucas."[3] One week later, Saperstein was not so certain, saying, "There are legal problems involved" with the Pipers' reinstatement in the ABL.

The commissioner of the shrunken league said all ABL teams had been asked to post performance bonds and a cash deposit in the amount of $100,000 to defray the expenses of opening a second campaign. "About half the teams have already done so," Saperstein said. "Cleveland is one of those who haven't [sic]. But there's still time."[4]

It was fast running out, though.

Ineradicable as a weed now that the ABL had lurched to its feet like a dazed fighter, McKeon said: "Everything is roses as far as my proceeding with the Pipers, but nothing is finalized."[5]

Nothing ever would be, either. On August 29, amid reports that the New York Knicks were offering Lucas a two-year, $150,000 contract, the Pipers went out of business in the ABL too, with Steinbrenner scrambling unsuccessfully to come up with the money to the end.

The next day, Lucas announced that he would not play basketball at all in the 1962–63 season but would concentrate on finishing his schooling at Ohio State. He signed a three-year personal services contract with the Marks agency for $30,000 per year. The personal services contract was a strategy Steinbrenner considered as long as the Pipers drew breath because the Royals attempted to expand the NBA's definition of a territorial draft choice. Cleveland might fall under that definition as a matter of NBA expediency, but territorial imperatives could not infringe on a personal services contract.[6]

"The ill feeling that seems to exist between myself and Cincinnati is there, but I didn't create it," said Lucas, all innocence. "The sportswriters there [in Cincinnati] just seemed to feel a resentment towards me when I chose to attend Ohio State. I'll never play for Cincinnati anymore, and I think they realize that." This was the next-to-last statement Lucas made in a Sudyk story that bore the headline: "Strange World of Jerry Lucas—Life of Confusion and Contradiction."[7]

Lucas had delivered this "final" rejection to Cincinnati on November 23, 1962. The last statement in Sudyk's story was made by Lucas on August 19, 1963, after he signed a Royals contract.

"I'm glad to join the Royals. I will move my family here and make Cincinnati my home," Lucas said.[8]

The Marks group tried unsuccessfully to buy the Arena and to obtain an NBA franchise. Future U.S. Senator Howard Metzenbaum lent a hand in their lobbying effort, but to no avail. The NBA was finished with Cleveland for eight long years when the expansion Cavaliers franchise began.

On September 7, 1962, Dick Barnett went back to the Syracuse Nats, who immediately traded him to the Lakers.

As the ABL wound down, Joe Gordon, who had worked for his first three months without pay in 1961 and had been hired solely because he could type, now became the general manager of the Rens. Gordon's first duty was to cut every player's salary in half—except that of Connie Hawkins. "Connie's salary stayed at $9,000," Gordon said.[9]

Kansas City owner Ken Krueger, originally rumored to be part of the Steinbrenner-McKeon partnership, was never really a player in Steinbrenner's attempt to get a sneaker in the door of the NBA because he too lacked the cash on the barrelhead. "By then, Krueger was tapped out," said Cleary, who returned to go down with the franchise in Kansas City.[10]

A distraught Tormohlen walked into Krueger's office late in December 1962, took out a passbook account that contained his life savings of $3,700, and laid it on Krueger's desk. "If this will keep us going another week, it's all yours," said Tormohlen.[11]

NBA scouts came to ABL games in droves, circling the dying league like vultures, evaluating the players who would be out of a job soon. Boston coach Red Auerbach attended a game in Kansas City, at which a huge fight broke out.

The Steers' George Pruitt ran to the bench, grabbed a towel, wrapped his shooting hand in it, then ran back onto the court, and, in Cleary's words, "cold-cocked about half of the other team."

"What shocked me was how prepared he was, how he ran to get the towel so he wouldn't hurt himself," said Cleary. "He had done this before. It wasn't his first rodeo."[12]

The last rodeo was on New Year's Eve 1962, when Saperstein wired the death notice to the surviving teams (Long Beach had replaced the long-gone Los Angeles Jets after relocating from Hawaii).

The Steers were declared to be champions, although it was an empty honor without the crucible of playoff competition. They received rings with the University of Texas Longhorn logo engraved on the side after the school gave its permission. "They cost about $35 each," said Cleary.

"I couldn't believe it had ended so quickly," said Gordon. "You had such great relations with the players. You partied with them. Everybody was just thrilled to be part of it. It was an opportunity that did not exist for those guys before—the chance to continue to play basketball."[13]

Years later with the Steelers, Gordon was in Phoenix to sign a free-agent quarterback. Hawkins had won a court suit that allowed him to play in the NBA and had become an All-Star with the Suns.

"Even then, free agents had agents. While I was there, the agent took me to a Suns game," said Gordon. "We were sitting in the front row. As the Suns warmed up, Connie saw me and came off the layup line to give me a big hug."[14]

Steinbrenner eventually paid off all his investors, buying an ore boat and giving all of the profits from it to them. In some ways, he emerged stronger than ever because he made good on what they had lost by trusting him. It was, again, part of his attempt at redemption through remuneration. Occasionally, it held for those outside his circle of Table 14 regulars and establishment money too.

Cleveland Press photographer Tony Tomsic—famous in later years as the *Sports Illustrated* photographer at whom the Cleveland Indians' Albert Belle threw a ball during warm ups, in objection to Tomsic's shots with a long-range lens—had made a number of publicity photos for the Pipers before the ABL season began. But Tomsic never received his promised $250.

Called back to active duty in the Army Reserves when the Berlin Wall went up in August 1961, Tomsic served his stint at Fort Bragg, North Carolina, and returned home broke. There, he read a *Plain Dealer* story about the Junior Chamber of Commerce naming Steinbrenner its "Man of the Year." There, he also heard from Flieger, his former *Press* colleague, that the Pipers' telephone bills had finally been paid.

Enraged, Tomsic bulled his way into the team president's office.

"You owe me $250 for those pictures. I've spent the last months serving my country in the Army, I'm out now, I'm broke, and I want my money!" Tomsic shouted.

"The check's in the mail," said Steinbrenner sharply.

"Yeah, you say that to everybody," fumed Tomsic.

The check arrived soon afterward. "George paid me $500," said Tomsic.[15]

CHAPTER 29

Postmortem

A fter the ABL's death, its quality of play became a matter of debate. The absence of big men and superstars are the reasons detractors cite for downgrading the ABL. A scouting report about the Pipers in their NIBL stage by the Detroit Piston's Philip "Ciney" Sachs summed up this argument well:

> I'm guessing Swartz and Adams at 6–4 are just too short to play forward in our league. As a general rule, we want men from 6–6 to 6–10 up front and they can't be just tall. They've got to have ability too. Why St. Louis' Clyde Lovellette can kill you with one handers from 30 feet out fast.
>
> I've heard it said the only difference between the NBA and NIBL is the superstars and big men.
>
> But what a difference. If they played just a couple of games, they'd find out fast. The NIBL doesn't have Elgin Baylor, Bob Cousy, Oscar Robertson, Dolph Schayes, Cliff Hagan, Frank Ramsey, Tom Gola, Paul Arizin or a dozen more I could name. Sam Jones, who can't play first string with the Celtics, would be the best guard in the league. Bill Russell is absolutely the finest defensive player I've ever watched. And Wilt Chamberlain is no man, he's a monster.[1]

Barnett, however, who was not on the NIBL Pipers, was the best backcourt player in the ABL. As he proved by starting on the Knicks' fabled 1970 NBA champions, he was better than most he faced.

Jack Adams, asked how a merged Pipers-Steers team with Lucas would fare, had no illusions. "They would be mediocre," he said.[2]

This overlooks how effective Lucas, even in the twilight of his career, was with the Knicks on their 1972–73 NBA championship team, playing so well in tandem with Willis Reed that writers called the two-headed, hybrid center "Willis Lucas."

Cleary's views are strongly positive and so were Joe Gordon's and Sudyk's.

"There was a wealth of talent. The league itself was merely excellent. It was at a much higher level than college basketball," said Gordon. "It was unfortunate it didn't have the finances to survive. I think they could very easily have done what the AFL did in football."[3]

"I think the play was very good," said Sudyk. "Barnett certainly became one of the best players in the game."[4]

Abe Saperstein, vacillating as usual, did not decide to keep the ABL going until September 1962. Any ABL player not offered a contract by August 15 automatically became a free agent. A simple registered letter of intent to sign the players would have bound them to the ABL for the coming season under the reserve clause.

Instead, Barnett averaged 18 points per game for the Los Angeles Lakers in the 1962–63 season and played 14 years in the NBA in all, averaging 15.8 points.

John Barnhill averaged 11.7 for the St. Louis Hawks the next season and played eight years in the NBA, averaging 8.6 points.

Johnny Cox played the 1962–63 season with the Chicago Zephyrs, averaging 7.2 points.

Larry Siegfried was unable to catch on with another team in the season after the Pipers folded.[5] The greatest relic of the ABL, though, was not the debate about the caliber of its players. Nor, given the reluctance of the NBA for years to embrace the three-point shot, would the impact of the bonus-point shot be appreciated for a generation. At the end, as controversial as Steinbrenner was, as reviled as he was at times by the players he could not afford to pay, he still became the dominant figure of the ABL's short, stormy existence.

The $17 paycheck for the Finals didn't even sour Barnett's opinion. "George could have been a great commander in the army. He was almost a great promoter," said Barnett. "He was extroverted. He wanted publicity. He obviously had a knowledge of finance as a shipping magnate. He had the entrepreneurial spirit. All of the traits that led to his success and controversies with the Yankees were present."[6]

In an interview in the wake of Steinbrenner's death, Barnett said, "I always talk about the limitlessness of human possibilities. If you take it to an extreme, if you take it to Kitty Hawk, North Carolina, where the Wright Brothers insisted that a man could fly like a bird in the sky . . . well, everybody thought Orville and Wilbur were crazy. But what they believed was plausible."[7]

Barnett seemed unaware that such comments could more readily apply to his rise from academic indifference to college professor. "The point is," he said, "I was never surprised by George Steinbrenner's ambition and determination." It did not mean Steinbrenner knew much about basketball, though. "As far as I could ascertain, no. But that didn't stop him from participating, and he did participate," Barnett said. Asked how, Barnett quipped, "By assuming the position that he was always right."[8]

"My impression overall was positive," said Gordon. "I thought, here was a guy who would get things done. Little did I recognize all he would get done [in baseball]."[9]

"After the ABL, everything he touched turned to gold," said Hamilton.[10]

In a typewritten reminiscence given to the author of this book, Sudyk shared the story of his reconciliation with Steinbrenner.[11]

Long after the Pipers folded, Sudyk was walking down Euclid Avenue in downtown Cleveland when he heard a familiar voice calling, "Sudyk! Sudyk!"

Steinbrenner rushed up and threw his arms around the writer.

"I've been trying to reach you," he said.

"You told me to never speak to you again," Sudyk said,

"Let's go to the Mug and talk," said Steinbrenner.

An invitation to meet George Steinbrenner at the Pewter Mug was the "golden ticket," the passport to Willie Wonka's chocolate factory, the seat at Table 14. It was usually reserved for Steinbrenner's closest associates.

As Steinbrenner sipped a 7-Up with a maraschino cherry, he said he was only kidding about trying to get Sudyk fired. Sudyk still didn't see the humor in it, but the two talked deep into the night.

"I was out of control. Maybe it was my youth. I was under a lot of pressure to meet the bills," Steinbrenner said.

"I was on my players because I felt they weren't giving their all. Professional athletes are emotional creatures. They've been pampered all their lives. That breeds complacency they aren't even aware of. A little turmoil, a little anxiety can bring more out of them."

This was close to the view of Ohio State football coach Woody Hayes, for whom George had once worked. "Show me a good guy that the players love all the time, and I'll show you a loser," Hayes said.[12]

This philosophy was absorbed by the young Steinbrenner and expounded upon and enlarged with the thoroughness of his own mercurial personality.

"When a player is busting his butt, he won't hear a word out of me," said Steinbrenner. "I think I can get more out of people by pushing them. I can't be a nice guy about it. Nobody will ever follow me out of affection. They follow me because they think I can come up with the answers. That is my only shot as a leader. I've got a favorite saying: The speed of the pack is determined by the leader."

The alpha dog of any alphabet anywhere, Steinbrenner then acknowledged his unpopular reputation in town. "Some people call me a tyrant and a meddler. I was brought up to be deeply involved, and I don't apologize for that. I got mad as hell when my team blew a game, just like a fan. But if I own the team, I can do something about it."

George said he never forgot old Henry's saying: "It's better to be the hammer than the nail." What nails had been pounded, what wood broken, what loyalties torn with a screech from their moorings, a few of them to be driven even more securely into place, by that hammer?

"Sure, I'm tough to work for," said Steinbrenner. "I wouldn't like to work for me. I don't think anybody ever reaches his potential. We all have 10 percent more to give."

Sudyk and Steinbrenner remained friends for the rest of George's life after that night.

The last time Cleary saw Steinbrenner, it was at a black-tie dinner at the Waldorf-Astoria Hotel in Manhattan. "I had heard rumors that the butter was slipping off his biscuit," said Cleary, alluding to Alzheimer's disease. Surprisingly, Steinbrenner recognized him.

"Mike, how ya doing?" Cleary's old boss said, reaching out with one hand to touch Cleary's shoulder while pointing with his other hand in his old habit.

No Pipe dreams were left to sell. Only human contact between old friends remained.

"Mike, you were always loyal," Steinbrenner said. It was the last thing Cleary ever heard him say.[13]

Before that, Tormohlen ran into Steinbrenner at the racetrack in Tampa. "The only sure way to win a championship is to buy one, like I did with the Yankees," Steinbrenner told him.[14]

Or you could win it after the team owner's tirade about establishing a curfew following the very first game of the season; and after he traded a player at halftime to the opposing team; and after the team lost the league's best rebounder for 10 games due to injury; and after the team's best player missed the first 30 games because of a court order; and after the same player later drove his car into a ditch on icy road; and after the owner stormed into the locker room to berate the players; and after he issued a win-or-else ultimatum to the first coach at a public function; and after he withheld the players' paychecks following a painful playoff defeat; and after the team threatened to boycott a game; and after he threatened in turn to fold the team; and after he forced out the team's respected and popular first coach; and after he rented a second coach with the team buried in last place with two wins in nine games; and after the team was nearly expelled from the league; and after the owner actively sought to leave the league through a merger, any merger; and after a key player's fear of flying caused him to miss a critical late-season trip to the West Coast; and after the team survived two sudden-death playoff games before the Finals; and after it lost the first two games of that best-of-five Finals; and after it won three straight do-or-die games, two of them at the buzzer.

That led to the owner achieving the nearly impossible feat of signing college basketball's biggest star, and then, with a team that was dead-broke when he bought it, almost making it all the way to the NBA with a team that could have been a contender, made up as it was of the best parts of the league he had left behind.

Maybe someone really should remember the Pipers.

Notes

INTRODUCTION

1. Paul Hornung, "Lucas Goes into Minors, Not in a Major League Way," *Columbus Dispatch,* May 16, 1962.

I. CASTLES IN THE AIR

1. Mike Cleary, interview with author, Mar. 2012, National Association of College Directors of Athletics offices (NACDA), Westlake, Ohio.

2. News conference with Bob Knight and other players, 50th anniversary celebration, 2010 at Ohio State's Value City Arena, www.cleveland.com/livingston/index.ssf/2010/01/often_harsh_in_competition_bob.html.

3. Wayne Emby, telephone interview with author, Mar. 2012.

4. Bob Ryan, "The One and Only Siggy," *Boston Globe,* Oct. 16, 2010.

5. Cleary, interview.

6. Tina Siegfried, telephone interview with author, Mar. 2014.

7. Jack Adams, telephone interview with author, 2012.

8. Siegfried, interview.

9. Siegfried, interview.

10. Author's personal recollection of McMahon's comments as Philadelphia 76ers assistant coach.

11. Mike Cleary, interview with author, Apr. 2012, NACDA, Westlake, Ohio.

12. Cleary, interview, Mar. 2012.

13. Cleary, interview, Mar. 2012.

14. Cleary, interview, Mar. 2012.

2. ED SWEENY'S PIPE DREAM

1. Mike Cleary, interview with author, Feb. 2014, NACDA, Westlake, Ohio.

2. Cleary, interview, Mar. 2012.

3. Cleary, interview, Feb. 2014.

4. Cleary, interview, Feb. 2014

5. Cleary, interview, Feb. 2014.

6. Cleary, interview, Feb. 2014.

7. Cleary, interview, Apr. 2012.

8. Jack McMahon, in discussion with author.

9. Cleary, interview, Apr. 2012.

10. Cleary, interview, Mar. 2012.

11. Chuck Heaton, "McLendon Free to Look for Job," *Plain Dealer,* Apr. 8, 1961.

12. "John McLendon: A League of His Own," unproduced television documentary.

13. Ron Hamilton, telephone interview with author, Apr. 2014.

14. Cleary, interview, Feb. 2014.

15. "John McLendon: A League of His Own."

3. FROM RUSSIA, WITH FEAR AND GRUMBLING

1. Adams, interview.

2. Adams, interview.

3. Cleary, interview, Mar. 2014.

4. Adams, interview.

5. Cleary, interview, Apr. 2012.

6. Ben Flieger, *Cleveland Press,* May 13, 1961.

7. Cleary, interview, Mar. 2012.

4. GEORGE

1. Mike Roberts, telephone interview with author, Mar. 2012.

2. Roberts, interview.

3. Roberts, interview.

4. Roberts, interview.

5. Cleary, interview, Feb. 2014.

6. Cleary, interview, Feb. 2014.

7. Author interview with eyewitness who requested anonymity, 2012.

8. Cleary, interview, Apr. 2012.

9. Stephen A. Blossom, "Forty Years with the Steinbrenners Is Like 400 with Anyone Else," *Plain Dealer,* Oct. 1, 1965.

10. Cleary, interview, Feb. 2014.

11. Adams, interview.

12. Bob Sudyk, memo to author, 2014.

13. Adams, interview.

5. JOHN

1. Douglas Bates, e-mail message to author, 2014.

2. Bates, e-mail message.

3. Milton S. Katz, *Breaking Through: John B. McLendon: Basketball Legend and Civil Rights Pioneer* (Fayetteville: Univ. of Arkansas Press, 2007).

4. Embry, interview.

5. Katz, *Breaking Through.*

6. Cleary, interview, Feb. 2014.

7. "New Coach with an Old Goal: Pipers Import from South Aims to Revive Basketball Interest Here," *Plain Dealer Sunday Magazine,* Dec. 6, 1959.

8. Ibid.

9. Ibid.

10. Cleary, interview, Apr. 2012.

11. Jimmy Doyle, *Plain Dealer,* Nov. 18, 1961.

12. Cleary, interview, Apr. 2012.

13. Cleary, interview, Apr. 2012.

14. Cleary, interview, Feb. 2014.

15. Adams, interview.

16. Cleary, interview, Feb. 2014.

17. Gene Tormohlen, telephone interview with author, Mar. 2012.

18. Tormohlen, interview.

6. GEORGE AND JOHN

1. Gene Tormohlen, telephone interview with author, Apr. 2012.

2. "The Noble Experiment; Branch Rickey and the First Interview," PBS, accessed Dec. 16, 2014, www.pbs.org/wnet/aaworld/history/spotlight_august2.html.

3. Adams, interview.

4. Adams, interview.

5. "New Coach with an Old Goal," *Plain Dealer.*

6. Dick Barnett, telephone interview with author, Mar. 2012.

7. Cleary, interview, Feb. 2014.

7. THE LEAGUE OF EXTRAORDINARY ASPIRATION

1. Cleary, interview, Mar. 2012.

2. Cleary, interview, Mar. 2012.

3. Cleary, interview, Mar. 2012.

4. Chuck Heaton, "Pipers to Face Ex-Big Ten Cagers," *Plain Dealer,* Dec. 13, 1961.

5. Gordon Cobbledick, "Plain Dealing: Coach Lists Rules Changes That Should Make Pro Basketball More Interesting," *Plain Dealer,* Feb. 13, 1962.

6. Ibid.

7. Chuck Heaton, "Pipers Seek 6th Straight," *Plain Dealer,* Mar. 21, 1962.

8. Ibid.

9. Associated Press, "Three-Pointer Makes Hit in Pro Cage," Apr. 15, 1962.

10. Heaton, "Pipers Seek 6th Straight."

8. THE RIVALS

1. Adams, interview.

2. Phil Musick, "Remembering a Man and His Craft," *Pittsburgh Post-Gazette,* June 6, 1977.

3. Chuck Heaton, "We Have Some Catching Up to Do," *Plain Dealer,* Nov. 7, 1961.

4. Embry, interview.

5. Joe Gordon, telephone interview, Mar. 2014.

6. Chuck Heaton, "New Piper Was Weakling—Just Look at Him Now," *Plain Dealer,* Oct. 1961.

7. Bob Sudyk, "Pipers Small, but on the Ball," *Cleveland Press,* Dec. 12, 1961.

8. "Hawkins Was Precursor to Dr. J, Jordan," ESPN SportsCentury Biography, accessed Jan. 5, 2105, http://espn.go.com/classic/biography/s/Hawkins_Connie.html.

9. Gordon, interview.

10. David Wolf, *Foul! The Connie Hawkins Story* (New York: Holt, Rinehart and Winston, 1972).

11. Ibid.

12. Ibid.

13. Cleary, interview, Mar. 2012.

14. Author's personal recollection.

15. Author's personal recollection.

16. Gordon, interview.

17. Gordon, interview.

18. Wolf, *Foul!*

19. Cleary, interview, Mar. 2012.

20. Cleary, interview, Mar. 2012.

21. Cleary, interview, Feb. 2014.

22. Bob Sudyk, "KC Coach Raps Refs in Loss to Pipers," *Cleveland Press,* Nov. 30, 1961.

23. Bob Sudyk, "Ben Warley, Only 6–7, Tops League Rebounders," *Cleveland Press,* Nov. 30, 1961.

24. "Pipers Have Foes All Fouled Up," *Cleveland Press,* Mar. 17, 1961.

25. Cleary, interview, Feb. 2014.

26. Cleary, interview, Feb. 2014.

27. Fritz Kreisler, interview with author, May 2014.

28. Kreisler, interview.

9. CONTROVERSIES AND A STAR FOR CHRISTMAS

1. Katz, *Breaking Through.*

2. Adams, interview.

3. Chuck Heaton, "Pipers Notch Sixth, 91–74," *Plain Dealer,* Nov. 22, 1961.

4. Ron Thomas, *They Cleared the Lane: The NBA's Black Pioneers* (Lincoln, NE: Bison Books, 2004).

5. Bill Madden, *Steinbrenner: The Last Lion of Baseball* (New York: Harper-Collins, 2011).

6. Thomas, *They Cleared the Lane.*

7. Frank Gibbons, "Success of Pipers Only Artistic So Far," *Cleveland Press,* Dec. 13, 1961.

8. Peter Golenbock, *Wild, High and Tight: The Life and Death of Billy Martin* (New York: St. Martin's Press, 1994).

9. Hal Lebovitz, "Pipers Use Fast Break to Drub Rens," *Plain Dealer,* Nov. 27, 1961.

10. Cleary, interview, Apr. 2012.

11. Bob Sudyk, *Cleveland Press,* "Ben Warley, Only 6–7, Tops League Rebounders," Nov. 30. 1961.

12. Bob Dolgan, "Pipers, Majors at Arena Tomorrow," *Plain Dealer,* Dec. 12, 1961.

13. Bob Sudyk, "All's Well that Ends Well; Pipers to Selves Were True," *Cleveland Press,* Dec. 22, 1961.

14. Ibid.

15. Golenbock, *Wild, High and Tight.*

16. Ibid.

17. Bob Sudyk, telephone interview with author, Feb. 2014.

10. THE UNORTHODOX SHOT AND UNEXPECTED LIFE OF DICK BARNETT

1. Cleary interview, Mar. 2012.

2. Cleary, interview, Mar. 2012.

3. Cleary, interview, Mar. 2012.

4. Cleary, interview, Mar. 2012.

5. Cleary, interview, Mar. 2012.

6. Cleary, interview, Mar. 2012.

7. Cleary, interview, Mar. 2012.

8. Embry, interview.

9. Gene Tormohlen, telephone interview with author, Feb. 2014.

10. William Rhoden, "Too Late; Fall Back, Baby," *New York Times,* Feb. 26, 1991.

11. Barnett, interview.

12. William Leggett, "A New Knick With a Knack," *Sports Illustrated,* Jan. 10, 1968.

13. Cleary, interview, Apr. 2012.

14. Cleary, interview, Mar. 2012

15. Bob Dolgan, "Barnett Now Big Man for Pipers," *Plain Dealer,* Jan. 3, 1962.

16. Cleary, interview, Feb. 2014.

17. Bob Sudyk, "Barnett Finds Self in Basketball Exile," *Cleveland Press,* Dec. 20, 1961.

18. "Piper Surprise in Court," *Plain Dealer,* Dec. 20, 1961.

19. Ben Flieger, "Pipers Face Court Fight for NBA Star," *Cleveland Press,* Aug. 19, 1961.

20. "Barnett Is Lost to Pipers," *Cleveland Press,* Dec. 21, 1961.

21. Jack Clowser, *Cleveland Press,* Dec. 22, 1961.

22. Bob Sudyk, "Barnett Set to Face Rens," *Cleveland Press,* Dec. 22, 1961.

23. Bob Dolgan, "Barnett Now Big Man for Pipers," *Plain Dealer,* Jan. 3, 1962.

24. Jerry West and Jonathan Coleman, *West by West: My Charmed, Tormented Life* (New York: Little, Brown, 2011).

25. Madison Square Garden Network video on Dick Barnett, www.youtube.com/watch?v=g5cTBV22mJE.

26. Madison Square Garden Network video on Barnett.

11. CAGE FIGHT

1. Jack Clowser, "Trouble at Top Endangering Pipers," *Cleveland Press,* Dec. 27, 1961.

2. Ibid.

3. Chuck Heaton, "M'Lendon's Job in Jeopardy," *Cleveland Press,* Dec. 28, 1961.

4. Ibid.

5. Ibid.

6. Ibid.

7. Ibid.

8. "McLendon to Stay, Says Piper Prexy," *Cleveland Press,* Dec. 28, 1961.

9. Ibid.

10. Heaton, "M'Lendon's Job in Jeopardy."

11. Ibid.

12. Gordon Cobbledick, *Plain Dealer,* Jan. 3, 1962.

13. Ibid.

12. THE AMAZING JERRY LUCAS

1. Jack Clowser, "Off-Court Lucas—A Serious Scholar," *Cleveland Press,* Feb. 13, 1962.

2. Ray Cave, "The Unassuming Ways of an Indispensable Man," *Sports Illustrated,* Jan. 8, 1962.

3. Ibid.

4. Ibid.

5. Frank Gibbons, "Jerry Lucas Aims Beyond Cage Court," *Cleveland Press,* Jan. 2, 1962.

6. Cleary, interview, 2014.

7. Adams, interview.

8. Cleary, interview, Mar. 2012.

9. Cleary, interview, Mar. 2012.

10. Cleary, interview, Mar. 2012.

11. Cleary, interview, Mar. 2012.

12. Chuck Heaton, "Pipers Win, Draft Three Ohio State Aces, Dischinger," *Plain Dealer,* Mar. 25, 1962.

13. "A TEAM DIVIDED"

1. "Pipers Play Chicago in Akron Tonight," *Plain Dealer,* Jan. 1, 1962.

2. Bob Dolgan, "Barnett Now Big Man for Pipers," *Plain Dealer,* Jan. 3, 1962.

3. Bob Dolgan, "Pipers in 1st-Place Tie; Win," *Plain Dealer,* Jan. 5, 1962.

4. Bob Dolgan, "Pipers Are Halted at 4 Straight," *Plain Dealer,* Jan. 7, 1962.

5. Bob Dolgan, "All Cox Does for Pipers Is Score Points," *Plain Dealer,* Jan. 5, 1962.

6. Ibid.

7. Bob Sudyk, "Pipers Seek 4th Straight in Hall Clash with Majors," *Cleveland Press,* Jan. 3, 1962.

8. Bob Dolgan, "McLendon Stays as Pipers Coach," *Plain Dealer,* Jan. 9, 1962.

9. Bob Dolgan, "Pipers, KC Open Title Play Tonight," *Plain Dealer,* Jan. 12, 1962.

14. THE FIRST HALF PLAYOFFS—"HEADS WILL ROLL!"

1. Fritz Kreisler, "Hot Herd Thunders In," *Kansas City Star,* Jan. 13, 1962.

2. Frank Gibbons, "Success of Pipers Only Artistic So Far," *Cleveland Press,* Dec. 13, 1961.

3. Fritz Kreisler, "Kansas City Wins First Pro Sports Championship in Nine Years as Herd Whips Cleveland 120–104, to Win ABL Play-Off," *Kansas City Star,* Jan. 15, 1962.

4. Fritz Kreisler, "Herd Rests—But Relaxation Stops with Start of Second Half Race," *Kansas City Star,* Jan. 15, 1962.

5. Cleary, interview, Feb. 2014.

6. Chuck Heaton, "Pipers Fall in Title Game, 120–104," *Plain Dealer,* Jan. 15, 1962.

7. Bob Sudyk, "No Timeout for Regrets—Pipers Hit the Road, *Cleveland Press,* Jan. 16, 1962.

8. Barnett, interview.

9. Golenbock, *Wild, High and Tight—The Life and Death of Billy Martin.*

15. THE PLAYERS REVOLT

1. Tormohlen, interview, Feb. 2014.

2. Tormohlen, interview, Feb. 2014.

3. Cleary, interview, Feb. 2014.

4. Cleary, interview, Mar. 2012.

5. Bob Sudyk, interview with author at Sudyk's home, May 2014.

6. Sudyk, interview, May 2014.

7. Bob Sudyk, "Pipers Near Revolt over Late Pay," *Cleveland Press,* Jan. 16, 1962.

8. Ibid.

9. Bob Sudyk, "No Timeout for Regrets—Pipers Hit the Road," *Cleveland Press,* Jan. 16, 1962.

10. Bob Sudyk, "Pipers Hit the Road, Look for Center," *Cleveland Press,* Jan. 18, 1962.

11. Chuck Heaton, "Piper Deal May Bring NBA Here," *Plain Dealer,* Jan, 18, 1962.

12. Golenbock, *Wild, High and Tight.*

13. Adams, interview.

14. Tormohlen, interview, Mar. 2012.

15. "Pipers Here Saturday in Double Bill," *Plain Dealer,* Jan. 29, 1962.

16. HEADS ROLLED

1. "McLendon Resigns in Clash with Piper Prexy—A Statement," *Cleveland Press,* Jan. 29, 1962.

2. Ibid.

3. "A Charge of Coercion," *Cleveland Press,* Jan. 29, 1962.

4. Sudyk, interview, Feb. 2014.

5. "A Charge of Coercion," *Cleveland Press,* Jan. 29, 1962.

6. Ibid.

7. Ibid.

8. Ibid.

9. Adams, interview.

10. Frank Gibbons, "Pipers' Boss Puts Self on Hot Seat," *Cleveland Press,* Jan. 29, 1962.

11. Ibid.

12. Gordon, interview.

13. Hamilton, interview.

14. Bill Pennington, *Billy Martin: Baseball's Flawed Genius* (New York: Houghton Mifflin Harcourt, 2015).

15. Harvey Greene, interview with author, Jan. 4, 2014, Fort Lauderdale.

17. BILL SHARMAN, THE METICULOUS, GENEROUS, VIOLENT BASKETBALL VISIONARY

1. Gordon, interview.

2. Sean Kirst, "The Passing of NBA Hall of Famer Bill Sharman: A Syracuse Legend Recalls a Friendship that Transcended Barriers," Oct. 26, 2013, www.syracuse.com/kirst/index.ssf/2013/10/post_551.html.

3. Gene Shue, telephone interview with author, Apr. 2014.

4. Shue, interview.

5. Terry Pluto, *Tall Tales: The Glory Years of the NBA in the Words of the Men Who Played, Coached and Built Pro Basketball* (New York: Simon & Schuster, 1992).

6. Earl Lloyd and Sean Krist, *Moonfixer: The Basketball Journey of Earl Lloyd* (Syracuse, NY: Syracuse Univ. Press, 2010).

7. Sean Kirst, "The Passing of NBA Hall of Famer Bill Sharman."

8. Bob Sudyk, "He Never Got in Game—But Was Tossed Out of One," *Cleveland Press,* Mar. 23, 1962.

18. SHARMAN TAKES OVER

1. Burt Graeff, "Sharman Has Tasty Cleveland Reunion," *Plain Dealer,* Feb. 8, 1997.

2. Cleary, interview, Apr. 2014.

3. Bob Sudyk, *Cleveland Press,* Feb. 3, 1962.

4. Bob Sudyk, *Cleveland Press,* Mar. 1962.

5. Sudyk, "He Never Got in Game—But Was Tossed Out of One."

6. Chuck Heaton, "Sharman, Ex-Celt, New Pipers Coach," *Plain Dealer,* Jan. 31, 1962.

7. Bob Sudyk, "No Rebound Help in Sight for Pipers," *Cleveland Press,* Feb. 5, 1962.

8. Bob Sudyk, "Mutt & Jeff Act Clicks for Pipers," *Cleveland Press,* Feb. 8, 1962.

9. Ibid.

10. Bob Sudyk, "Abe Rejects Piper Protest," *Cleveland Press,* Feb. 13, 1962.

11. Chuck Heaton, "Tapers Loom as Big Threat for Pipers," *Plain Dealer,* Feb.17, 1962.

19. TO THE BRINK OF EXPULSION

1. "Pipers in New Rhubarb," *Cleveland Press,* Feb. 17, 1962.

2. Bob Sudyk, "NBA Won't Admit Pipers," *Cleveland Press,* Feb. 20, 1962.

3. "Pipers in New Rhubarb."

4. Sydyk, "NBA Won't Admit Pipers."

5. Cleary, interview, Apr. 2014.

6. Chuck Heaton, *Plain Dealer.*

7. Sydyk, "NBA Won't Admit Pipers."

8. Ibid.

9. Cleary, interview, Feb. 2014.

10. Bob Sudyk, "Pipers Confident of Re-instatement," *Cleveland Press,* Feb. 21, 1962.

11. Julius Erving, *Dr. J: The Autobiography* (New York: HarperCollins, 2013).

12. Chuck Heaton, "Pipers Expulsion Threat Lifted," *Plain Dealer,* Feb. 21, 1962.

13. Bob Sudyk, "Who Owns the Pipers?" *Cleveland Press,* Feb. 21, 1962.

20. "WE STILL HAVE A CHANCE"

1. Bob Sudyk, "Barnett Injury Blow to Pipers," *Cleveland Press,* Feb. 23, 1962.

2. Chuck Heaton, "Keller Is Hero on Defense," *Plain Dealer.* Feb. 26, 1962.

3. Wolf, *Foul!*

4. Chuck Heaton, "Tapers Defeat Pipers," *Plain Dealer,* Feb. 28, 1962.

5. Bob Sudyk, *Cleveland Press,* Mar. 5, 1962.

6. Bob Sudyk, "Pipers Face Saints in Grudge Set," *Cleveland Press,* Mar. 6, 1962.

7. Bob Sudyk, *Cleveland Press,* Mar. 7, 1962.

8. Bob Sudyk, "Pipers Try for Repeat," *Cleveland Press,* Mar. 9, 1962.

9. Chuck Heaton, "Still Chance for Pipers—Sharman," *Plain Dealer,* Mar. 13, 1962.

10. Chuck Heaton, "Dierking Is Back to Bolster Pipers," *Plain Dealer,* Mar. 12, 1962.

21. COCHAMPIONS

1. Bob Sudyk, "Pipers Survive Cage Gang War," *Cleveland Press,* Mar. 15, 1962.

2. Chuck Heaton, "Pipers Beat Majors," *Plain Dealer,* Mar. 15, 1962.

3. Ibid.

4. Ibid.

5. Ibid.

6. Chuck Heaton, "Pipers Top Chiefs to Take Lead," *Plain Dealer,* Mar. 18, 1962.

7. Chuck Heaton, "Pipers Gamble on Lucas as Top Draft Pick," *Plain Dealer,* Mar. 20, 1962.

8. Bob Sudyk, "Piping-Hot Pipers Seek Seventh Straight Victory," *Plain Dealer,* Mar. 22, 1962; Sudyk, interview, 2104.

9. Chuck Heaton, "Pipers 1 Short of Title Tie," *Plain Dealer,* Mar. 25, 1962.

10. Chuck Heaton, "Pipers Win, Draft Three Ohio State Aces," *Plain Dealer,* Mar. 26, 1967.

22. THE BUCKEYES' MARCH SADNESS

1. Paul Hornung, *Columbus Dispatch,* May 12, 1962.

2. Dick Otte, "Bucks Gun for 22nd," *Columbus Dispatch,* Mar. 3, 1962.

3. Dick Otte, "Badgers' Boss Overjoyed," *Columbus Dispatch,* Mar. 4, 1962.

4. Dick Otte, "Wisconsin Snaps Buck Streak," *Columbus Dispatch,* Mar. 4, 1962.

5. Dick Otte, "A Slight Sprain," *Columbus Dispatch,* Mar. 24, 1962.

6. Dick Otte, "Ohio State Bows to Cincinnati; Bearcats Capture Second Straight NCAA Cage Title," *Columbus Dispatch,* Mar. 25, 1962.

7. Ibid.

8. AP, "We Showed 'em—Jucker," *Columbus Dispatch,* Mar. 25, 1962.

9. Dick Otte, "Lucas Insists Knee Was OK: Taylor Praises Bearcats," *Columbus Dispatch,* Mar. 25, 1962.

10. Ibid.

23. THE SUDDEN-DEATH TOURNAMENT

1. Chuck Heaton, "Pipers Win, Seek Place in Finals," *Plain Dealer,* Mar. 31, 1962.

24. CHAMPIONS

1. Fritz Kreisler, "Steers Get Rough—McMahon Likes It," *Kansas City Star,* Mar. 30, 1962.

2. Fritz Kreisler, "On a Bonus Tear—Pipers Get Back into Game on Three-Point Shooting by Cox," *Kansas City Star,* Apr. 2, 1962.

3. Ibid.

4. Fritz Kreisler, "Steers Work Hard to Hold Upper Hand," *Kansas City Star,* Apr. 3, 1962.

5. Tormohlen, interview, Apr. 2012.

6. "It's Not Over, Says M'Mahon," *Kansas City Star,* Apr. 4, 1962.

7. Ibid.

8. Bob Sudyk, "Trotters Share Stage with Pipers Tomorrow," *Cleveland Press,* Apr. 4, 1962.

9. Bob Sudyk, "Unbelievable Shot Gives Pipers Life," *Cleveland Press,* Apr. 6, 1962.

10. Chuck Heaton, "Pipers Buoyed by Home Fans," *Plain Dealer,* Apr. 6, 1962.

11. Sudyk, "Unbelievable Shot Gives Pipers Life."

12. Ibid.

13. Cleary, interview, Apr. 2014.

14. Fritz Kreisler, "Too Many Easy Shots," *Kansas City Star,* Apr. 6, 1962.

15. Associated Press, "Bridges Is Top Steers Threat," Apr. 7, 1962.

16. Kreisler, "Too Many Easy Shots."

17. Ibid.

18. Ibid.

19. Bob Sudyk, "Pipers Out to Fry Steers," *Cleveland Press,* Apr. 7, 1962.

20. Ibid.

21. Cleary, interview, Feb. 2014.

22. Cleary, interview, Feb. 2014.

23. Fritz Kreisler, "ABL Labels Itself as B-U-S-H League," *Kansas City Star,* Apr. 9, 1962.

24. Kreisler, "Doubt Clouds Play-Off Final," *Kansas City Star,* Apr. 8, 1962.

25. Ibid.

26. Ibid.

27. Sudyk, "Muddled Windup Has Pipers at KC," *Cleveland Press,* Apr. 9, 1962.

28. Gordon, interview.

29. Gordon, interview.

30. Gordon, interview.

31. Chuck Heaton, "Pipers Nip Steers to Tie Series," *Plain Dealer,* Apr. 8, 1962.

32. Sudyk, "Muddled Windup Has Pipers KC."

33. Kreisler, "ABL Labels Itself as B-U-S-H League."

34. Ibid.

35. Ibid.

36. Sudyk, "Muddled Windup Has Pipers KC."

37. Kreisler, interview.

38. Cleary, interview, Feb. 2014.

39. Cleary, interview, Feb. 2014.

40. Cleary, interview, Feb. 2014.

41. Cleary, interview, Feb. 2014.

42. Cleary, interview, Feb. 2014.

43. "Cleveland Personnel Proves Its Worth," *Kansas City Star,* Apr. 10, 1962.

44. Cleary, interview, Feb. 2014.

45. Cleary, interview, Feb. 2014.

46. Bob Sudyk, "Will Pipers Be Back? It May Depend on Lucas," *Cleveland Press,* March 13, 1962.

25. A CONTRACT THAT OVERSHADOWED WILT'S

1. Cleary, interview, Apr. 2014.

2. Jerry Lucas, telephone interview with author, Apr. 2012.

3. Gordon, interview.

4. Hal Lebovitz, "Lucas Listens to Cage Offers, but Won't Turn Pro," *Plain Dealer,* Apr. 10, 1962.

5. "Why I'm Turning Pro," *Sports Illustrated,* May 21, 1962.

6. Chuck Heaton, "Champion Pipers to Remain Here, Play at Arena," *Plain Dealer,* Apr. 11, 1962.

7. Bob Sudyk, "Pipers' Bid for Lucas Called Largest Ever," *Cleveland Press,* Apr. 10, 1962.

8. Hal Lebovitz, "Ask Hal, the Referee," *Plain Dealer,* Apr. 13, 1962.

9. Chuck Heaton, "Pipers Awaiting Lucas Decision," *Plain Dealer,* Apr. 25, 1962.

10. Ibid.

11. "Why I'm Turning Pro," *Sports Illustrated.*

12. Ibid.

13. Ibid.

14. Chuck Heaton, "Lucas Signs 2-Year Pact," *Plain Dealer,* May 16, 1962.

15. Hornung, "Lucas Goes into Minors, Not in a Major League Way."

16. Chuck Heaton, "Landing of Lucas Is Shot in Arm for Pipers," *Plain Dealer,* May 16, 1962.

17. Ibid.

18. Frank Gibbons, "Signing of Lucas Is a Job Well Done," *Cleveland Press,* May 16, 1962.

19. Ibid. Parentheses were in the original column.

20. Associated Press, "Lucas Signing Like Bomb," May 16, 1962.

21. Cleary, interview, Feb. 2014.

22. Jimmy Doyle, "The Sport Trail," *Plain Dealer,* May 23, 1962.

23. Jim Flanagan, "Lucas Again Avers 'No Suitcase Living,'" *Plain Dealer,* Apr. 14, 1962.

24. Hornung, "Lucas Goes into Minors."

25. Ibid.

26. Ibid.

27. Ibid.

28. Ibid.

29. Jack Clowser, "Lashes at Writers for Lucas Attacks," *Cleveland Press,* May 23, 1962.

30. Ibid.

26. INTO THE NBA

1. Arthur Daley, "NBA Wanted Lucas so Pipers Get Franchise," *New York Times,* July 13, 1962.

2. Ibid.

3. Ibid.

4. Murry Nelson, *Abe Saperstein and the American Basketball League, 1960–1963: The Upstarts Who Shot for Three and Lost to the NBA* (Jefferson, NC: McFarland, 2013).

5. Chuck Heaton, "Rival NBA Eyes Pipers and Lucas," *Plain Dealer,* July 7, 1962.

6. Cleary, interview, Feb. 2014.

7. Cleary, interview, Feb. 2014.

8. Cleary interview, Feb. 2014.

9. This sentence was inspired by "Not Unfriendly," an unpublished poem by Marcus Bales of Cleveland, Ohio.

10. Cleary, interview, Feb. 2012.

11. Sudyk, interview, May 2014.

12. Cleary, interview, Feb. 2014.

13. Cleary, interview, Feb. 2014.

14. "Lucas Mum on Switch," *Plain Dealer,* July 8, 1962.

15. Chuck Heaton, "Pipers Will Play in NBA," *Plain Dealer,* July 11, 1962.

16. Bob Sudyk, "Lucas Knew Pipers' NBA Plans at Start," *Cleveland Press,* July 17, 1962.

17. Gordon Cobbledick, "Cleveland Now Has Big League Basketball but Will Fans Remain Cool," *Plain Dealer,* July 12, 1962.

27. OUT OF THE NBA

1. Bob Sudyk, "Saperstein Says Pipers 'Pirated,'" *Cleveland Press,* July 13, 1962.

2. Bob Sudyk, "Sharman Believes Pipers Can Reach NBA Playoffs," *Cleveland Press,* July 14, 1962.

3. Bob Sudyk, "Cincinnati Contends Not Yet a Member of NBA," *Cleveland Press,* July 20, 1962.

4. Ibid.

5. Associated Press, "McMahon Takes Zephyrs' Post; Spurns Pipers," *Plain Dealer,* July 25, 1962.

6. Cleary, interview, Feb. 2014.

7. Associated Press, "ABL to Sue if Cleveland Enters NBA," July 26, 1962.

8. Bob Sudyk, "Piper NBA Entry in Doubt as Major Backer Withdraws," *Cleveland Press,* July 27, 1962.

9. Hal Lebovitz, "New Bid Offered to NBA," *Plain Dealer,* July 28, 1962.

10. Ibid.

11. Bob Sudyk, "ABL to Sue," *Cleveland Press,* July 27, 1962.

12. Lebovitz, "New Bid Offered."

13. Bob Sudyk, "Piper Boss Says Group Tried Steal," *Cleveland Press,* July 28, 1962.

14. Ibid.

15. Hal Lebovitz, "Fate of Pipers Due for Airing," *Plain Dealer,* July 29, 1962.

16. Dick Schaap, *Steinbrenner!* (New York: Putnam, 1982).

17. Pat Harmon, "NBA Backs Royals, Rejects Podoloff Deal with Jerry Lucas; Pipers Out of League," *Cincinnati Enquirer and Times-Star,* July 30, 1962.

18. Ibid.

19. Ibid.

20. Ibid.

21. Ibid

22. Hal Lebovitz, "Pipers Rejected by NBA, Intend to Keep Trying," *Plain Dealer,* July 31, 1962.

23. Hamilton, interview, 2014.

24. Gordon Cobbledick, "Pipers Learn that the Best Way to Get Talked about Is to Foul Things Up," *Plain Dealer,* Aug. 1, 1962.

25. Bob August, "The Sorry State of the Pipers," *Cleveland Press,* Aug. 1, 1962.

28. ENDGAME

1. Hal Lebovitz, "Pipers and Lucas to Stay in ABL," *Plain Dealer,* Aug. 13, 1962.

2. Bob Sudyk, "Pipers Fail to Pay Lucas," *Cleveland Press,* July 31, 1962.

3. Hal Lebovitz, "Cleveland Stays in ABL Says Abe," *Plain Dealer,* Aug. 5, 1962.

4. "Status of Pipers Is Uncertain," *Plain Dealer,* Aug 12, 1962.

5. Hal Lebovitz, "Lucas Sues Lane in Libel Charge," *Plain Dealer,* Aug. 14, 1962.

6. Ibid.

7. Bob Sudyk, "Strange World of Jerry Lucas—Life of Confusion and Contradiction," *Cincinnati Enquirer and Times-Star,* Aug. 20, 1962.

8. Ibid.

9. Gordon, interview.

10. Cleary, interview, Feb. 2012.

11. Tormohlen interview, Mar. 2012.

12. Cleary, interview, Mar. 2012.

13. Gordon, interview.

14. Gordon, interview.

15. Tony Tomsic, telephone interview with author, 2014.

29. POSTMORTEM

1. Ben Flieger, *Cleveland Press,* May 1961.

2. Jack Adams, follow-up telephone interview with author, 2014.

3. Gordon, interview.

4. Sudyk, interview, May 2014.

5. Bob Sudyk, "Former Pipers Doing Well in New NBA Surroundings," *Cleveland Press,* Oct. 31, 1962.

6. Barnett, interview.

7. Bud Poliquin, "One Old Syracuse National, Dick Barnett, Recalls 'The Boss' . . . and, Yes, He Does So Fairly Fondly," Syracuse.com, July 20, 2010, www.syracuse.com/poliquin/index.ssf/201%7/one_old_syracuse_nat_dick_barn.html.

8. Barnett, interview.

9. Gordon, interview.

10. Hamilton, interview.

11. Sudyk, memo to author.

12. Cleary, interview, 2012.

13. Cleary, interview, 2012.

14. Tormohlen, interview, Mar. 2012.

Suggested Readings

BOOKS AND MAGAZINES

Erving, Julius, and Karl Taro Greenfeld. *Dr. J: The Autobiography.* New York: HarperCollins, 2013.

Golenbock, Peter. *George: The Poor Little Rich Boy Who Built the Yankee Empire.* Hoboken, NJ: Wiley, 2008.

———. *Wild, High and Tight: The Life and Death of Billy Martin.* New York: St. Martin's Press, 1994.

Katz, Milton S. *Breaking Through: John B. McLendon, Basketball Legend and Civil Rights Pioneer.* Fayetteville: Univ. of Arkansas Press, 2007.

Madden, Bill. *Steinbrenner: The Last Lion of Baseball.* New York: HarperCollins, 2011.

Nelson, Murry R. *Abe Saperstein and the American Basketball League, 1960–1963: The Upstarts Who Shot for Three and Lost to the NBA.* Jefferson, NC: McFarland Press, 2013.

Pennington, Bill. *Billy Martin: Baseball's Flawed Genius.* New York: Houghton Mifflin Harcourt, 2015.

Pluto, Terry. *Tall Tales: The Glory Years of the NBA in the Words of the Men Who Played, Coached and Built Pro Basketball.* New York: Simon & Schuster, 1992.

Roberts, Michael D. "Last Call." *Cleveland Magazine,* November 2011.

Ryan, Bob. *The Pro Game: The World of Professional Basketball.* New York: McGraw-Hill, 1975.

Schaap, Dick. *Steinbrenner!* New York: Putnam, 1982.

Thomas, Ron. *They Cleared the Lane: The NBA's Black Pioneers.* Lincoln, NE: Bison Books, 2004.

West, Jerry, and Jonathan Coleman. *West by West: My Charmed, Tormented Life.* New York: Little, Brown, 2011.

Wolf, David. *Foul! The Connie Hawkins Story.* New York: Holt, Rinehart and Winston, 1972.

INTERNET RESOURCES

For Dick Barnett background

Legget, William. "A New Knick with a Knack." *Sports Illustrated* online. January 17, 1966. www.si.com/vault/1966/01/17/607804/a-new-knick-with-a-knack.

"MSGProFiles Nicks #12 Dick Barnett." Uploaded July 31, 2010 by Harrison McClendon. www.youtube.com/watch?v=g5cTBV22mJE.

Poliquin, Bud. "One Old Syracuse National, Dick Barnett, Recalls 'The Boss' . . . and, Yes, He Does so Fondly." Syracuse.com. July 20, 2010. www.syracuse.com/poliquin/index.ssf/2010/07/one_old_syracuse_nat_dick_barn.html.

Rhoden, William. Sports of the Times: "Too Late; Fall Back, Baby." *New York Times* online. February 26, 1991. www.nytimes.com/1991/02/26/sports/sports-of-the-times-too-late-fall-back-baby.html.

For Bill Sharman background

Friedman, David. "Remembering Bill Sharman, Star Player and Coaching Innovator." *20 Second Timeout* (blog). November 5, 2013. http://20secondtimeout.blogspot.fr/2013/11/remembering-bill-sharman-star-player.html.

Kirst, Sean. "The Passing of NBA Hal of Famer Bill Sharman: A Syracuse Legend Recalls a Friendship That Transcended Barriers." Syracuse.com. October 26, 2013. www.syracuse.com/kirst/index.ssf/2013/10/post_551.html.

Noland, Clare, and Jerry Crowe. "Bill Sharman, Hall of Fame Basketball Player, Lakers Coach, Dies at 87." *Los Angeles Times* online, October 25, 2103. www.latimes.com/local/obituaries/la-sp-sn-bill-sharman-hall-of-fame-basketball-player-and-laker-coach-dies-at-87–20131025-story.html.

Preston, J. G. "No, Bill Sharman Was Never Ejected from a Major League Baseball Game as a Member of the Dodgers." *The J. G. Preston Experience* (blog). October 28, 2013. https://prestonjg.wordpress.com/2013/10/28/no-bill-sharman-was-never-ejected-from-a-major-league-baseball-game-as-a-member-of-the-dodgers/.

Rosen, Charley. "NBA Backstage." Espn.com. December 4, 2004. http://espn.go.com/page2/s/rosen/021204.html.

Sharman, Bill, biography. NBA Encyclopedia Playoff Edition. www.nba.com/history/players/sharman_bio.html.

For Jerry Lucas background

Cave, Ray. "Jerry Lucas, Sportsman of the Year." *Sports Illustrated* online, January 8, 1962. www.si.com/vault/1962/01/08/590444/jerry-lucas.

Lucas, Jerry, biography. NBA Encyclopedia Playoff Edition. www.nba.com/history/players/lucasj_bio.html.

———. "Why I Am Turning Pro." May 21, 1962. *Sports Illustrated* online.

For Larry Siegfried background

Ryan, Bob. "The One and Only Siggy." Boston.com. October 16, 2010. www.boston. com/sports/columnists/bob_ryan_blog/2010/10/the_one_and_onl_1.html.

For John McLendon background

Beschloss, Michael. "Naismith's Choices on Race, From Basketball's Beginnings." *New York Times* online. May 2, 2014. www.nytimes.com/2014/05/03/upshot/ choices-on-race-even-from-basketballs-beginnings.html?_r=0.

"John McLendon: A League of His Own, Cleveland State." Unproduced television documentary by the late Cleveland film producer Tom Sweeney. The John McLendon Foundation currently owns the rights.

For the Theatrical Grill

Mosbrook, Joe. "Part 93: The Theatrical Grill." January 13, 2005. www.cleveland. oh.us/wmv_news/jazz93.htm.

For a contrarian view of the Harlem Globetrotters

Musick, Phil. "Remembering a Man and His Craft." *Pittsburgh Post-Gazette,* June 6, 1977. http://news.google.com/newspapers?nid=1129&dat=19770606&id =q39IAAAAIBAJ&sjid=U2oDAAAAIBAJ&pg=3055,627289.

For Connie Hawkins background

Hawkins, Connie, biography. NBA Encyclopedia Playoff Edition. www.nba.com/ history/players/hawkins_bio.html.

For details on basketball when it was played in a cage

Peterson, Robert W. "When the Court Was a Cage in the Early Days of Pro Basketball." *Sports Illustrated* online. November 11, 1991. www.si.com/ vault/1991/11/11/125381/when-the-court-was-a-cage-in-the-early-days-of- pro-basketball-the-players-were-segregated-from-the-fans.

NEWSPAPER ARTICLES

Associated Press. "Three-Pointer Makes Hit in Pro Cage." April 15, 1962.

Daley, Arthur. "NBA Wanted Lucas so Pipers Get Franchise." *New York Times.* July 13, 1962.

Harmon, Pat. "NBA Backs Royals, Rejects Podoloff Deal with Jerry Lucas; Pipers Out of League." *Cincinnati Post and Times-Star.* July 30, 1962.

SPORTSWRITERS

Cleveland Plain Dealer
Gordon Cobbledick
Bob Dolgan
Jimmy Doyle
Chuck Heaton
Hal Lebovitz

Cleveland Press
Bob August
Jack Clowser
Lou Darvas
Ben Flieger
Frank Gibbons
Bob Sudyk

Columbus Dispatch
Dick Otte
Paul Hornung

Kansas City Star
Fritz Kreisler
Dick Mackey

Index

Abdul-Jabbar, Kareem, 33

Abe Saperstein and the American Basketball League, 1960–1963 (Nelson), 42, 190

Adams, Jack: first half of season games, 101, 106; first half playoffs and, 110; McLendon and, 36; Pipers' legacy and, 208–9; Pipers in NIBL and, 12, 16; Pipers' rivals and, 57, 67; second half of season games, 116, 117; in Soviet Union, 17, 18–19, 20; Steinbrenner and, 26–27, 69, 71, 74, 76, 120, 122–23; with Tapers, 135; views on McLendon, 39

Akron Tramonte Black Label (team), 182

Allain, Jack, 137

Amateur Athletic Association (AAU), 5

American Basketball Association (ABA), xiii, 32, 44, 55, 68, 75, 127, 128, 132, 143

American Basketball League (ABL): draft system of, 153, 155; financial problems of, 43; legacy of, 44, 52–56; officiating by, 51–52; Pipers move from NIBL to, 21, 25; Pipers' NBA plans and, 189–95, 196–202; Pipers' rival teams and players, 57–68; Pipers threatened with expulsion from, 140–43; player honors by, 154; Saperstein and, 42–47, 48, 51, 53, 55–56 (*see also* Saperstein, Abraham M.); short tenure of, xi–xiv; teams and venues of, 47–51. *See also individual names of teams*

"Anchorage" (Steinbrenner homes), 3

Arizin, Paul, 208

Attles, Al, 46

Auerbach, Red, 128, 205

August, Bob, 53, 79, 80, 120, 201–2

Barnett, Dick, 78–87; biographical information, 80–81, 83, 87; "fall back, baby!" catchphrase and, 81; first half of season games, 102, 103, 105; first half playoffs and, 108–11; injury of, 144, 145, 147, 148; with Lakers, 205; Lucas and, 181; McLendon and, 31, 32, 39, 40, 91; move from Syracuse to Cleveland by, 46; Pipers' championship, 166, 168–70, 176–78; Pipers' legacy and, 209–10; Pipers' NBA plans, 192, 193–94; Pipers' rivals and, 64; second half of season games, 115, 150–51, 152, 154, 155; Sharman's coaching and, 134, 135, 137, 139; "Skull" nickname of, 78; Steinbrenner and, 70; sudden-death series games, 162, 163

Barnhill, John "Rabbit": Army service of, 103; Barnett and, 83; fans of, 70; first half of season games, 72; first half playoffs, 109–10; injuries of, 88, 144, 146; Lucas and, 182; Pipers' championship, 166, 168, 176–77; Pipers formation and, 8, 40, 72, 76; Pipers' legacy and, 209; Pipers' NBA plans, 194; race relations and, 37; second half of season games, 117, 152, 154–55; Sharman's coaching and, 134; in Soviet Union, 17, 19; sudden-death series games, 161, 163

18–20; Steinbrenner and, 70; sudden-death series games, 162–63; with Tapers, 135–36, 139

Sweeny, Ed, 11–16, 33, 34, 123

Syracuse Nationals (Nats), 77, 78, 83–85, 115–16, 134, 181, 192, 205

Taylor, Chuck, 30

Taylor, Fred, 158–59, 180

Taylor, Roger, 16, 17, 20, 37, 59, 70, 105, 117, 122, 135, 162–63

Tennessee State University Tigers, 5, 6, 29–30, 32, 82, 133–34

Terwilliger, Wayne, 127

Texas Western University, 30

Thacker, Tom, 158–59

Theatrical Grill (Cleveleand), 22–23

They Cleared the Lane (Thomas), 72

Thomas, Isiah, 45

Thomas, Ron, 72

Thompson, David, 86

three-point shot, ABL and, 52–56

Tittle, Y. A., 46–47

tobacco use, by basketball players, 73–74

Tomsic, Tony, 206–7

Tormohlen, Gene: ABL demise and, 205; Barnett and, 82; first half playoffs and, 110; late-season team injuries and, 146; Pipers' championship, 165–68, 171; Pipers' legacy and, 212; Pipers' NBA plans, 193; Pipers in NIBL and, 12–13, 14; Pipers' rivals and, 64, 65; on race, 37; second half of season games, 112, 118, 151; Steinbrenner and, 70; sudden-death series games, 161; traded by Steinbrenner, 38

Truitt, Frank, 197

Truman, Harry, 112–13

Turner, Herschell, 76, 150, 154, 194

"two in a corner" delay game, 32

Twombley, Wells, 58

Uline Arena, 48–49

University of Cincinnati Bearcats, 34

University of Iowa Hawkeyes, 57

University of Kentucky Wildcats, 30, 34, 104

University of San Francisco Dons, 48

U.S. State Department, 33

Vann, Bryce, 108, 110

Vaughn, Govoner, 138

Veeck, Bill, 45

Walsh, Thomas, 35

Warley, Ben: career of, 74–76; first half of season games, 105, 106; first half playoffs and, 109; late-season team injuries and, 147; Lucas and, 182; McLendon and, 40, 88, 92; Pipers' championship, 167; Pipers formation and, 8; Pipers' NBA plans, 193–94; Pipers in NIBL and, 16; Pipers' rivals and, 67; second half of season games, 115, 117, 150–51; Sharman and, 137; in Soviet Union, 17; Steinbrenner and, 69, 70; sudden-death series games, 162

Warley, Carlin, 75

Washington Capitols, 127, 130

Washington Coliseum, 48–49

Washington Generals, 45, 74

Washington Tapers, 43, 49, 54, 61, 88, 91

Webster, Ruth E., 26

Wessels, John, 52

West, Jerry, 7, 14, 81, 82, 86, 96, 129, 131–32

West by West (West), 86

White, Hubie, 155

White, Jo Jo, 73

Wilfong, Win, 73–74, 167, 193

Wilkens, Lenny, 31, 128

Williams, Pat, 46

Willis, Bill, 31

Wilson, Pepper, 186, 197

Wilson, Ralph, 115–16, 134, 141, 143, 182

Wisconsin Badgers, 158

Wolf, David, 52, 62, 65, 146, 148, 178

Wooden, John, 128, 131, 158

Woolpert, Phil, 48

Wright, Leroy, 62

Yardley, George, 46, 70

Zagar, Ron, 153